D0152142

GEORGE ORWELL

Recent Titles in
Contributions to the Study of World Literature
Series Adviser: Leif Sjoberg

Klaus Rifbjerg
Charlotte Schiander Gray

Scenarios of Modernist Disintegration: Tryggve Andersen's Prose Fiction
Timothy Schiff

Guido Gezelle: Flemish Poet-Priest
Hermine J. van Nuis

Voices of the Storyteller: Cuba's Lino Novás Calvo
Lorraine Elena Roses

Lessing and the Enlightenment
Alexej Ugrinsky, editor

Dostoevski and the Human Condition After a Century
Alexej Ugrinsky, Frank S. Lambasa, and Valija K. Ozolins, editors

Russian Romantic Criticism: An Anthology
Lauren Gray Leighton, editor and translator

The Literary Heritage of Childhood: An Appraisal of Children's Classics in the
Western Tradition
Charles Frey and John Griffith

Goethe in the Twentieth Century
Alexej Ugrinsky, editor

The Stendhal Bicentennial Papers
Avriel Goldberger, editor

The Writer Written: The Artist and Creation in the New Literatures
Jean-Pierre Durix

Becoming True to Ourselves: Cultural Decolonization and National
Identity in the Literature of the Portuguese-Speaking World
Maria Luisa Nunes

GEORGE ORWELL

Edited by
COURTNEY T. WEMYSS
and
ALEXEJ UGRINSKY

Prepared under the auspices of Hofstra University

Contributions to the Study of World Literature, Number 23

Greenwood Press
New York • Westport, Connecticut • London

Library of Congress Cataloging-in-Publication Data

George Orwell.

(Contributions to the study of world literature,
ISSN 0738-9345 ; no. 23)
Includes index.
1. Orwell, George, 1903-1950—Criticism and
interpretation. I. Wemyss, Courtney T. II. Ugrinsky,
Alexej. III. Series.
PR6029.R8Z639 1987   828'.91209   87-15053
ISBN 0-313-26079-6 (lib. bdg. : alk. paper)

British Library Cataloguing in Publication Data is available.

Copyright © 1987 by Courtney T. Wemyss and Alexej Ugrinsky

All rights reserved. No portion of this book may be
reproduced, by any process or technique, without the
express written consent of the publisher.

Library of Congress Catalog Card Number: 87-15053
ISBN: 0-313-26079-6
ISSN: 0738-9345

First published in 1987

Greenwood Press, Inc.
88 Post Road West, Westport, Connecticut 06881

Printed in the United States of America

(∞)™

The paper used in this book complies with the
Permanent Paper Standard issued by the National
Information Standards Organization (Z39.48-1984).

10 9 8 7 6 5 4 3 2 1

ROBERT MANNING
STROZIER LIBRARY

AUG 26 1988

Tallahassee, Florida

Copyright Acknowledgments

The editors and publisher gratefully acknowledge permission to use portions of the following:

Today the Struggle by K. B. Hoskins, University of Texas Press, 1969.

The Road to 1984 by William Steinhoff. Copyright © by The University of Michigan, 1975.

The Aerodrome by Rex Warner, Oxford University Press, 1982.

The Will to Believe by R. Johnstone, Oxford University Press, 1984.

*On a Ruined Farm Near the His Master's Voice Gramophone Factory, Coming Up for Air,
Nineteen Eighty-Four, The Collected Essays, Journalism and Letters of George Orwell,* and
Down and Out in Paris and London by George Orwell courtesy of the Estate of the late Sonia
Brownell Orwell and Secker and Warburg Ltd. for British Commonwealth and world rights.

Excerpt from "On a Ruined Farm Near the His Master's Voice Gramophone Factory" in
The Collected Essays, Journalism and Letters of George Orwell, Volume I, copyright © 1968
by Sonia Brownell Orwell. Reprinted by permission of Harcourt Brace Jovanovich, Inc.

Excerpts from *Coming Up for Air* by George Orwell. Reprinted by Permission of Harcourt
Brace Jovanovich, Inc.

Excerpts from *Nineteen Eighty-Four* by George Orwell, copyright 1949 by Harcourt Brace Jovanovich, Inc.; renewed 1977 by Sonia Brownell Orwell. Reprinted by permission of the publisher.

Excerpts from *The Collected Essays, Journalism and Letters of George Orwell*, Volumes 1-4, edited by Sonia Orwell and Ian Angus, copyright © 1968 by Sonia Brownell Orwell. Reprinted by permission of Harcourt Brace Jovanovich, Inc.

Excerpts from *Down and Out in Paris and London*, copyright 1933 by George Orwell; renewed 1961 by Sonia Pitt-Rivers. Reprinted by permission of Harcourt Brace Jovanovich, Inc.

From George Orwell's works:
"Charles Dickens," "Such, Such Were the Joys," "Literature and Totalitarianism," "The Prevention of Literature," "England Your England," "Culture and Democracy," "Inside the Whole," and "The Road to Wigan Pier," courtesy of the Estate of the late Sonia Brownell Orwell and Secker and Warburg Ltd. for British Comonwealth rights. U.S. rights by permission of Harcourt Brace Jovanovich, Inc.

The Idea of Clerisy in the Nineteenth Century by Ben Knights, Cambridge University Press, 1978.

"Fatalism of George Orwell," by D. S. Savage in *The Present, New Pelican Guide to English Literature*, Vol. 8, Boris Ford, editor, Penguin, 1983.

"George Orwell, 19th Century Liberal," by George Woodcock. Courtesy of George Woodcock. Previously published in *Politics*, December 1946, and in *George Orwell: The Critical Heritage*, Jeffrey Meyers, editor, London: Routledge and Kegan Paul, 1975.

Excerpt from *Whigs and Hunters: The Origin of the Black Act* by E. P. Thompson, Pantheon Books, a division of Random House, Inc., 1975.

Excerpt from *Industry and Empire* by Eric J. Hobsbawm, Penguin Books, 1969.

Poem by the late Major Michael Davis O'Donnell from the book *Dear America: Letters Home from Vietnam*, edited by Bernard Edelman, New York Vietnam Veterans Memorial Commission, Norton, 1985.

"To a Melancholy Lady" by Mary Elizabeth Mahnkey from *Ozark Lyrics*. Courtesy of her son, Douglas Mahnkey, and The School of the Ozarks, Missouri.

The Road to Wigan Pier by George Orwell. Reprinted by permission of Harcourt Brace Jovanovich, Inc., 1958.

"*Nineteen Eighty-Four* and the Constitution," by W. Russel Gray from *Laws of Our Fathers: Popular Culture and the U.S. Constitution*, Ray B. Browne and Glen J. Browne, editors, Popular Press, Bowlng Green State University, Ohio, 1986.

"Slouching Toward Relevance, or What to Do with 1984 until 1984," by W. Russel Gray, in *English Journal*, April 1983. Reprinted by permission of the National Council of Teachers of English.

"Poetics and Linguistics," by George Steiner from *Extraterritorial*, Peregrine, 1975.

Quotes from Orwell's works and three unpublished letters courtesy of A. M. Heath on behalf of Mrs. George Orwell and Secker and Warburg Ltd.

Every reasonable effort has been to trace the owners of copyright materials in this book, but in some instances this has proven impossible. The publishers will be glad to receive information leading to more complete acknowledgments in subsequent printings of the book, and in the meantime extend their apologies for any omissions.

Contents

GEORGE ORWELL

Preface

I think it important that the life and works of George Orwell come to hold a secure, proper niche in the noble body of literature which has been generated in the English tongue over many centuries. Mention of his name in the far future should evoke in educated men that same breed of respect which the names Fielding, Goldsmith, and Sterne evoke in us. These names suggest the rank to which I trust Orwell will be assigned by scholars of other ages.

To my mind Orwell's niche is at risk because of the current over-emphasis of some facets of the man at the expense of certain others, these latter being of a more enduring quality. My fear is that Orwell the Patron Saint of Poverty and Bard of Apocalypse will, in the long run, tire people of the future and consequently subvert them into neglecting Orwell the ligand — the connection between the higher and lower grades of literature — and of Orwell the preserver of the twentieth-century milieu.

I have long been struck by the fact that Orwell is a much more significant figure than his mere literary accomplishments — which are modest — suggest. Furthermore he is honored here and elsewhere this year because of a novel which is not his best. The greatest virtue of Nineteen Eighty-Four — this taut, well-brewed, and commanding horror story — is that it directs us or should direct us to his other offerings. Then the other novels (Burmese Days, Coming up for Air, etc.), the superb literary criticism (Kipling, Dickens, etc.) the book reviews, the documentaries (Down and Out in London and Paris, The Road to Wigan Pier, Homage to Catalonia) will bring forth to us the English milieu of the first half of this century with at least the accuracy with which Pepys presented the milieu of the Restoration — without, I judge, the particular intent of diarist himself.

Burmese Days, fine novel that it is, cannot touch Coming up for Air, Orwell's best ever, of which one seldom hears mention today or, for that matter, heard mention of forty years back. Yet in it we meet England about to face Hitler — the Vlad Dracula of modern Europe. We also meet George Bowling, the incarnate spirit of the decent Englishmen who shortly afterward made "a pact of death" (These apt words are, alas, those of A. J. P. Taylor and not my own) with Winston Churchill.

These works also contrive to send us up to Swift, over to Defoe and Chesterton, and down to Jack London and George Gissing. George Orwell's works are, in short, marvelous points of departure. His BBC broadcast of 1941 or thereabouts in which he analyzed Gerard Manley Hopkins' poem "Felix Randal" is of a quality such as to inspire the interested young to take up the study of prosody.

His 1941 essay on the mind of H. G. Wells -- written because Wells a month or so earlier had been so foolish as to tell the press that the Wehrmacht was finished and that Herr Hitler had shot his wad -- not only accounts for the mentality which could reach such a fatuous conclusion but also, at least by implication, explains the intellectual lesions of Sidney and Beatrice Webb, George Bernard Shaw, and others of that kidney.

In putting down someone whose notions were not rooted in reality, Orwell frequently resorted to the flat, unadorned statement; "He does not know how things work." He then set out to prove as much, almost always successfully. Among the notable instances are those of Wells, Dickens, and, in lesser degree Kipling. His regard for Jack London (such as it was) stemmed from the fact that London clearly realized that bravery was not a monopoly virtue of fighters in righteous causes.

As far as I know, Orwell never addressed himself to the works of Anthony Trollope, who did indeed know how things work and who never mentioned matters the workings of which he did not understand. I wish to God that Orwell had turned his attention to Trollope.

To conclude, preoccupation with his immediate importance should not ultimately cause scholars of the future to underrate George Orwell.

Part I

The Man of Letters

1.
G. K. Chesterton and
Nineteen Eighty-Four
LOUIS C. BURKHARDT

Scholars of the works of both G. K. Chesterton and George Orwell agree
that Orwell was well-read in Chesterton. As a schoolboy Orwell report-
edly quoted Chesterton frequently. As late as 1945 Orwell remarked that
Chesterton was "a writer of considerable talent."(1) But at the same
time Orwell also criticized Chesterton's tendency to allow Roman Catholicism to suppress "both his sensibilities and his intellectual honesty."
The following year, in a letter to Herbert Rogers, Orwell objected to
Chesterton's naive political program, which entailed distributing a small
piece of private property to every man.(2) At the time Orwell wrote
Nineteen Eighty-Four he still appreciated the imagination of a writer in
whom he reveled as a youth, but he could no longer tolerate Chesterton's
political optimism. Orwell's ambivalent feelings toward Chesterton generated a tension toward him that seems to be discernible in several
striking parallels between Ninteen Eighty-Four and three early Chesterton
novels, The Napoleon of Notting Hill, The Ball and the Cross, and The Man
Who Was Thursday.
    Scholars who have commented on parallels between Chesterton's writ-
ings and Nineteen Eighty-Four commonly begin by observing that The Napoleon of Notting Hill opens in the year 1984.(3) Published in 1904, The
Napoleon of Notting Hill proclaims, "When the curtain goes up on this
story, eighty years after the present date, London is almost exactly what
it is now."(4) This statement is modestly proposed to explain Orwell's
choice of the year 1984 as his title, although there is no proof Orwell
read The Napoleon of Notting Hill. All we know with certainty is that
Orwell read much of Chesterton and that Orwell's remark that "Chesterton,
in a less methodical way, predicted the disappearance of democracy and
private property, and the rise of a slave society which might be called
either capitalist or Communist,"(5) best describes The Napoleon of Notting Hill, which states, "Democracy was dead; for no one minded the governing class governing" (NNH, p. 25).(6)
    More significant than the use of the year 1984 are the political
problems portrayed in The Napoleon of Notting Hill. Although these problems prove solvable, whereas those in Nineteen Eighty-Four are not, both
governments at the outset are similar collective despotisms. The England
of The Napoleon of Notting Hill has become a "great cosmopolitan civilization," absorbing all cultures and societies. Since absorption entails
the abolition of individuality, freedom means nothing. As Adam Wayne,
the heroic liberator of Notting Hill, remarks,

> What a farce is this modern liberality. Freedom of speech
> means practically in our modern civilization that we must
> only talk about unimportant things. We must not talk about

religion, for that is illiberal; we must not talk about bread
and cheese, for that is talking shop. (NNH, p. 149)

Oceania also suffers from a lack of liberty, including the loss of freedom of speech, as is evidenced by the constant chatter concerning the
lottery. The Thought Police, moreover, enforce great suppression, but
the effects in both societies are essentially the same: the people do
not know enough to realize their predicament. As Kierkegaard often emphasized, the only thing worse than being lost is being lost and not
knowing one is lost.   Orwell asserts this truth in "Toward European
Unity," where he writes: "The greatest difficulty of all is the apathy
and conservatism of people everywhere."
    Both Adam Wayne and Winston Smith become distinguished in their ef-
forts to rise above this state of apathy -- Wayne by lifting his sword;
Smith, his pen. It is fitting that Winston Smith resorts to the isolated
act of writing a diary instead of urging revolution among the proles.
They knew so little history and so much propaganda that the likelihood of
a prole-based revolution was as slim as the possibilty that Winston Smith
would obtain a satisfactory answer from the old man in the pub. Whereas
apathy in Orwell's book results primarily from ignorance, in Chesterton's
book it results in belief in social evolution. People felt that if they
must change, they must "'change slowly and safely, as the animals do'"
(NNH, p. 21). It is noteworthy that Wayne, who resorts to violent means,
succeeds in altering the spirit of the age, whereas Smith, who only con-
templates the use of violence, fails altogether.
    Winston Smith's inertia may partly result from Orwell's disdain of
Chesterton's apparent delight in bloodshed. Chesterton easily lets his
characters die, as in the following instance: "'The banner of Notting
Hill stoops to a hero,' and with the words he drove the spear-point and
half the flag-staff through Lambert's body and dropped him dead upon the
road below, a stone upon the stones of the street" (NNH, p. 243). Yet
armed with knowledge of Chesterton's gentle temperament, a sympathetic
reader understands that fighting is symbolic of caring. After battling,
Adam Wayne sincerely exclaims, "'We have won. . . . We have taught our
enemies patriotism!'"(NNH, p. 243) It was better, according to Chesterton, for one to lose a limb than for one's whole mind to be cast into
hell.   Orwell, though, lacked the sympathy to read Chesterton's use of
violence as an expression of human decency. His antipathy toward the unrestrained shedding of blood by Chesterton's heroes perhaps contributed
to his portrayal of Winston Smith's revolutionary impotence. Orwell endowed the Party with the monopoly of power, as is evident by the inquisi-
torial nature of the tortures Smith received, thereby ensuring the book's
fatalistic conclusion.
    In allowing Winston Smith to fail, Orwell departed not only from
Chesterton's symbolism and plot but also from the latter's metaphysical
suppositions. Smith foresees his doom from the beginning because his
entire world is against him -- from the neighborhood children to the
Thought Police. Only Julia supports him as a person. Wayne, on the
other hand, realizes his hope because transcendental powers assist him.
The book ends with him walking off into the twilight of some cosmic
afterlife.
    On the surface the conclusion of Nineteen Eighty-Four appears to be
much more believable than that of The Napoleon of Notting Hill, yet Nineteen Eighty-Four is so dependent on causality that once a reader detects
a fault in the sequence, the entire vision is rendered unbelievable. Being structured around the syllogism that (1) no individuality can exist
with the Party; (2) Winston Smith becomes an individual; (3) therefore,
Winston Smith ceases to exist, Nineteen Eighty-Four is only as credible
as its major premise. The Napoleon of Notting Hill is fantastic from the
start (with such phrases as "When the curtain goes up on this sto-

ry . . ."), but the supposition that a man's love for the particular is capable of transcending all political obstructions is certainly more palatable than Orwell's major premise and is also easier to verify historically. The Napoleon of Notting Hill depicts a revolution that fits a historical pattern long established by occurrences such as the American and French revolutions; Nineteen Eighty-Four depicts a reign that cannot be documented: the unending domination of mankind by a totalitarian government.

One weakness in the major premise is the means of the Party's success in blotting out history and in mesmerizing citizens through propaganda. Once the possibility of such technological control is doubted, Orwell's syllogism totters. None of this is to say that The Napoleon of Notting Hill is free from stumbling blocks. A belief in Fairyland, as Chesterton called it, is required of the reader. Fairyland is presumably that place or state where spiritual values such as love and courage are found. It is both what is being threatened by modern materialism and what enables Adam Wayne to defeat materialism. Being enigmatic and flexible, Fairyland sustains the hopeful plot of The Napoleon of Notting Hill; being systematic and rigid, the technocracy sustains the fateful plot of Nineteen Eighty-Four.

This tendency in Orwell to glean from Chesterton valuable conceptions while rejecting the hope Chesterton offers is also apparent in The Ball and the Cross, a book in which MacIan, the theist, battles Turnbull, the atheist, only to discover their common enemy is modern indifference. Recall the comic scene from Nineteen Eighty-Four in the pub where Winston Smith attempts to get a "truthful account of conditions in the early part of the century." The old man with "pale blue eyes," a strong appetite for beer, and an inability to think abstractly frustrates Smith with meaningless responses such as "'The beer was better,'" and "'Lackeys . . . Now there's a word I ain't 'eard ever so long.'" In a similar episode from The Ball and the Cross, MacIan also seeks what is "right" from a common man, a half-tipsy yokel with "bleared blue eyes." As was Smith's man, this old man is incapable of coherent dialogue; when asked about the invisible Church, he refers to an abandoned church building. Similar as the two scenes are, Smith and MacIan reach contrary conclusions. Smith realizes that the crucial question, "'Was life better before the Revolution than it is now?'" is "unanswerable even now, since the few scattered survivors from the ancient world were incapable of comparing one age with another."(7) This mental impotence of the proles adds credibility to the bleak conclusion that the Party will never be overthrown. Conversely, MacIan is encouraged by the yokel's final incoherent response: "'When I sees a man, I sez 'e's a man.'"(8) MacIan believes that the yokel understands something modern thinkers have failed to grasp: that man is a man, not an animal, an angel, or anything else. This emphasis on the supremacy of the common man resonates throughout the book. In the end, M. Durand, the man who lights the saving fire, is described as "merely a man" (BC, p. 138).

The second most striking similarity between the books is the prison scenes. Both MacIan and Turnbull are locked in a windowless building specially designed to cure mental problems, as is the case with Winston Smith. Just as in Nineteen Eighty-Four looms the dreaded room 101, so in The Ball and the Cross room A carries the same mystique: it is a cell without a door, and in it the monk, Michael, has been sealed by Lucifer, the scientist. The allegorical nature of Chesterton's writings surfaces in that the prison is admittedly representative of ideological bondage (BC, p. 212). Likewise, the naturalism of Orwell's book remains steady as he narrates Smith's experience in the Ministry of Love -- solid concrete, blinding lights, and prolonged tortures. When Smith leaves the prison he remains a prisoner of himself, whereas the prisoners in The Ball and the Cross escape all ills, probably too easily, by the powers of Fairyland.

The intolerable confusion Smith suffered in prison is largely a re-sult of his ambiguous relationship with O'Brien. He is haunted by ambiv-alent feelings toward O'Brien, even after he is sure O'Brien belongs to the Thought Police. "He was the tormentor, he was the protector, he was the inquisitor, he was the friend" (Nineteen Eighty-Four, p. 247). He was most likely the man in the dark room who had promised Smith, "'We shall meet in the place where there is no darkness.'" And there in the sterile white chambers of the Ministry of Love, Smith met his friend for frequent tortures. The cosmic irony of a dream about light leading him into darkness and of his ally turning out to be his mortal enemy worked on Smith's mind until he could no longer distinguish between good and evil, or between four fingers and five.

A similar eerie relationship exists in The Man Who Was Thursday, a book Orwell mentioned in a review. Syme, the protagonist, also hears a voice in the dark room, the voice of the "chief" who commissions him to oppose the anarchists. The terms of membership which the mysterious chief presents to Syme are echoed in O'Brien's initial meeting with Julia and Winston. Syme is told, among other things, "'I am condemning you to death.'"(9) O'Brien states, "'You will work for a while, you will be caught, you will confess, and then you will die'" (Nineteen Eighty-Four, p. 177). The parallel continues as Syme realizes that the voice he heard in the dark belongs to Sunday, the head anarchist. To Syme Sunday is at once a mortal enemy and an ally, as O'Brien is to Smith.

The similarities between O'Brien and Sunday stop when Syme realizes that inexplicably he had always seen Sunday from the back, and that un-like his hideous back, Sunday, who represents Nature, is filled with goodness. Hence the voice Syme heard in the dark room was genuinely good, whereas the voice Smith heard in his dream was deceptively evil. Once again, Orwell borrows certain dramatic elements from Chesterton but stops short of Chesterton's hope.

In connection with the chief who spoke to Syme in the dark lies a final example of Chesterton's limited influence on Orwell. Like O'Brien's connection with the Thought Police, this chief heads the philo-sophical policemen, whose job it is to discover mental crimes: "'We dis-cover from a book of sonnets that a crime will be committed. We have to trace the origin of those dreadful thoughts that drive men at last to in-tellectual fanaticism and intellectual crime'" (MWWT, p. 42).

It is doubtful Chesterton considered the oppressive nature of such an organization. Far from detecting heresy in others, the philosophical police are bewildered about their relationship with Sunday throughout the book. Although they consider themselves a special task force, they actu-ally represent the common man's temptation to despair of finding meaning in life. Only at the brink of despair do the philosophical police stum-ble upon the goodness hidden in Sunday. Chesterton said that when he wrote The Man Who Was Thursday he had recently developed a form of opti-mism based on a minimal amount of good. It could be charged that Orwell wrote Nineteen Eighty-Four out of a pessimism based on a maximal amount of evil. His omniscient Thought Police are a hardened, treacherous ver-sion of Chesterton's naive policemen. Instead of discovering the meaning of life for the common man, the Thought Police bar it from him forever, as is consistent with Orwell's major premise.

It is tempting, but not quite accurate, to conclude that Orwell was a pessimist and Chesterton an optimist. True, Orwell gleaned many scenes and settings from Chesterton while consistently rejecting Chesterton's redemptive themes. Nevertheless Orwell still believed life was worth redeeming. He lacked only belief in Fairyland, which for Chesterton in-cluded every imaginable possibility, whether natural or supernatural in origin. What Chesterton's concept of reality excluded was unimaginable events, as he explains: "You cannot imagine two and one not making three. But you can easily imagine trees not growing fruit; you can imagine them growing golden candlesticks or tigers hanging on by the tail."(10) Nineteen Eighty-Four presents the antithesis of Fairyland. Not even the possibility of a political revolution is admitted, much less of trees growing golden candlesticks. The one thing excluded from Fairyland enters into Nineteen Eighty-Four: the mental impossibility of two plus two fingers equaling five. Miracles, no; absurdities, yes. For Orwell was convinced of man's almost infinite capacity for evil.

Yet Orwell was not simply a pessimist. In spite of his disbelief in Fairyland, he was exactly what Chesterton considered himself: a Patriot of Life. Optimistic and pessimistic thoughts alike were reasons to fight for the human race. For it is the only human race that exists, too good to abandon, too corrupt to accept passively. This universal patriotism explains an apparent inconsistency in Orwell: he condemned author James Burnham for his fatalistic predictions of the Communist threat, yet he allowed Winston Smith — and humanity with him — to expire under totalitarianism. For in Burnham's writings Orwell sensed something foreign to this patriotism, a spirit of compromise. Although he agreed with the grim realities cited by Burnham, he could not accept Burnham's proposed solutions, such as starting a preventive war. Neither could he trust Fairyland to make all things well. With his mind he agreed with Burnham, but with his heart he concurred with Chesterton. He was constrained to hand Winston Smith over to the Party, although he was not convinced Nineteen Eighty-Four represented the future. He wrote Nineteen Eighty-Four in an effort to bring Britain and Western Europe one step closer to uniting as a socialist state (the United States of Europe), hoping that men would dedicate themselves to the improbable alternative of undefiled socialism once they were faced with a clear picture of totalitarianism. Orwell, of course, derived his moral strength and his literay elements from many sources, but Chesterton's influence on his imagination and on his emotions is appreciable, to say the least.

NOTES

1.   George Orwell, "Notes on Nationalism," in the Collected Essays (London: Secker and Warburg, 1961), p. 285.

2.   George Orwell, In Front of Your Nose, Vol. IV of The Collected Essays, Journalism, and Letters of George Orwell, Sonia Orwell and Ian Angus eds. (London: Secker and Warburg, 1968), p. 102.

3.   Among those who noted and commented on the shared use of the year 1984 are Ian Boyd, The Novels of G. K. Chesterton: A Study in Art and Propaganda (London: Paul Elek, 1975), p. 16; Christopher Hollis, in A Study of George Orwell (London: Hollis and Carter, 1956), pp. 177-79 and in The Mind of Chesterton (London: Hollis and Carter, 1970), p. 111; and William Steinhoff, George Orwell and the Origins of 1984 (Ann Arbor: University of Michigan Press, 1975), pp. 16-17. Among those who found reason to contrast The Napoleon of Notting Hill to Nineteen Eighty-Four but made no mention of the shared date are Dudley Barker, G. K. Chersterton: A Biography (New York: Stein and Day, 1973); p. 41; and Kenneth Hamilton, "G. K. Chesterton and George Orwell: A Contrast in Prophecy," Dalhousie Review XXXI (1950), 198-205. Finally, Hollis noted similarities between Nineteen Eighty-Four and The Ball and the Cross in The Mind of Chesterton, pp. 94-95, and Steinhoff noted similarities between Nineteen Eighty-Four and The Man Who Was Thursday in George Orwell and the Origins of 1984, pp. 16-19.

4.   G. K. Chesterton, The Napoleon of Notting Hill (Torquay: Devonshire Press, 1904), p. 20; hereafter cited in the text as NNH.

5.   George Orwell, "James Burnham and the Managerial Revolution," in In Front of Your Nose, p. 163.

6.   Of four other theories explaining Orwell's choice of title, the most obvious states that he simply inverted the last two digits of 1948, the year he completed Nineteen Eighty-Four. A second theory points out that a footnote in Jack London's The Iron Heel (a book Orwell reviewed) marks 1984 as the year Asgard, a totalitarian capital, was completed (David Richards, "Orwell's Nineteen Eighty-Four: His Choice of the Date," The Explicator 35, No. 1 [1976], 8). The third theory, a highly speculative one, states that 1949, the year Nineteen Eighty-Four was published, lay halfway between 1914 ("a key year in twentieth-century history") and 1984 (Richard Frothingham, "Orwell's Nineteen Eighty-Four Part I, Chapter VIII," The Explicator 29 [1971], item 37). The fourth theory, also highly speculative, works on the assumption that Orwell titled the book in answer to the "time-honored refrain, 'What will the world be like in fifty -- or a hundred -- years?' or 'What will the world be like when he's my age?'" The latter question is then related to the date of Richard Orwell's adoption, June 1944 (Bernhard J. Sussman, The Explicator 38, No. 4 [1980], 32).

7.   George Orwell, Nineteen Eighty-Four (New York: Harcourt Brace Jovanovich, 1949), p. 92; cited as Nineteen Eighty-Four.

8.   G. K. Chesterton, The Ball and the Cross (Beaconsfield: Darwen Finlayson, 1910), p. 93; this book was serialized in part in 1905-1906 and is hereafter cited in the text as BC.

9.   G. K. Chesterton, The Man Who Was Thursday (New York: Dodd, Mead, 1908), p. 47; hereafter cited in the text as MWWT.

10.   G. K. Chesterton, Orthodoxy (New York: John Lane Co., 1915), p. 88.

2.
Past and Present in
Coming up for Air and
Nineteen Eighty-Four:
A Comparison with Rex Warner's
The Aerodrome

MARIA TERESA CHIALANT

> The acid smoke had soured the fields,
> And browned the few and windworn flowers
> But there, where steel and concrete soar
> In dizzy, geometric towers
> . . . .
> There is my world, my home; yet why
> So alien still? For I can neither
> Dwell in that world, nor turn again
> To scythe and spade, but only loiter
> Among the trees that smoke has slain.
> -- G. Orwell, On A Ruined Farm Near the
> His Master's Voice Gramophone Factory
> (1934)

The question of the relation between past and present is crucial in Or-well's fiction. Recurring motifs in his novels are the meaning of his-tory, considered as both a personal and a collective experience; the im-portance of memory, as part of the identity of the individual and of a nation; the destruction of the past theme, with man struggling against an authoritarian State.

These are central issues of two novels in particular, Coming up for Air and Nineteen Eighty-Four, which are so closely related to each other that the former can be read as a first draft of the latter.(1) George Bowling's premonitions of the war forebode the nightmare experience of Winston Smith; the apocalyptic atmosphere of certain parts of Coming up for Air becomes the dominant mode and tone of Nineteen Eighty-Four. The evocations of the past of the two characters show it to be better than the present and the future. George Bowling's nostalgic excursion into Lower Binfield takes place in a year (1938), when England, like the rest of Europe, was under the threat of war. The past becomes the Golden Country of Winston Smith's recollections of childhood, a period of his life and of English history when family ties, love, and friendship still counted and human individuality was respected. The present, instead, means only the blind acceptance of the inhuman power of the Party.

A novel written in Orwell's time that presents striking analogies with the two books just mentioned is Rex Warner's The Aerodrome. Pub-lished in 1941, it is now enjoying some success after a most timely re-print in 1982 and a film dramatization screened on British television in December 1983. But apart from a couple of brief mentions of Nineteen Eighty-Four accompanying this rediscovery,(2) no closer comparison has been yet made, which seems to me worth attempting.

Rex Warner belonged to the group of those left-wing intellectuals of the thirties (Auden, Isherwood, Day Lewis, Upward, Lehmann, etc.) who took an active part in the British response to the Spanish Civil War and used the literary medium to denounce Fascism and to envision a new society.

In his autobiography, where he gives a fascinating account of the atmosphere of those years, John Lehmann maintains that Warner's novels published between the thirties and the early forties, together with others of the period, "though not immediately concerned with the war, had been written or finished at least under its influence, and had a deep symbolic or allegoric relation to it."(3) The most influential ones, according to Lehmann, were Virginia Woolf's Between the Acts and Rex Warner's The Aerodrome.

The six novels Warner wrote in the span of about twenty years have been variously described as allegories, fairy tales, or political fantasies.(4) They deal, like Orwell's, with crucial ideological and ethical dilemmas of the time: the cult of power and the dangers of totalitarianism, the inadequacy of liberalism, and the inefficiency of bourgeois democratic institutions.(5) In both Orwell's and Warner's works one can breathe the intellectual and political atmosphere of the thirties, which determined the subject matter and the tone of a relevant part of the literature of that decade and of the following one, characterized by a sense of impending doom.

Coming up for Air (1939), The Aerodrome (1941), and Nineteen Eighty-Four (1949) are, respectively, a premonition of the looming threat of war, a warning against the various forms of totalitarianism that were consolidating all over Europe, and a dramatization of an authoritarian future that already had its roots in the present. All three novels look back to a recent past, prior to World War I, nostalgically evoking a piece of British history and a way of life that appear irremediably lost. The apprehension of the imminent disaster, the actuality of the European conflict, and the political effects of the postwar partition of power are, both in history and in these fictions, successive stages in the same escalation toward a worldwide catastrophe.

But I intend neither to look at these novels as dystopias or prophetic books nor to single out influences or derivations. What interests me here is to examine certain fictional elements, such as the narrative modality of presenting an issue in terms of contrast, in order to detect continuities and connections with a common cultural tradition.

The contrast, as we have seen, is enacted in a recognizable historical context: a tenderly remembered past, situated between the 1890s and 1914, is opposed to a threatening present, with the spreading of Nazism and the outbreak of World War II, and to an even more appalling future, the aftermath of the war.

In The Aerodrome the two poles of the antithesis are embodied in a forlorn, old-fashioned English village and a new, highly organized aerodrome that has been implanted at its outskirts. The village, womblike and protective, stands for tradition, while the aerodrome, metallic and aggressive, stands for the new order. But although the former can be taken as representative of the life of natural man and the latter of the mechanized life of the modern state — an impersonal power reminiscent of Kafka's castle(6) — the village is not idealized. Its backwardness, hypocrisy, and stagnation are no less criticized than the ruthless efficiency of the aerodrome.

The dialectical relationship between the spatial structures of the novel is effectively rendered by the movement of the protagonist, young Roy, who partakes of the life and values of both worlds, divided as he is between them. His first-person narration contributes to dramatize the contrast. Indeed, it is one of the strengths of the text that the individual and the historical levels subtly intertwine: personal relationships find their counterpart in political questions of wider implication.

The village, which is a community founded on such English institutions as the Rector, the Squire, and the pub, is shattered by the new principles imposed by the Air Vice-Marshal and his officers. Their first objective is to destroy the individual and collective memory of the people in the village. It is significant, in terms of narrative structure, that the search for identity is a central problem in the protagonist's personal history.

As the novel begins Roy, on his twenty-first birthday, has just been informed by the Rector (whom he and everybody else thought was his father) that in fact he is a foundling. Later a new version of the mystery surrounding his origins is disclosed to him until in the end, in a melodramatic sequence of revelations about mistaken parenthood, confused identity, and final recognition, it is discovered that Roy is the Air Vice-Marshal's son. This is no sensationalistic device, though. The "intricacies of deception" in which Roy feels himself lost are the expression of a more dangerous and far-reaching lie: the web of falsehood and hate which entangles the people of the village.

But also the law of the aerodrome, in order to be enforced, requires new lies and destruction: the obliteration of family ties and of that sense of identity that is built up through connections with people, property, and place. The words that have been banned by the language of the aerodrome are, in fact, "parenthood,", "marriage," "ownership," "locality," and even "future." "These words are without wings," says the Air Vice-Marshal in a memorable speech to the young recruits, the would-be airmen. According to these principles time must be frozen in an eternal present, which implies the negation of history and freedom from the bondage of time. This is the reason that the men of the aerodrome are forbidden to procreate; hence woman is lowered to the level of a mere "source of pleasure," from the comparatively nobler role of childbearer, and is despised because "the construction of her body must inevitably make her much more a prisoner of time" than man is.(7)

The great myth of the aerodrome is freedom, symbolized by "the first flyers, the race of birds," a superior race because it is endowed with wings -- although the only wings the aerodrome can provide its men are the artificial wings of airplanes. But this ancient and powerful myth is used paradoxically here. The new order contains its own defeat: the new race of "free" men is fatally bound to extinguish itself through its own philosophy that denies the possibility of a descent. So also the idea of immortality is baffled.

In terms of plot, the end of the aerodrome comes as a consequence of an act of sabotage; the aircraft piloted by the Air Vice-Marshal crashes during takeoff having been damaged by one of his officers, the Flight-Lieutenant, who is also a son of his. But the real element of disruption in the aerodrome is love rather than hate: the opposition to a blind inhuman power can only come from something whose force lies not in aggression but in surrender. The discovery of friendship and of genuine affection and respect for a woman is the feeling the new order dreads most. In asserting his right to become a father Roy breaks the law, saving himself and the village from the invaders. This act of rebellion against the Air Vice-Marshal -- at once father and dictator -- is the springboard for change in the protagonist's life and the end of the totalitarian society.

From what we have seen so far Warner's novel, predating Nineteen Eighty-Four by eight years, depicts an authoritarian state that is founded on most of the principles that rule Oceania. One of the Party's aims is to do away with the past, both by destroying the memory of the people and by rewriting the official history of the nation. Without memory the individual is not a human being but an animal; without history a nation is in the same state. "Witness how quickly the past recedes from the thoughts of the beasts of Animal Farm," a critic has rightly pointed out.(8)

The values the Party tries to suppress are those that convey a feeling of continuity and the sense of history that cannot simply be erased by the Ministry of Truth: privacy, love, and friendship. As in the aerodrome, sex is encouraged but love is despised, and although procreation is not forbidden in Oceania, family ties are not only ignored but scorned.

Things are different with the Proles, who as a class are more tied to tradition and still preserve vestiges of the past. But neither Orwell nor Warner, in spite of their socialist loyalties, idealizes the working classes in these novels.

In The Aerodrome the degradation of the Proles is shown in two episodes that take place in the local pub. The protagonist's attitude is different on the two occasions. Before joining the aerodrome Roy attends the pub regularly and, like everybody else, apparently enjoys its noisy crowd and vulgar jolliness. After Roy has become an airman himself, he is annoyed by the coarseness and utter stupidity of the people in the pub, which now appears to him "as a somewhat sordid and uninteresting place." But at the end of the novel, when his enthusiasm for the aerodrome has thoroughly waned, he can look at the pub with new eyes, being more aware of his true desires: "From behind the door I could hear the voices of men whom I used to know, and these voices were strangely attractive to me."(9)

From all this we understand that the pub, for all its vulgarity and squalor, embodies positive values, since it constitutes a subversive form of culture that is opposed to the new order.

The same contradictory connotations characterize the pub in Nineteen Eighty-Four. Although it is the only place where the Proles can communicate freely, it is described as a rather shallow ambience where silly talk about lottery goes on together with interminable games of darts and too much noise and drinking. Being one of the few areas where proletarian culture still survives -- in spite of the new impersonal name the Party has given to it, "drinking shop" -- it is here that Winston Smith tries to get some information about what life was like before the Revolution. But the old man he attempts to interview proves too drunk and lost in irrelevant details to be of any use. The pub, like the Proles themselves, belonging to a past that has lost its function in the collective memory of the people, can no longer be an expression of the community or a meaningful institution in the new society of the total state. And if we think of the sociological and anthropological value of the pub in Mass-Observation writing of the thirties,(10) we easily understand its centrality in both Orwell's and Warner's novels.

Another significant place in Nineteen Eighty-Four that is endowed with a highly symbolic value is Mr. Charrington's junk shop. This character is himself a link with a tradition -- that of the English novel -- in which the author seems to situate his own text in an attempt to rescue it from the obliteration to which the literature of the past is condemned by the Party -- an ironic attempt, however, in light of the fact that Mr. Charrington proves to be a spy. But the place is important because it has all the flavor of "the old curiosity shop" of Dickensian memory:

> It was a little old man with long grey hair, whose face and figure as he held the light above his head and looked before him as he approached, I could plainly see. . . . The place through which he made his way at leisure was one of those receptacles for old and curious things which seem to crouch in odd corners of this town and to hide their musty treasures from the public eye in jealousy and distrust. . . . The haggard aspect of the little old man was wonderfully suited to the place; he might have groped among old churches and tombs and deserted houses and gathered all the spoils with his own hands.(11)

> He was a man of perhaps sixty, frail and bowed, with a long, benevolent nose, and mild eyes distorted by thick spec-

tacles.   His hair was almost white, but his eyebrows were
bushy and still black. . . .   His voice was soft, as though
faded, and his accent less debased than that of the majority
of proles. . . .   He led a ghostlike existence between the
tiny, dark shop, and an even tinier back kitchen. . . . Wandering about among his worthless stock, with his long nose
and thick spectacles and his bowed shoulders in the velvet
jacket, he had always vaguely the air of being a collector
rather than a tradesman.(12)

In Mr. Charrington's shop Winston finds such precious objects as the
diary, the old print of St. Clement's church, and the glass paperweight
with its air "of belonging to an age quite different from the present
one," its apparent uselessness, its absolute beauty.
   The second part of Nineteen Eighty-Four widens the theme of memory
and desire, introducing the reader to the world of pastoral romance, represented by an unpolluted piece of nature that seems to allow an escape
into the past.(13)   The Theme of past versus present is, in fact,
reasserted and emphasized by the opposition between the country and the
city.   Nature represents the only alternative to a dehumanized society:
the smells, colors and sounds of the English countryside evoke the world
of childhood and are associated with the good life.
   The country is the first place where Winston and Julia escape, re-
treating not only physically from the telescreens but from the loss of
individuality and from the feeling of not belonging to themselves but to
the Party.   The bluebells Winston picks while waiting for Julia at their
first meeting, the "old, close-bitten pasture with a footpath wandering
across it and a molehill here and there,"(14) the thrush singing in the
afternoon hush — this is the landscape that, through a series of Prous-
tian associations, reminds Winston of the Golden Country of his dream, of
his mother and sister.   So it is no surprise to find barren soil and
leafless shrubs at Winston and Julia's last desperate meeting.
   The same kind of sensations bring the past back to the protagonist
of Coming up for Air:

      . . . in a manner of speaking I am sentimental about my
      childhood — not my own particular childhood, but the civili-
      zation which I grew up in and which is now, I suppose, just
      about its last kick. And fishing is somehow typical of that
      civilization. . . . There's a kind of peacefulness even in
      the names of English coarse fish. Roach, rudd, dace, bleak,
      barbel, bream, gudgeon, pike, chub, carp, tench. They're
      solid kinds of names.(15)

George Bowling's attempt to recapture the past takes shape in the
recalling of a language whose euphony and semantics were still coincidental; then the gap between the language as it was and the language as it
is will become one of Winston's main concerns.   While in Coming up for
Air it is still possible to pronounce the words that were once part of
everyday life, in Nineteen Eighty-Four the old linguistic system is com-
pressed and deformed into the new crazy synthesis of Newspeak.(16)
   George Bowling's pleasure in ticking off a list of fishes is similar
to the delight Roy feels while he is lying in the marsh near a small pond
outside the village on a spring evening.   The first four pages of The
Aerodrome are a minute, loving description of the natural surroundings in
which the protagonist has grown up.   Birds and trees are named with the
utmost precision. With a writer like Warner, who has always disclaimed
realism as a narrative method, it is worth noticing the felicitous rendering of the differing calls of the birds ("the fierce, broken snarls of
an owl . . . , the confident whistle of the redshank . . . , the outland-
ish scream of a lapwing") and of the multifarious shapes and shades of

plants and flowers ("sedge and willows, polyanthus and honesty, the huge lilac bush and the gigantic horse-chestnuts, the libocedrus, the cedar tree and the lime tree, daffodils and bushes of laurel and lauristinus"). At the end of this description the first-person narrator comments, as if to stress its centrality to the overall economy of the novel: "I know every inch of this garden; the feel and taste of branches and twigs; the smell of leaves and grass in rain and sunshine; the consistency and colour of the soil in different parts."(17)

The narrative treatment of the countryside ties Orwell and Warner to a long tradition in the English novel and, more generally, to the town-country opposition that in British culture can be traced back to the seventeenth century. R. Williams has explained in his essay The Country and the City (1973) how a series of complex feelings and meanings have clustered around these words. The contrast needs to be situated in its historical context; new concepts develop around new experiences and cultural formations. So it happened that the idea of the sheep enclosures, in the period in which the Industrial Revolution was beginning, shifted attention from the real history and became an element of that very powerful myth of modern England — that of the "organic" community as opposed to the organized society founded on technological progress, or of the rural past versus urban industrialism.(18)

The opposition is important because it is connected to the debate around two crucial concepts of nineteenth-century thought: culture and civilization. The debate [explored by R. Williams again(19)] started with Coleridge, went on with M. Arnold, and continued in this century with T. S. Eliot and F. R. Leavis, influencing a great part of the literary and cultural production of the twenties and thirties. After World War I a new body of popular literature flourished, books "in search of England" (by H. V. Morton, P. Gibbs, F. J. H. Darton, E. Shanks, A. Bryant, C. Henry Warren) but also such sophisticated novels as those written by E. M. Forster (such as Howards End and The Longest Journey) celebrating old rural England and its glorious tradition.

The American historian Martin J. Wiener, who has explored the English ambivalence toward modern industrial society, has included R. Warner in this line of thought that demonstrates hostility toward industrialism and economic growth.(20) The inclusion is important but needs to be questioned.

The Aerodrome is no pastoral dream: the conclusion leaves no doubt about the protagonist's feelings of uncertainty and his awareness of the complexity of life. No simplistic contrasts, no clear-cut definitions; for Roy new questions arise with the destruction of the aerodrome, thinking "of how the new order . . . had been broken and the old order could never be restored, of the vices and virtues of each."(21) One of the strengths of this text lies in its ambiguity and restraint, which surround places and characters from the physical structure of the aerodrome itself ("The long hangars . . . were so disposed and camouflaged that . . . they appeared merely as rather curious modifications of the natural contours of our hills") to the personality of the Air Vice-Marshal, whose force and efficiency appeal even to young Roy, dissatisfied as he is with the weakness and confusion of his own people. His apprehensions about the future of the village (and of England, then) are mitigated by his love for nature, but contradictions are not easily resolved.(22)

The same borderline position and alien attitude (which is so effectively stated in Orwell's poem at the beginning of this paper) emerge in Coming up for Air. George Bowling's return to his home town, in order to recapture the sense of individuality and emotional security associated with the days "before the war," not only proves utterly disappointing because of the changes the place has gone through but shows him that it is impossible to go back to the past and forget about the inevitability of the new war:

War is coming. 1941, they say. . . . I'll tell you
what my stay in Lower Binfield had taught me, and it was
this. It's all going to happen. All the things you've got
at the back of your mind, the things you're terrified of, the
things that you tell yourself are just a nightmare or only
happen in foreign countries. The bombs, the food-queues, the
rubber-truncheons, the barbed wire, the coloured shirts, the
slogans, the enormous faces, the machine-guns squirting out
of bedroom windows.(23)

The protagonist's pilgrimage to his birth-place leads him to the
realization that "his understanding of himself is based upon a reality
that no longer exists, and may indeed never have existed."(24)

Yet the total effect of the novel, however bewildering, is not depressing. The epigraph, "He's dead but he won't lie down," could apply
not only to the protagonist but to British society in the thirties. The
final optimism of Coming up for Air, however, "rests in the indomitable
qualities of the 'common man' rather than in any sense of the 'inevitability of the revolution.'"(25) The orthodox Left tended to identify
these two concepts, as did Warner in his first novel, The Wild Goose
Chase (1937), which has been rightly defined as a Marxist folktale.
Orwell had criticized those intellectuals who had wanted to be anti-
Fascist without being anti-totalitarian. If this was once true of Warner, The Aerodrome reveals an important change of attitude that puts him,
as a writer, much closer to Orwell. In this novel he shares the same
hope in the fundamental "decency" of the common people and the refusal of
dogmas and abstract principles, in spite of the deep involvement in ideological and ethical issues of the time. Here lies the 'Englishness' of
the two writers, their belonging to a common tradition. To the works of
both can apply, I believe, the words A. Burgess used to describe The
Aerodrome:

. . . The language breathes England -- not just the flowers
and the grass but also the common-sense pragmatism and decency which will defeat, we think, any encroachment of totalitarian aerodromes. But we must not forget the quite uncom-
monsensical complexity.(26)

NOTES

1.   S. Hynes, The Auden Generation (London: The Bodley Head,
1976), p. 375.

2.   A. Burgess, "Introduction," in The Aerodrome (Oxford: Oxford
University Press, 1982), pp. 8-12; P. Kemp, "New Styles of Architecture,
a Change of Heart," Times Literary Supplement, December 23, 1983 (this is
the review of the TV film shown on BBC 1).

3.   John Lehmann, I Am My Brother (London: Longmans, 1960), p. 224.

4.   Rex Warner's novels are The Wild Goose Chase: An Allegory
(1937), The Professor: A Forecast (1938), The Aerodrome: A Love Story
(1941), Why Was I Killed?: A Dramatic Dialogue (1943), Men of Stones: A
Melodrama (1950), and Escapade: A Tale of Average (1953). Warner has
also written poetry (Poems, 1937; Poems and Contradictions, 1945), a collection of essays (The Cult of Power, 1946), literary criticism, and
journalism. He is also a well-known classicist.

5.   A. L. McLeod, Rex Warner: Writer (Sidney: Wentworth Press,
1964), p. 45.

6.   G. Woodcock, "Kafka and R. Warner," Focus One, ed. B. Rajan and A. Pearse (London: D. Dobson, 1945), p. 63.

7.   Warner, The Aerodrome, p. 183.

8.   W. Steinhoff, The Road to Nineteen Eighty-Four (London: Weidenfeld and Nicolson, 1975), p. 131.

9.   Warner, The Aerodrome, p. 259.

10.   See in particular The Pub and the People, published by V. Gollancz in 1943, which Orwell reviewed as soon as it came out. He also wrote an article in 1946, "The Moon and the Water," in which he sketched his ideal pub. G. Orwell, Collected Essays, Journalism and Letters (London: Secker & Warburg, 1968), III: 44-47.

11.   Charles Dickens, The Old Curiosity Shop (Harmondsworth: Penguin, 1972), pp. 46-47.

12.   George Orwell, Nineteen Eighty-Four (Harmondsworth: Penguin, 1967), pp. 78, 123.

13.   See C. Pagetti, "Nineteen Eighty-Four: cronache del dopobomba," in AA.VV., Orwell. "Nineteen Eighty-Four": il testo (Palermo: Aesthetica, 1984), p. 50.

14.   Orwell, Nineteen Eighty-Four, p. 101.

15.   George Orwell, Coming up for Air (Harmondsworth: Penguin, 1967), p. 74.

16.   See S. Manferlotti, Anti-utopia: Huxley, Orwell, Burgess (Palermo: Sellerio, 1984), p. 96.

17.   Warner, The Aerodrome, p. 16.

18.   R. Williams, The Country and the City (Frogmore: Paladin, 1975), p. 121.

19.   R. Williams, Culture and Society 1780-1950 (London: Chatto & Windus, 1958).

20.   Martin J. Wiener, English Culture and the Decline of the Industrial Spirit 1850-1980 (Cambridge, Cambridge University Press, 1982), pp. 75-77.

21.   Warner, The Aeordrome, p. 298.

22.   McLeod, Rex Warner, p. 22.

23.   Orwell, Coming up for Air, pp. 223-224.

24.   R. Johnston, The Will to Believe. Novelists of the Nineteen Thirties (Oxford: Oxford University Press, 1984), p. 120. See also F. Ferrara, La lotta contro il Leviatano (Napoli: Pironti, 1981), pp. 69-70.

25.   K. B. Hoskins, Today the Struggle (Austin and London: University of Texas Press, 1969), p.123.

26.   Burgess, "Introduction," p.12.

3.
"Sugarcandy Mountain": Thoughts on George Orwell's Critique of the Christian Doctrine of Personal Immortality

JAMES CONNORS

In a 1946 book review George Orwell described Winwood Reade's Martyrdom of Man as an "unhonoured masterpiece."(1) Unfortunately, in the years since Orwell's death Reade and his book have remained, among Orwell scholars, unhonored -- indeed, totally neglected.(2) This is regrettable for several reasons. The review contains statements indicating that Orwell's youthful exposure to Reade may have contributed greatly to his abandonment of Christianity.

> I well remember its effect on me when I first read it at
> the age of about seventeen. . . . It was a curiously liber-
> ating experience. Here was somebody who neither accepted
> Jesus as the Son of God, nor, as was the fashion at that
> time, as a Great Moral Teacher, but simply presented him as a
> fallible human being like any other -- a noble character on
> the whole, but with serious faults, and, in any case, only
> one of a long line of very similar Jewish fanatics.

Orwell's concluding observations on Reade's contribution to and relevance for the socialist movement suggest that Reade may have helped to shape Orwell's approach to the socialist struggle. He called Reade "an irregular ally of the Socialist movement, fighting chiefly on the religious front." Significantly, throughout his career Orwell himself, did a great deal of fighting on the "religious front." And the chief target of his many forays was precisely the same as Reade's -- the Christian doctrine of personal immortality.(3)

In the remainder of this paper I shall examine Orwell's critique of the Christian doctrine of immortality, relate this critique of some of his major concerns as a socialist reformer, and finally touch briefly on his rather tentative speculation on secular replacements for the Christian doctrine of immortality.

Orwell's fable, Animal Farm, offers the most convenient entry to my subject. The two passages featuring Moses the Raven's efforts to promote the belief among animal workers that an eternal life of bliss on Sugarcandy Mountain will more than compensate for the hardships endured during their present existence clearly spring from Orwell's conviction that historically the Christian concept of heaven propagated by a variety of Christian churches had served to rationalize the cynical exploitation of the common man by government. Several years earlier, in a "Notes on the Way" essay, Orwell had written that Christianity, by

> the nineteenth century . . . was already in essence a
> lie, a semi-conscious device for keeping the rich rich and

> The poor were to be contented with their poverty, because it
> would all be made up to them in a world beyond the grave. .
> . . Ten thousand a year for me, two pounds a week for you,
> but we are all the children of god.(4)

It is worth noting that Moses serves both tyrants in the fable, Farmer
Jones and Napoleon. At the outset he is Jones's special pet and chief
apologist: he is the only animal to flee the farm when Jones's regime is
toppled. His return to the farm coincides with the emergence of a new
tyranny. Orwell writes:

> He was quite unchanged, still did no work, and talked in
> the same strain as ever about Sugarcandy Mountain. . . . "Up
> there comrades," he would say solemnly . . . "up there, just
> on the other side of that dark cloud that you can see —
> there it lies, Sugarcandy Mountain, that happy country where
> we poor animals shall rest forever from our labours". . . .
> Many of the animals believed him. Their lives, they now
> reasoned, were hungry and labourious; was it not right and
> just that a better world should exist somewhere else? A
> thing that was difficult to determine was the attitude of the
> pigs towards Moses. They all declared contemptuously that
> his stories about Sugarcandy Mountain were lies, and yet they
> allowed him to remain on the farm, not working, with an al-
> lowance of a gill of beer a day.(5)

This passage clearly foreshadows one of Orwell's major future anxi-
eties — an opportunistic alliance between the Catholic church and a despotic, reactionary form of socialism. In his 1947 essay, "Towards European Unity," he wrote:

> The dangerous thing about the Church is that it is not reac-
> tionary in the ordinary sense. . . . It is perfectly capable
> of coming to terms with Socialism, or appearing to do so,
> provided that its own position is safeguarded. But if it is
> allowed to survive as a powerful organization, it will make
> the establishment of true Socialism impossible, because its
> influence is and always must be against freedom of thought
> and speech, against human equality, and against any form of
> society tending to promote earthly happiness.(6)

On occasion Orwell was expansive enough to concede (albeit with
great reluctance and numerous qualifications), that some Christians —
even Catholics — were sincerely interested in social and economic progress. But even on these occasions he invariably withdraws the concessions on the grounds that Christianity, thanks to the doctrine of personal immortality, is fundamentally otherworldly. His essay, "The Christian
Reformers," a segment of a four-part essay written for the Manchester
Evening News in 1946, offers an excellent example of my point. The bulk
of the essay is a fairly straight forward description of some of the main
figures in Christian progressive thought. This description, however, is
severely qualified by the opening and concluding paragraphs, in which Orwell analyzes the two powerful obstacles in the path of erstwhile Christian reformers. There is an institutional problem. The major Christian
churches — the Anglican, Catholic, and Lutheran — are wedded to social
orders that are rooted in the private property system. In Orwell's view
this made these churches at best very doubtful allies of those Christians
who desired far-reaching social and economic change. The other problem
derives directly from the Christian doctrine of personal immortality.

Christian thinkers . . . have to face [a] problem. They
claim rightly, that if our civilization does not regenerate
itself morally it is likely to perish. . . . But the Christian religion includes, as an integral part of itself, doctrines which large numbers of people can no longer be brought
to accept. The belief in personal immortality, for instance,
is almost certainly dwindling. If the Church clings to such
doctrines, it cannot attract the great mass of the people --
but if it abandons them, it will have lost its raison d'être
and may well disappear. This is merely to say over again
that Christianity is of its nature "otherworldly" while socialism is of its nature "this worldly."(7)

As the foregoing passage indicates, Orwell believed the conviction
of personal immortality to be declining among Europeans. While he regarded this trend as probably irreversible and salutary, he acknowledged
that the immediate and short-term consequences were nothing short of appalling. These consequences were apparent in the behavior and attitudes
of people who had been contaminated by money and power, the two major
corrupting forces in modern life. More precisely, Orwell believed that
there was virtually no crime that the bulk of the European intellectual
community and the vast majority of the members of the European business,
religious, and political establishments would not either commit or con-
done. In a 1944 "As I Please" column he put this fashionable ruthless
realism into broad perspective:

Western civilization, unlike some oriental civilizations, was founded partly on the belief in individual immortality. If one looks at the Christian religion from outside,
this belief appears far more important than the belief in
God. The Western conception of good and evil is very difficult to separate from it. There is little doubt that the
modern cult of power worship is bound up with modern man's
feeling that life here and now is the only life there is. If
death ends everything, it becomes much harder to believe that
you can be in the right even if you are defeated. . . . Sup-
posing that one can separate the two phenomena, I would say
that the decay of the belief in personal immortality has been
as important as the rise of machine civilization.(8)

In light of this statement it is not surprising that Orwell should
have devoted an entire novel, Clergyman's Daughter, to an exploration of
the consequences of abandoning faith in Christianity, or that it should
have contained a number of strategically placed passages dealing with the
problem of living a decent life in the face of the certain knowledge that
there is no afterlife.(9) Nor should it be surprising that Orwell al-
lotted as much space to the subject of personal immortality as he did in
what might be called his miscellaneous prose -- an assortment of essays,
book reviews, and editorials totaling over eight hundred items.

For illustrative purposes I would like to examine one small group of
these latter prose efforts in detail. In terms of both substance and
style, not to mention spirit, it reveals a great deal about Orwell's
moral vision, his strategies as a controversialist in behalf of socialism, and what Raynor Heppenstall has described as Orwell's extreme lit-
eral-mindedness.(10) The writings I wish to examine all relate to a controversy that erupted in the Tribune shortly after Orwell became its literary editor in late 1943.

On February 4, 1944, the Tribune printed a thoroughly tasteless
review of Victoria Sackville-West's The Eagle and the Dove by Charles
Hamblett. Part of it read: "This book is crammed with facts about Holy

Freaks who have capered elliptically Godwards."(11) A week later a Catholic <u>Tribune</u> reader, Mary Murphy, wrote a letter protesting the vulgarity
of Hamblett's review. Orwell, in his capacity as literary editor, wrote
in defense of Hamblett and received a still stronger letter of protest
from Murphy. On March 3, 1944, Orwell made the question of personal immortality the major topic of his "As I Please" column. Using the alleged
miraculous activity of Christian saints as a springboard, Orwell went on
to charge that Christian intellectuals were involved in a pathetic game
of self-deceit: they concealed their own disbelief in doctrines such as
personal immortality from themselves by the transparently thin argument
that such doctrines do not have to be taken literally.(12) Orwell's editorial provoked considerable correspondence, pro and con, from other
<u>Tribune</u> readers, and a rejoinder from the prominent Anglican apologist,
Sidney Dark, in the <u>Malvern Torch</u>. Dark maintained that "'seventy-five
percent (of the British population) would confess to a vague belief in
survival.'" Orwell responded to Dark's argument in his April 14, 1944,
"As I Please" column:(13)

>   The point Mr. Dark has missed is that the belief [in im-
>   mortality], such as it is, hasn't the actuality that it had
>   for our forefathers. Never, literally never in recent years,
>   have I met anyone who gave me the impression of believing in
>   the next world as firmly as he believed in the existence of,
>   for instance, Australia. Belief in the next world does not
>   influence conduct as it would if it were genuine. With that
>   endless existence beyond death to look forward to, how triv-
>   ial our lives would seem. Most Christians profess to believe
>   in Hell. Yet have you ever met a Christian who seemed as
>   afraid of Hell as he was of cancer? Even very devout Chris-
>   tians will make jokes about Hell. They wouldn't make jokes
>   about leprosy, or RAF pilots with their faces burnt away; the
>   subject is too painful.

At this point in his essay Orwell quoted from memory a comic poem by G.
K. Chesterton on the consequences of selling one's soul. Part of the
poem read:

>   It's a pity that Poppa has sold his soul,
>   It makes him sizzle at breakfast so.
>   The money was useful, but still on the whole,
>   It's a pity that Poppa has sold his soul.

Orwell's gloss on the poem was scathing:

>   Chesterton, a Catholic, would presumably have said that he
>   believed in Hell. If his next-door neighbour had been burnt
>   to death, he would not have written a comic poem about it,
>   yet he can make jokes about somebody being fried for millions
>   of years. I say that such belief has no reality. It is sham
>   currency, like the money in Samuel Butler's Musical Banks.

Orwell's essay elicited another barrage of letters from <u>Tribune</u> readers, including one from a minor versifier, A. M. Currie. Currie announced that he, not Chesterton, was the author of the poem quoted by
Orwell. He declared himself, moreover, an agnostic and in full agreement
with Orwell's arguments regarding the declining belief in personal immortality. Orwell's response is revealing: he apologized for the false
attribution but stubbornly maintained that the mere fact that Chesterton
had printed the poem in his own periodical, <u>G. K.'s Weekly,</u> bore out his

(Orwell's) main contention that Christians were frivolously insincere on the question of the reality of Hell.(14)

The question of Christian self-deceit and insincerity on the matter of personal immortality is directly linked to the larger moral issue that preoccupied Orwell throughout his life: orthodoxy and lying. It is too often overlooked that Orwell usually included Christian intellectuals, especially Catholic intellectuals, in his comprehensive indictments of the English and European intellectual class. To Orwell the mind-sets of Communists and Catholics were remarkably similar. "Queer," he wrote in Road to Wigan Pier, "that Comrade Mirsky's spiritual brother should be Father _____ . The Communist and Catholic are not saying the same thing, in a sense they are even saying opposite things, and each would gladly boil the other in oil if circumstances permitted; but from the point of view of an outsider they are very much alike."(15) What created the similarity for Orwell was orthodoxy -- complete orthodoxy, the great-est menace to the integrity of modern intellectual life.

Orthodoxy in Orwell's view led to dishonesty. In 1942 he wrote:

> In theory it is still possible to be an orthodox reli-gious believer without being intellectually crippled in the process; but it is far from easy, and in practice books by orthodox believers usually show the same cramped, blinkered outlook as books by orthodox Stalinists or others who are mentally unfree.(16)

A few months earlier he had made the same point in a blazing rage. "The Catholic gang, the Stalinist gang. . . . My case against all of them is that they write mentally dishonest propaganda."(17) Of all the lies told by Christian intellectuals the biggest lie, the most serious lie, con-cerned the doctrine of personal immortality. To be sure, Orwell was a-ware that the actual decline in the belief in personal immortality had had frightening results. At the same time, he insisted that the reasons for this development needed to be faced squarely and courageously. The Christian intellectual, however, in defending the indefensible was not only compromising his own intellectual integrity, but was obscuring the extent and seriousness of Europe's moral crisis. He was therefore con-tributing to the postponement of the day when Europeans would identify and accept a suitable secular replacement. In 1944 Orwell wrote:

> What I want to point out is that its disappearance has left a big hole. . . . Reared for thousands of years on the notion that the individual survives, man has got to make a considerable psychological effort to get used to the notion that the individual perishes. He is not likely to salvage civilization unless he can evolve a system of good and evil which is independent of heaven and hell. . . . One cannot have any worthwhile picture of the future unless one realizes how much we have lost by the decay of Christianity. Few so-cialists seem to be aware of this. And Catholic intellectu-als who cling to the letter of the Creeds while reading into them meanings they were never meant to have, and who snigger at anyone simple enough to suppose that the Fathers of the Church meant what they said, are simply raising smoke-screens to conceal their own disbelief from themselves.(18)

Although Orwell spent a lifetime attacking the Christian doctrine of personal immortality, he recognized the authenticity of the human need that underlay the doctrine. Commenting in 1940 on the distortion of Marx by many of his modern disciples, Orwell noted that too often the impres-sion is conveyed that Marx viewed religion as merely a drug. The line,

"Religion is the opium of the people," said Orwell, needed to be placed in context with the previous line "Religion is the sigh of the soul in a soulless world." The two lines together, Orwell argued, showed that Marx saw religion as "something the people created for themselves to supply a need that he recognized to be a real one."(19) From Orwell's other writings it seems clear that he believed that this need would still exist even after massive economic reforms had been realized. "Any thinking socialist," he wrote in 1943, "will concede to the Catholic that when economic injustice has been righted, the fundamental problem of man's place in the universe will still remain."(20) Put somewhat differently, Orwell seems to have felt that some secular replacement for the Christian heaven was required as part of a meaningful European moral reform.

Actually he believed that such secular replacements had been in the process of formation for a number of years. In a 1940 "Notes on the Way" essay Orwell commented at length on Malcolm Muggeridge's The Thirties, a book in which the author had argued that the only solution for the moral anarchy spreading throughout Europe was to return to the traditional doctrines of Christianity. Orwell disagreed and built his argument on a line from one of Kipling's poems, "Who dies if England lives." Two questions, said Orwell, were central to the problem of moral reform in Europe. Could human beings develop a sense of community without believing in God as a common father? Could a viable secular morality be created without reliance on otherworldly forms of immortality? Orwell answered yes to both questions. People, he said, were already developing a sense of community in a fragmentary fashion -- nation, race, and class -- and were merging their desire for immortality with the hope and expectation that such communities would endure far into the future.

> Man is not an individual, he is only a cell in an ever-lasting body, and he is dimly aware of it. . . . 'Who dies if England live' sounds like a piece of bombast, but if you alter England to whatever you prefer, you can see that it expresses one of the main motives of human conduct. People sacrifice themselves for the sake of fragmentary communities. . . . A very slight increase in consciousness, and their sense of loyalty could be transferred to humanity itself.(21)

Although Orwell never discussed the secular replacements for the Christian heaven in such a direct way again, these replacements do figure in many of his subsequent writings. Habitually Orwell censures that which promotes a narrow, sectarian loyalty and praises that which enlarges the boundaries of human loyalty and concern. In his essay "Notes of Nationalism" (1945), it is the concept of a single humanity that sustains his assault on those whose moral vision is limited to a particular group.(22) Significantly, both narrow and broad secular replacements for the Christian heaven are present in Orwell's final work, Nineteen Eighty-Four. O'Brien at one point tells Winston Smith that the only way to escape the failure that death brings is to make "utter submission" and to merge himself in the Party. "Can you not understand that the death of the individual is not death? The Party is immortal."(23) Yet O'Brien's way is not the only way. The yearning for immortality can also be satisfied by a broad loyalty to suffering humanity. Winston's final reflection on the Proles, where he is deeply moved by a sense of solidarity among all exploited peoples, captures the core of Orwell's own secular humanist faith and provides a fitting conclusion to my presentation.

> It was curious to think that the sky was the same for everybody, in Eurasia or Eastasia as well as here. And the people under the sky were also very much the same -- everywhere, all over the world, hundreds and thousands of millions

of people just like this [Prole woman]. . . . If there was
hope it lay in the Proles! . . . The future belonged to the
Proles. . . . Sooner or later it would happen: strength
would turn into consciousness. The Proles were immortal:
you could not doubt it when you looked at the valiant figure
in the yard. In the end their awakening would come. And until that happened, though it might be a thousand years, they
would stay alive against all odds, like birds, passing on
from body to body the vitality which the Party did not share
and could not kill.(24)

NOTES

1.   Review of Winwood Reade's The Martyrdom of Man in Collected Essays, Journalism and Letters, IV, pp. 116-120. Hereafter cited as CEJL.
Except for notes 10 and 11, all citations are to Orwell's writings.

2.   Neither Stansky and Abrahams nor Bernard Crick mentioned Reade.
The omission I believe reflects a reluctance to confront directly the extent and significance of Orwell's hostility to Christianity.

3.   It is worth noting that Orwell was aware of H. G. Wells's deep
admiration for Reade. Reade is a major cultural hero in some of the novels Wells wrote while Orwell was at Eton. See, for example, the testimony of various characters in Joan and Peter (1918) to Reade's salutary
influence on their lives. For the Reade-Wells connection, see Orwell's
obituary essay on Wells in the Manchester Evening News, August 14, 1946.

4.   "Notes on the Way" in CEJL, II: 15-19.

5.   Animal Farm, (New York: New American Library), edition, p.
109.

6.   "Toward European Unity" in CEJL, IV: 370-375.

7.   "The Christian Reformers" in Manchester Evening News, February
7, 1946, p. 2.

8.   "As I Please," March 3, 1944, in CEJL, III: 101-104.

9.   See Clergyman's Daughter, pp. 315-318, where Dorothy confronts
the problem of living a life of service to her father's congregation
knowing that death ends everything.

10.   Heppenstall, who roamed briefly with Orwell during 1935,
writes: "The distinctiveness of print meant a great deal to Orwell. He
would praise or condemn people on the evidence of a single sentence that
they could be shown to have written." See his Four Absentees, p. 62.

11.   Charles Hamblett, review of Victoria Sackville-West's The Eagle
and the Dove in Tribune, February 4, 1944.

12.   CEJL, III: 101-104.

13.   CEJL, III: 119-122.

14.   For Currie's letter and Orwell's response, see Tribune, May 26,
1944.

15.   Road to Wigan Pier, pp. 177-182.

16.   Review of T. S. Eliot's Burnt Norton in CEJL, II: 236–242.

17.   Letter to the Partisan Review in CEJL, II: 229.

18.   "As I Please," March 3, 1944, in CEJL, III: 101–104.

19.   "Notes on the Way" in CEJL, II: 15–19.

20.   "As I Please," December 24, 1943, in CEJL, III: 63–65.

21.   "Notes on the Way," CEJL, II: 15–19.

22.   "Notes on Nationalism" in CEJL, III: 361–380.

23.   Nineteen Eighty-Four (New York: Harcourt Brace and World Edition), pp. 117–119.

24.   Ibid., p. 98.

4.
Beyond Orwell: Clarity and the English Language
MADELYN FLAMMIA

George Orwell's novel <u>Nineteen Eighty-Four</u> presents the catastrophic outcome of a perversion of language by politics and politics by language. But it is the classic essay, "Politics and the English Language," that pretends to finger the inner mechanisms effecting that perversion of plain sense. Because the English profession at large has, over the years, massively accepted -- seemingly without question — the Orwellian diagnosis and recommended cure of the odd disease infecting the alliance of English and politics (this is quite likely the most frequently encountered text in freshman readers!), the essay is due for a reexamination in the light of structuralism and poststructuralism. What these developments bring most into question is the pedagogic feasiblity of any simple set of absolute "rules" that pretend to describe a model style by static abstractions: clarity, brevity, variety, vitality, imagination.

Orwell particularly stresses the importance of clarity and refers to it repeatedly throughout the essay. He refers to the way he intends to make things "clear" for his readers. He makes statements such as the following: "by that time the meaning of what I have said here will have become clearer."(1) Discussing the "defence of the English language" he says, "It (the defence) has nothing to do with correct grammar and syntax, which are of no importance so long as one makes one's meaning clear, or with the avoidance of Americanisms, or with having what is called a 'good prose style.'"

However, a "good prose style" is, of course, clear. Orwell's rules tell a writer how to achieve this indispensable "clarity." Yet before one accepts them wholeheartedly, the notion of clarity itself must be examined more closely. "Since Aristotle," writes Richard Lanham, "it has figured as a central goal for verbal expression. Theorists, without giving the matter special thought, seem to have considered clarity a property of the text."(2) Similarly meaning is believed to reside within the "word."

Although Orwell points out in his first paragraph the fallacy of the belief "that language is a natural growth and not an instrument which we shape for our own purposes," he seems to overlook the implications of this realization in his essay. He discusses language in terms of "concreteness" and makes the statement "The whole tendency of modern prose is away from concreteness" as a criticism. Orwell suggests that good writing uses words that call up images of "concrete" objects and not abstract notions. He belongs to a school that thinks, as Coward and Ellis say, "in terms of a real world 'out there' which is accessible to reason, rather than a world which is produced by the whole ensemble of social activities, including that of conceptualisation in language."(3)

Orwell seems to believe that words that refer to concrete objects are in some way less removed from those objects and therefore less deceptive or dishonest. For someone like Jacques Derrida, who takes a view of language radically opposed to Orwell's, this makes no sense. Derrida's problematic and rather extreme view of language is that every word is as potentially misleading as the next. Derrida's disturbing theory is, in fact, diametrically opposed to Orwell's. He states:

> The written signifier is always technical and representative. It has no constitutive meaning. This derivation is the very origin of the notion of the 'signifier.' The notion of the sign always implies within itself the distinction between signifier and signified, even if, as Saussure argues, they are distinguished simply as the two faces of one and the same leaf.(4)

Orwell, however, speaks of the importance of letting "the meaning choose the word, and not the other way about." Again he seems to be implying that the relationship between the signifier and the signified is stable and dependable for some classes or groups of words but not for others. He makes the error of believing that thought predates language and fails to see that people are enmeshed in their language system.(5) Coward and Ellis state that "the human subject is constructed by a structure whose very existence escapes his gaze."(6) Orwell, on the other hand, sees people as potentially always in charge unless they let their guard down and give in (due to laziness). "In prose, the worst thing one can do with words is to surrender to them."

When he speaks in the following sentences of putting off "using words as long as possible" and getting "one's meaning as clear as one can through pictures or sensations," he actually seems to be reaching back to the origin of written language use when pictures were used to communicate experience to those not present. To quote Derrida:

> The same content, formerly communicated by gestures and sounds, will henceforth be transmitted by writing, by successively different modes of notation, from pictographic writing of the Egyptians and the ideographic writing of the Chinese.(7)

Derrida's essay "Signature Event Context" discusses the "absence of referent" as well as the way in which the written sign "breaks with its context."(8) For Orwell the break from context occurs because of failure on the writer's part and a weakness in the writing. From Derrida's troubling perspective, however, the "breaking force is not an accidental predicate but the very structure of the written text."(9)

Orwell attacks certain kinds of writing, particularly political writing, for being deliberately misleading. This writing is considered misleading primarily because it moves in the direction of abstraction rather than concreteness — it refuses to be clear! Yet even when one rejects Derrida's extremist deconstruction or destruction of language, a real problem remains. The notion of "clarity" must be looked at contextually, as must Orwell's essay itself.

First of all, the written sign is believed to have a "real context." For Orwell this context is one always controlled consciously by the writer: "Afterwards one can choose -- not simply accept -- the phrases that will best cover the meaning, and then switch round and decide what impression one's words are likely to make on another person." Communication is facilitated by language because language is "an instrument for expressing and not for concealing or preventing thought." The only conceivable problem is that someone will attempt to use the instrument in a clumsy or dishonest way.

Orwell fails to take into account the occasional inadequacy of the "instrument" itself. He does not see the fact that by its very nature language is alway lending itself to confusion and duplicity. Again Derrida takes this problem of context to the extreme by suggesting that it begins simultaneously with the production of written language. Derrida believes that language by its very nature has the potential of being cut off from referents or signifieds and thereby from its context and from communication. This calls into question the possibility of any communication in a way too disturbing to embrace. However, it also serves effectively to contrast with the picture Orwell presents. Orwell sees the problem in the way language is used (hence his rules to prevent misuse) rather than in language itself. He, too, sees language in absolute terms; he believes it is potentially capable of one hundred percent clear communication.

The second problem with context applied not to the slipperiness of language in general but to the relationship between context and style in particular. Orwell states didactically that "it is clear that the decline of a language must ultimately have political and economic causes." He assumes not only that political writing is more "hackneyed" and "abstract" than other kinds of discourse but also that in its fall from grace it can bring both the current state of the English language and of all modern thought tumbling down after it.

One must react to Orwell's assumption in several ways, the first of which has to do with style. He holds political language up as "especially bad" because "the concrete melts into the abstract." Political writing consists "less and less of words chosen for the sake of their meaning." The five examples Orwell gives the reader to "illustrate various of the mental vices" are predominantly drawn from political rhetoric.

Orwell treats political rhetoric as though it were the same as all other kinds of discourse. He then judges its style to be "bad" primarily on the basis of a single criterion -- clarity. Two objections may be raised at this point. First, even if one does not question the possibility of attaining clarity in language use, as Derrida does to an extreme, one may very well question whether clarity has always been and should be the intention of language use.

Second, Orwell sees "clarity" as a constant. If one writes something clear today, it will be clear forever. As already noted, the problem of "essential drift" may come into play, although not to the degree of unintelligibility that Derrida suggests. Another problem is that of context. As Lanham states, "Clarity no more permits objective standards than custom itself."(10) One man's jargon is another man's clarity. In fact Orwell's own clarity may be jargon to students reading the 1946 essay some 38 years later. As Cleo McNelly points out in her essay "On Not Teaching Orwell": "his dire warnings on the use of cliche and jargon do not even cover his own writing, which is in some ways a highly sophisticated tour de force predicated on the ability to employ them both."(11)

Orwell admits this himself by saying to the reader, "Look back through this essay, and for certain you will find that I have again and again committed the very faults I am protesting against." This admission, which may do something for the writer's ethos, leaves students perplexed as to how to proceed in their own writing. It is bad enough to give students advice that boils down to "Do as I say but not as I do," but it is intolerable to suggest "Do as I say, not as I do -- some of the time." Now the student is in a real double bind.

The problem is further complicated when clarity is exposed as something less than the god it was traditionally held to be. The task for Orwell and the student alike lies in recognizing political rhetoric for what it is and being aware of the possibility of an even more subtle deception taking place under the guise of clarity. Lanham has noted this paradox:

> Rhetorical style seems less miraculous because it does not hide the amplifying powers of language, it waves them in our faces. The real deceiver is the plain stylist who pretends to put all his cards on the table. Clarity, then, is a cheat, an illusion.(12)

Political rhetoric is, in many cases, self-conscious language use. Repetition of key phrases is used to establish conformity and arouse emotions. It does not pretend to objectivity but rather draws attention to its desire to create identification and persuasion in the audience being addressed.

There exists another kind of rhetoric that is more damaging than the obvious bombast of the Communist pamphlet quoted by Orwell. It is a rhetoric not of revolution but of the status quo. Although he does not discuss this aspect of political writing directly, his rule four ("Never use the passive where you can use the active") applies aptly to the kind of writing intended to uphold the current system. The passive voice suggests that what is being described is simply the way things are. This kind of political ideology strives to produce a "natural attitude" so the "existing relations of power are not only accepted but perceived precisely as the way things are, ought to be and will be."(13)

This ideology is perhaps one of the most valuable weapons that leaders and oppressors have at their disposal. Conversely, the realization by the oppressed that what they are experiencing "is not a given destiny but the result of an unjust order"(14) is often a powerful means toward achieving liberation. Paulo Freire stresses the necessity of teaching the oppressed to think critically. This is, of course, something invaluable for students to learn also.

It is therefore the more subtle and insidious kind of rhetoric, the rhetoric that does not call attention to itself as rhetoric at all, that must be looked at more critically. Orwell's own essay may be reexamined and, perhaps, recontextualized in this light.

Orwell would have the reader believe that his main concern, his only concern, is with the decay of the English language. He gives five examples of "bad" English at the beginning of his essay. Surprisingly at least two of these examples explicitly discuss their concerns with the decrepit state of the language. It is possible to write badly about how bad written English has become on the whole.

It is also possible to frame an argument about the decline of language in general in such a way that it becomes an attack on political rhetoric and Marxism in particular. It seems Orwell cannot help but reveal his own motives in the Burkean sense when he attempts to "unmask" his adversaries.(15) Orwell takes exception to certain tired political phrases such as "iron heel, blood-stained tyranny, free peoples of the world." He dismissed them as jargon (rule five) and therefore enemies of good standard English.

Yet the reader senses that Orwell's real concern is with something much deeper. As Lanham has noted in a discussion of style and clarity, "When we call a style inappropriate, we mean that we don't like the reality it creates, that we find that reality incoherent or jejune . . . we should recognize the disagreement as with reality, not style."(16)

Orwell wishes to attack Marxism; his "disagreement" is with dialectical materialism that can be said to attack or disprove certain of his own cherished notions about language. He attempts to discredit Marxist political language by showing it to be and to do what political language is and does by definition. As Burke says, "You can even attack a thing

on the grounds that it is exactly what it claims to be." (17)   The rules
Orwell lays down which seem to be of questionable value for students may,
if each one is reversed or negated, serve as rules or guidelines for bud-
ding political writers, ending with the marvelously apt: "Sooner than
break any of the rules say something outright barbarous."

If students can be made to see Orwell's rhetorical motive and use
his piece as a model of argument, their acumen as both writers and critical readers may be enhanced. Students will probably benefit more from an
awareness of the context in which Orwell writes than even the brightest
and most conscientious among them could from an attempt to apply his misleading rules.

Nevertheless the real value of Orwell as a model -- and he does have
value -- is as a model of a particular kind of essay (argument) about a
particular kind of discourse (political). Orwell is concerned with per-
suading the reader that the English language is "in a bad way" because of
bad political writing, particularly Marxist writing. Being a good rhet-
orician, he will use any available means to persuade his audience. He
will break all his own rules rather than fail to convince his readers.
Orwell takes a "potshot" at the Marxist "jackboot" even while he tosses
off metaphors such as "sections of a prefabricated henhouse," metaphors
that often are like "tea leaves blocking a sink." The temptation becomes
irresistable and it is largely a matter of personal taste whether or not
"the cavalry horses answering the bugle" strike one as barbarous.

However, Orwell carries readers along by the sheer energy of his argument.   He displays the horrors of certain political realities even
while his manifest content is concerned with the "not un-formation." Orwell, writing in 1946, is expressing legitimate concerns regarding the
power of rhetoric to mislead the masses. One suspects that he would like
to "jeer" more than just a phrase or two into the "dustbin."

But Orwell's Achilles heel seems to be his belief in the neutrality
of language. Even as he uses it to gain his own position of advantage
with the reader he longs for sincerity in language. One may turn Orwell's own words against him to suggest that the "greatest enemy of sincerity is seemingly clear language." Orwell finds fault with political
language for doing what all language does to some degree -- being unclear
and misleading.

Students can be shown the mechanics of Orwell's subtle persuasion
juxtaposed both to the more obviously inflated rhetoric of politicians
and to political writings that are similarly subtle. Political discourse
can be seen as only gradation in a scale of advantage-seeking rhetoric.
The formulation of an awareness of manifest and latent contents across a
series of discourses is an intrinsic part of critical reading.

Orwell's "Politics and the English Language" may be shown to students not with the injunction "Go do this" but with the explanation "See
how this works and where it succeeds and fails." It may simply be used
as an example of argument. It also serves as an example of the inescapable fact that rhetoric, even in the hands of a great writer, always has
as one of its aims a desire to "gain advantage."(18)

Beyond its functioning as a model of argument, Orwell's essay may be
approached as an example of the necessity -- or, rather, the inescapa-
bility -- of viewing all texts in relation to one another; although Orwell himself might deny this fact. Tony Bennett in Formalism and Marxism
makes this point:

> The test is not the issuing source of meaning. . . .
> The social process of culture takes place not within texts
> but between texts, and between texts and readers: not some
> ideal, disembodied reader, but historically concrete readers
> whose act of reading is conditioned, in part by the text it

is true, but also by the whole ensemble of ideological relationships which bear upon the incessant production and repro-
duction of texts.(19)

Orwell's text is useful, then, when it is recontextualized, when it
is studied in relation to other pieces of political rhetoric both more
and less dogmatic than it is.   This rhetoric may range from Communist
pamphlets to the political speeches of presidential candidates in 1984.
Then the student will see that while the "in" term may be "build down" as
opposed to the once popular "jackboot," political rhetoric always ignores
Orwell's rules to a greater or lesser degree.   The composition student
too may choose to ignore Orwell's rules even while heeding the example of
Orwell's essay as a subtle, persuasive argument.

NOTES

1   George Orwell, "Politics and the English Language," in The Norton Reader, 5th ed. Arthur M. Eastman et al., ed., (New York: W. W. Norton & Company, 1980), pp. 369-380. All subsequent references will be to
this edition.

2.   Richard A. Lanham, The Motives of Eloquence (New Haven: Yale
University Press, 1976), p. 20.

3.   Rosalind Coward and John Ellis, Language and Materialism (London: Routledge & Kegan Paul, 1977), p. 36.

4.   Jacques Derrida, Of Grammatology, trans. Gayatri Chakravorty
Spivak (Baltimore: Johns Hopkins University Press, 1976), p. 11.

5.   Coward and Ellis, Language and Materialism, p. 23.

6.   Ibid., p. 20.

7.   Jacques Derrida, "Signature Event Context," in Glyph, ed.
Samuel Weber and Henry Sussman (Baltimore: Johns Hopkins University
Press, 1977), p. 176.

8.   Ibid., p. 182.

9.   Ibid., p. 182.

10.   Lanham, Motives of Eloquence, p. 21.

11.   Cleo McNelly, "On Not Teaching Orwell," College English 38, no.
6 (1977): 556.

12.   Lanham, Motives of Eloquence, p. 22.

13.   Coward and Ellis, Language and Materialism, p. 68.

14.   Paulo Freire, Pedagogy of the Oppressed, trans. Myra Bergman
Ramos (New York: Continuum, 1983), p. 28.

15.   Kenneth Burke, A Rhetoric of Motives (Berkeley: University of
California Press, 1969), p. 99.

16.   Lanham, Motives of Eloquence, p. 28.

17.   Burke, A Rhetoric of Motives, pp. 97-98.

18.   Ibid., p. 60.

19.   Tony Bennett, Formalism and Marxism (London: Methuen & Co. Ltd., 1979), pp. 174–175.

5.
The Rhetoric of *Down and Out in Paris and London*

JOHN P. FRAZEE

George Orwell's first published book, Down and Out in Paris and London
(1933), is a powerful piece of first-person reportage. Through vividly
detailed incidents Orwell presents a picture of the life he led on the
fringes of poverty, first as a dishwasher in Paris and then on the tramp
in London. However, Down and Out is not quite, as one critic has argued,
"straight autobiography."(1) We know, for example, that Orwell's experience in London actually preceded his Paris experience. This manipulation
of the facts points the way to my thesis: Orwell is less interested in
the facts of his experience than in the lesson he learned from it, a lesson alien to the assumptions and experience of his liberal educated middle-class English audience. To bring his alien and alienating message
home to this audience, Orwell transforms the raw material of his experience into an artful rhetorical construction, some details of which I propose to examine.(2)

Apart from the change in chronology, the most important aspect of
the rhetoric of Down and Out is the creation of a narrator who resembles,
and by resembling gains the trust of, Orwell's English, middle-class
reader.(3) The creation of this narrator, together with the use of other, overtly literary devices, draws readers into an experience designed
to awaken their sleeping conscience and shake their complacent, liberal
faith in social institutions to take care of human needs.

With the opening paragraphs of the book Orwell establishes important
qualities of the narrator and his relation to the audience. Down and Out
begins in the manner (and with approximations of the typographic conventions) of a play:

> The Rue du Coq d'Or, Paris, seven in the morning. A
> succession of furious, choking yells from the street. Madame
> Monce, who kept the little hotel opposite mine, had come out
> on to the pavement to address a lodger on the third floor.
> Her bare feet were stuck into sabots and her grey hair was
> streaming down.
> Madame Monce: "Salope! Salope! How many times have I
> told you not to squash bugs on the wallpaper? Do you think
> you've bought the hotel, eh? Why can't you throw them out of
> the window like everyone else? Putain! Salope!"
> The woman on the third floor: "Vache!"
> Thereupon a whole variegated chorus of yells, as windows
> were flung open on every side and half the street joined in
> the quarrel. They shut up abruptly ten minutes later, when a
> squadron of cavalry rode past and people stopped shouting to
> look at them.

> I sketch this scene, just to convey something of the
> spirit of the Rue du Coq d'Or. . . . Quarrels, and the deso-
> late cries of street hawkers, and the shouts of children
> chasing orange-peel over the cobbles, and at night loud sing-
> ing and the sour reek of the refuse-carts, made up the atmo-
> sphere of the street.(4)

The narrator of this "scene" is observant, unemotional, and unsentimen-
tal. His tone is reassuringly understated, humorously ironic. These
opening paragraphs invite readers to sit back in their front-row seats,
as it were, while the conventions of the dramatic mode place them in a
comfortably passive state, a voyeur secure in the hands of the narrator.
    Orwell then plunges readers into the lives of the people of the
scene described as the narrator suddenly finds himself "down and out."
The narrator's transition from observer to actor runs the risk of creating anxiety on the part of the audience, but Orwell manages the transition in such a way as to minimize the anxiety. For the narrator proves
as detached about his own actions as he has been about those of the people on the Paris street, giving only the most cursory and unemotional explanation for his sudden poverty. He simply states that as his money began to run out, he decided to look for a job. But then a lodger in his
boarding house made off with his money — all but forty-seven francs. He
comments laconically: "This put an end to my plans of looking for work.
I had now got to live at the rate of about six francs a day, and from the
start it was too difficult to leave much thought for anything else. It
was now that my experiences of poverty began" (p. 16). With this brief
explanation he launches into a detailed description of his first reactions to poverty almost with a sense of relief. One has the feeling that
the narrator has in no way exhausted the possibilities for employment or
other means to escape his imminent poverty. On the contrary, he seems to
seek his "experiences of poverty" as experience. His almost existential
attitude helps to minimize the reader's feelings of anxiety.
    Having created a narrator who can reliably present the experience of
poverty, Orwell makes him a reliable evaluator of that experience. The
narrator views his experiences from a distinctly English point of view,
measuring almost everything he described by English standards. He applies these standards in the most straightforward and the most subtle of
ways. For example, he consistently reduces the economic realities of the
Paris slum to their English equivalents. One can get drunk in a tiny
bistro "for the equivalent of a shilling" (p. 6). Moreover the atmosphere of these bistros compares quite favorably with that of their English equivalents: "I wish one could find a pub in London a quarter as
cheery" (p. 10). Yet the narrator's preoccupation with English standards
does more than provide a yardstick by which to measure his external observations. It also exerts a strong though subtle influence on his behavior. For example, his description of his first reactions to being
poor raises questions about his point of view that can be answered only
by referring to his English-ness:

> It is altogether curious, your first contact with pov-
> erty. You have thought so much about poverty. . . . You
> thought it would be quite simple; it is extraordinarily com-
> plicated. You thought it would be terrible; it is merely
> squalid and boring. It is the peculiar lowness of poverty
> that you discover first; the shifts that it puts you to, the
> complicated meanness, the crust wiping.
>   You discover, for instance, the secrecy attaching to
> poverty. . . . Sometimes, to keep up appearances, you have
> to spend sixty centimes on a drink, and go correspondingly
> short of food. (pp. 16-17)

The narrator continues in this vein for more than two pages, emphasizing the necessity of maintaining certain standards of sanitation, behavior, and appearance, even at the sacrifice of physical well-being. Given the situation, his scrupulosity seems strange: he is, after all, living in a slum where poverty is a way of life. Yet his first instinct is to "keep up appearance." The source of that instinct becomes clear if we examine the striking shift in style in the passage itself. Here for the first time the narrator describes his reactions not merely as his own but as "your" reactions. In fact, by my count the words "you" and "yours" are used over eighty times in the course of this two-page passage, and the repetition is not without effect. The "you" of this passage is, of course, Orwell's audience -- an English audience with English standards. This passage has a three fold effect. First, it illustrates in a compelling way the system of values that the narrator brings to his foreign experience. Second, it shows that these standards of value exert an integral and immensely powerful force on the narrator's and, by implication, the English reader's behavior. And third, the repetition of "you" draws the reader into more direct imaginative engagement with this experience and with the experiences that follow.

The reader's deepening engagement with the experience of the narrator and the narrator's (very English) insistence on the importance of appearances are both put to use in the major episode of the Paris segment of the book, when the narrator describes his experience as a plongeur, or dishwasher, in a fashionable French restaurant. Aside from being a shocking expose of French restaurants, the episode presents in microcosm a picture of the way Paris society operates:

> It was amusing to look round the filthy little scullery and think that only a double door was between us and the dining room. There sat the customers in all their splendour -- spotless table-cloths, bowls of flowers, mirrors and gilt cornices and painted cherubim; and here, just a few feet away, we in our disgusting filth. For it really was disgusting filth. (pp. 67-68)

The narrator goes on to describe in elaborate detail the nature and extent of the filth that lurks just below the surface of the life of the well-to-do in Paris. For a reader who shared the narrator's concern for appearances, this description invites the troubling recognition that his concern leaves him vulnerable to the kind of manipulation practiced by the staff on the wealthy patrons of this hotel. Orwell exploits this recognition in the London half of the book.

Another striking feature of this restaurant microcosm is that, for all the obvious differences between the two levels of society on either side of the restaurant wall, the organizations of the two societies mirror each other. The narrator describes in some detail what he calls "the elaborate caste system" (p. 70) of the hotel staff. At the very bottom is the plongeur, and it is his lot that particularly interests the narrator:

> Theirs is a job which offers no prospects, is intensely exhausting, and at the same time has not a trace of skill or interest. . . . They have no way of escaping from this life, for they cannot save a penny from their wages, and working from sixty to a hundred hours a week leaves them no time to train for anything else. . . .
> And yet the plongeurs, low as they are, also have a kind of pride. (p. 78)

The narrator finds the plongeurs' plight horrible, and in his analysis of "the social significance of a plongeur's life" (p. 116) denounces it as a form of slavery perpetuated by the educated classes, who "acquiesce in the process, because they know nothing about [the plongeur] and consequently are afraid of him" (p. 121). This fear is based, too, on the mistaken notion "that there is some mysterious, fundamental difference between rich and poor" (p. 120).

The stinging tone of his analysis indicates that a significant change has taken place in the detached, objective narrator of the opening pages of the book. Now deeply involved, he has acquired definite and (by middle-class standards) radical opinions about the significance of his experience — although he dismisses those opinions as "no doubt largely platitudes" (p. 121). But where does the narrator's altered attitude leave the reader who initially took some comfort in his detachment, objectivity, and middle-class English point of view?

The fact is that Orwell's rhetoric in this passage is carefully constructed to provide the reader with a way to deal with the potentially alienating force of the narrator's analysis, for his attack is aimed explicitly at those who are ignorant of the life of the stratum of society represented by the plongeur. But the reader has been presented with a detailed and reliable account of this kind of life. Accordingly the reader can join in the narrator's charge that "intelligent, cultivated people, the very people who might be expected to have liberal opinions, never do mix with the poor" (p. 120), secure in the knowledge that he now has a rather clear idea of what the life of the poor is like. Such a response by anyone who professes "to have liberal opinions" involves at least the acknowledgment that the problem of poverty exists. This acknowledgment is made easier because the experiences described and evaluated by the narrator do, after all, take place in the foreign slums of Paris. This fact leaves the door open to a self-righteous and condescending judgment on the part of Orwell's reader. "After all," the reader might say, "in England we have institutions that provide for the poor." Orwell is willing to allow such a judgment, being content for the time being with documenting the existence of the problem of poverty and establishing the responsibility of the educated, cultivated class to acknowledge it. For having informed them of the problem in a foreign environment, Orwell sets out to exploit his readers' growing awareness by examining the problem of poverty in the more familiar environment of England.

The narrator immerses himself in the poverty of London even more deliberately than he did the depths of Paris society. Finding the employment for which he comes to London delayed for a month, he decides that "it seemed hardly decent" to borrow sufficient money from his friend "B." to tide him over until his employment begins (p. 127). Accordingly at a local pawn shop the narrator exchanges his clothes for a shilling and "the sort of clothes you see on a bootlace seller, or a tramp" (p. 129) and joins the world of the London poor. He is immediately struck by the power of appearance to determine one's social relationships:

> My new clothes had put me instantly into a new world. Everyone's demeanour seemed to have changed abruptly. . . . For the first time I noticed, too, how the attitude of women varies with a man's clothes. When a badly dressed man passes them they shudder away from him with a quite frank movement of disgust, as though he were a dead cat. Clothes are powerful things. Dressed in a tramp's clothes it is very difficult . . . not to feel that you are genuinely degraded. You might feel the same shame, irrational but very real, your first night in prison. (p. 129)

As he did in his early encounter with poverty in Paris, the narrator pays considerable attention to maintaining appearances. If it seemed to be a somewhat irrational concern there, in London appearances are of real consequence. Also in much the same way as the double doors marked the thin boundary between the served and the servant classes in the Paris restaurant, the narrator's easy and apparently complete metamorphosis from gentleman to tramp merely by changing his clothes suggests just how little really separates the rich from the poor in English society.

As the narrator's small cache of money dwindles, he examines one by one the possibilities open to the London poor. As he does so, he systematically destroys the illusion entertained by the liberal-minded reader that England provides effective institutions to deal with poverty.

If in Paris one who is down and out is forced into a neurasthenic slavery that can be escaped only by the most extraordinary exertions and good luck, in England the poor become part of a system that guarantees there can be no escape. The "enlightened" English system has as its basic operating principle the institutionalized exploitation of the poor. The filthy, low-cost lodging houses exploit the old people who live on small government pensions, yet the narrator learns that these houses are "profitable concerns and are owned by rich men" (p. 133). He learns, too, that the tramps who receive charity handouts of meal tickets are consistently given less than the full value of their ticket in food, allowing the proprietor to bilk them "to the tune of seven shillings or more a week. This kind of victimisation is a regular part of a tramp's life" (p. 185).

But the most insidious form of exploitation of the poor is that committed by those who (like the reader, perhaps?) have a well-intended but misguided belief in the saving power of charitable and religious institutions. The poor who seek refuge in the casual wards are treated as if they are some lower form of life, "herded" about like "cattle" and fed a ration "which is probably not even meant to be sufficient" (p. 203). Moreover, the men are subject to visits by religious "slumming-parties" who deliver sermons that the men in self-defense pointedly ignore: "Presently the slummers gave it up and cleared out, not insulted in any way. . . . No doubt they consoled themselves by thinking how brave they had been, 'freely venturing into the lowest dens,' etc. etc." (p. 181). The narrator's comment on the episode points out again the artificial gulf that divides those who preach from those who are preached at: "It is curious how people take it for granted that they have a right to preach at you and pray over you as soon as your income falls below a certain level" (p. 181).

The situation proves to be no better in the private charitable institutions. In one such institution the narrator finds that to receive a cup of tea he must subject himself to the religious ministrations of "a lady in a blue silk dress" (p. 140). After the tea the tramps are required to kneel down and pray, saying "that we had left undone those things that we ought to have done, and done those things that we ought not to have done, and there was no health in us" (p. 141). The narrator concludes that the tea was "given in a good spirit, without any intention of humiliating us; so in fairness we ought to have been grateful — still, we were not" (p. 142).

Clearly the English system of dealing with the poor is wrong or, as the narrator says "evil." He provides a summary analysis of this evil, but an analysis full of passionate human involvement rather than cool institutional detachment. He isolates three "especial evils" that the reader needs to understand: hunger, lack of sexual companionship, and enforced idleness. These are faults of the systems, faults the narrator shows to have tremendous human consequences. Hunger destroys the tramp in body and mind, while the "entirely useless" waste of "innumerable foot-pounds of energy" (p. 205) in enforced idleness and the isolation from female contact utterly destroy the tramp's self-respect. However bad the lot of the Paris plongeur was, he at least ate decently and had a kind of pride in his work. The English system denies even these minimal concessions to its poor.

In the detached and analytic tone of the opening pages of the book, the narrator proposes certain reforms of the institutions that deal with poverty (such as giving the tramps money instead of meal tickets), as well as more sweeping changes in the economy of poverty. And as he had in the Paris section, in the penultimate paragraph of the book the narrator overtly denies the significance of this experience: "My story ends here. It is a fairly trivial story, and I can only hope that it has been interesting in the same way as a travel diary is interesting" (p. 213). But the last paragraphs of the book end on a different note:

> At present I do not feel that I have seen more than the fringe of poverty.
> Still I can point to one or two things I have definitely learned by being hard up. I shall never again think that all tramps are drunken scoundrels, nor expect a beggar to be grateful when I give him a penny, nor be surprised if men out of work lack energy, nor subscribe to the Salvation Army. . . . That is a beginning. (p. 213)

The emphasis of this paragraph is, in marked contrast to the opening paragraphs, on the personal evaluation of the narrator's experience, and the paragraph implicitly directs the reader's attention to what he as a person has learned from the experiences of the book.

With this contrast in mind we can now examine the rhetoric of Down and Out in light of Orwell's purposes. By creating a narrator with whom the educated Englishman can identify, and by placing him in a situation foreign both to him and to the English audience, Orwell forms a bridge between his own enlightened understanding and the reader's ignorance of or complacency about the problem of poverty. The narrator also bridges the gap between detachment and personal involvement, and between institutional theories and their human applications. Orwell's rhetoric directs his reader toward a recognition that is at once a far simpler and a potentially more radical solution to poverty than the complex task of reforming institutions, important as such reform might be. He wants his reader at least to be able to acknowledge "that a tramp is only an Englishman out of work . . . that they are ordinary human beings" (p. 202). That is, he wants his reader to realize that institutions and appearances create false distinctions between people that are just as meaningless as the double doors of the French restaurant or the suit of old clothes that can transform one from gentleman to tramp. Furthermore, he wants his reader to understand that any institution that denies the humanity of one human being denies the humanity of all.

The bridge that Orwell creates through the rhetoric of Down and Out in Paris and London, the bridge that connects all men, is made of nothing more or less than simple human decency. And awakening that quality in his reader, Orwell's achievement in his powerful first book, is, as he tell us, "a beginning."

NOTES

1.   Donald Crompton, "False Maps of the World -- George Orwell's Autobiographical Writings and the Early Novels," Critical Quarterly 16 (1974): 150.

2.   Orwell's use of various fictional methods and rhetorical strategies to tell his apparently artless story has received scant attention.

Gordon Beadle, "George Orwell's Literary Studies of Poverty in England," <u>Twentieth Century Literature</u> 24 (1978): 188-201, acknowledges its "semi-fictionalized" character (p. 190) but does not explore what it means for a work to be semifictionalized.   Only Roger Ramsey, "'Down in Paris': Orwell's First Novel," <u>Arizona Quarterly</u> 32 (1976): 154-170, considers in any detail Orwell's use of fictional techniques.   But Ramsey deals only with the Paris section of the book, dismissing the London half as "didactic" and not "novelistic."   As I hope to demonstrate, the two halves of <u>Down and Out</u> form, if not the "overall unity" that Ramsey seeks, at least a unity of rhetorical purpose and effect.

3.   In one sense, of course, <u>Orwell</u> is the narrator; however, the narrator is also Orwell's creation because Orwell the author has been transformed by the experiences recorded in the book.   Thus the narrator, who represents Orwell's former self, is in this sense distinct from the author.   I shall maintain a distinction between them throughout this discussion.

4.   George Orwell, <u>Down and Out in Paris and London</u> (New York: Harcourt Brace Jovanovich, 1961), p. 4.   Subsequent reference to this readily accessible edition will appear parenthetically in the text.

6.
Orwell: From Clerisy to Intelligentsia

JASBIR JAIN

In his essay on Dickens, Orwell referred to him as a "nineteenth-century liberal, a free intelligence."(1) A few years later George Woodcock used the same phrase to describe Orwell's work and found fault with it on the grounds of his having adopted the stance of a nineteenth-century liberal.(2) More recently D. S. Savage's attack works under a similar misconception.(3) Despite the countless references made to Orwell's liberalism, no serious attempt has been made to relate his evaluation of nineteenth-century liberalism to his view of the intellectual or to analyze what the term "free intelligence" meant to him, or to place his ideas in a historical perspective.

The nineteenth-century was predominantly a century of liberal thought and education, at least in England, and it did succeed in freeing the idea of the clerisy from its secluded and advisory roles, and by secularizing the concept widened its meaning and extended the role of the intellectuals to include social responsibility. As Ben Knights in The Idea of the Clerisy in the Nineteenth Century writes: "at the root of the theory of the clerisy was a conviction not merely that there was no discontinuity between the life of the mind and the practical life of society, but that the latter was vitally affected by the former."(4) It was this view of the influence of the intellectual which was responsible for the degree of faith men placed in cultural traditions and in the integrity of the men of learning, in the ability of the few to guide the many. Matthew Arnold's concept of the best self is aligned both to tradition and society and places the concept of culture above both class and state.(5) The clerisy was taken to be a body of learned men distinguished by the fact of their learning and, therefore, capable of objective behavior. Their learning also placed them above the narrow claims of the class of their birth, and as such they were well within the ruling class structure: an intellectual being a privileged insider and assured of freedom of space.(6)

The sociological changes of the present century have drastically affected both the position and the influence of the intellectual. From being a respected voice within the system, he has become an outsider.(7) This process of change crystallized in the dominant intellectual position of the 1930s when disaffection was the order of the day rather than the exception. In his essay "England Your England" (1944), Orwell traced this alienation partly to the morally reprehensible position of the ruling class.(8) In another essay, "Culture and Democracy" (written at about the same time but not easily available now), he squarely put the blame on the capitalistic society (and its imperialistic outlook), and proceeded to ask:

> Why is it that a weathly capitalistic society seems nat-
> urally to breed a discontented intelligentsia like a sort of
> wart on the surface? The reason is that in such a society as
> ours the intelligentsia is functionless. . . . The intelli-
> gentsia during the last twenty years could not take part in
> that process of administration because the Empire and all its
> workings were so out of date, so manifestly unjust that they
> would necessarily have revolted against it.(9)

Orwell's inroads into the working class and the world of the tramps were
attempts to be useful to society (not to the Establishment) and to do
something about the conditions he so much disliked. They should also be
viewed as his way of protesting against the alienation that was being
thrust upon the intellectual. The tramp, for him, is a symbol of the
contemporary intellectual who must needs be free of both commitment and
alienation as both destroy his integrity.(10)

The question of the intellectual's freedom and his role in society
was one that occupied his attention over the years. Obliquely critical
of Miller's passivity,(11) he elaborated upon the need for intellectual
freedom in "Inside the Whale" (1940), "The Frontiers of Art and Propaganda" (1941), "The Prevention of Literature" (1946), "Writers and Leviathan" (1948), and a number of other essays and book reviews. It was this
concern that formed the basis of his views on education which were directly opposed to the theorists of elitist concepts,(12) as well as on
machine civilization. Orwell was deeply concerned with language and its
relationship to human thought — both important to the writers — and
this led to his questionings about the nature of the human mind. An essay written shortly before his death and published posthumously, "Such,
Such Were the Joys,"(13) explains a great deal in Orwell's attitude as
does the novel <u>Nineteen Eighty-Four</u>. In both the individual is treated
as a microcosmic representative of society; and there is a tacit admission of the need to continue the process of questioning the nature of
reality.

The significance of "Such, Such Were the Joys" does not lie in its
autobiographical element; it lies in its expression of Orwell's opinions
about the relationship of the individual to the outer reality. Orwell
recounts how one experiences alienation in a strange place, which in its
turn may lead to a sense of insecurity and also a loss of control over
one's physical funtions,(14) and how external threat may superimpose control over the body through generating a greater sense of terror.(15) He
goes on to elaborate how guilt can originate simply from having deviated
from the norm. And more important than any realization of guilt is the
act of public confession, which in some way links the outer and inner
world, rendering the individual vulnerable and exposed.(16) Looking at
the superimposition of an external value structure from the individual's
point of view, Orwell records how the personal questioning of this process continues(17) and there is a recognition of the existence of these
two worlds in opposition to each other, a condition more suitably described as schizothymia than as schizophrenia:

> And yet all the while, at the middle of one's heart
> there seemed to stand an incorruptible inner self who knew
> that whatever one did — whether one laughed or snivelled or
> went into frenzies of gratitude for small favours — one's
> only true feeling was hatred.(18)

There is also an admission of the impossibility of any subjective conformity to the external pressures.(19) It is this nonconformist inner self
that Winston Smith in <u>Nineteen Eighty-Four</u> is anxious to protect, and toward this end he is anxious to create an area of privacy around himself

partly through memory and partly through withdrawal from the external world and proceeds to keep a diary. This act of recording is important to him, for through this, reality can be concretized. It also is indicative of the need to find a response to something other than the purely personal world of memory: a world to which he can return and verify his feelings experienced at some earlier time. It is both a substitute for an external world as well as an act of proclamation separated from the act of confession.(20)

Throughout the novel the world of the senses is contrasted with that of the mind: and through this contrast questions of a greater philosophical dimension are raised pertaining to the nature of reality and that of human perception. Winston Smith's reactions and opinions are based solely on sensual perception (and as such he is not purely in the empirical traditon). He proceeds on the basis of a number of a priori assumptions and recognizes the role of instinct. There is also an admission of how the rational can be invaded by the irrational and logic superseded by faith.(21) Further there is an acceptance of the existence of the unconscious which may at times be at variance with the conscious and often encroaches upon it. The main refrain of the novel — two plus two equals four — is not only an echo from the world of dystopian fiction beginning with Dostoevsky's Notes from the Underground and running through Zamyatin's We to Orwell's Nineteen Eighty-Four but also from the Kantian theory of knowledge. Kant categorizes mathematical judgments as synthetic a priori which, being universally valid and necessary, are independent of verification through experience.(22). The same is true of the principles of natural science.(23) The question that is further raised is whether the same is true of the nature of reality or not — that is, is it possible to make certain assertions about reality which in principle it is impossible, by any form of experience, either to verify or to falsify? Kant asserts that metaphysics consists, "at least in intention entirely of a priori synthetic propositions."(24)

Orwell's concern with language as revealed in Nineteen Eighty-Four is also Kantian in its basic concepts.(25) Newspeak is an attempt to narrow the range of human consciousness by limiting the range of words available and by eliminating their polysemic quality. When certain conceptual possibilities can find no correspondence in the external world, they are apt to become incommunicable, language being thus reduced to being one-dimensional.

When Winston Smith sits down to begin his diary, he is uncertain as to the date and time (p. 9), his awareness is mainly speculative, supported by some vague memory of the past. Time moves not in any linear fashion but in a cyclic movement, having a finite limit and a point from which to begin again. The very framework of his diary is an attempt on Winston's part to place his life within the historicity of time, which is a form of intuition, not a concept, as in Kantian terms: "Time is not a discursive or what is called a general concept, but a pure form of sensible intuition . . . of the intuition of ourselves and of our inner state."(26) Kant elaborates on this and stresses the subjective element in this awareness:

> It is nothing but the form of our inner intuition. If we
> take away from out of inner intuition the peculiar condition
> of our sensibility, the concept of time likewise vanishes; it
> does not inhere in the objects, but merely in the subject
> which intuits them.(27)

Winston's attempt is to transcend the confines of the present, but the Party desires to destroy the very idea of progression. The concept of change is being refuted, as is the idea of flux.

As the story progresses Winston increasingly realizes the impossibility of preserving his freedom in a world that offers him no external correspondence to his awareness and is forced to recognize the futility of trying to lead a schizophrenic existence. Earlier, in "The Prevention of Literature" (1946), Orwell had written that totalitarianism "does not so much promise an age of faith as an age of schizophrenia." In Nineteen Eighty-Four the ruling class is engaged in reversing all emotional and moral norms. Thus when the individual is stranded without the past and the future, in a little cubbyhole of the present, even schizophrenia fails to provide a permanent solution, for without the correspondence of inner awareness at some level — memory, history, or desire — the two worlds meet and dissolve into each other. Also schizophrenia is fatal to the idea of integrity so essential to the sustenance of any moral value or continuance of any intellectual life. And while fear and pain are actualized in experience, there are other concepts that have the possibility of actuality only in the future, or belong to the area of speculative knowledge, or have transcendental value, and these concepts, when condemned to loneliness and isolation, are stillborn and impotent. In order to be actualized they need to be discussed, expressed, and linked through language to the possibility of experience. It is not that pure ideas do not have any existence in Nineteen Eighty-Four. The Brotherhood is not an organization in the ordinary sense: "Nothing holds it together except the idea which is indestructible" (NEF, p. 143). But this idea is propagated and exchanged. When there is no link between subject and object, the life of the mind becomes limited. The purely rationalistic view that it is possible to evolve all truths from pure thought, independent of experience, loses its validity when discussion is forbidden. Finally it brings about a complete reversal in the situation: the unverifiable existence of Big Brother acquires a reality while the actual physical existence of the individual ceases to be. Here faith imposes itself on reason just as earlier reason is superimposed upon empirical reality. Winston wonders about the nature of existence: "Did not the statement, 'You do not exist', contain a logical absurdity?" (p. 208). It is a play on words, and reality is controllable through words. It is as Steiner emphasizes in "Linguistics and Poetics":

> Any true examination of meaning is, first and perhaps also in the final analysis, an examination of relevant grammar, of the instrumentalities of language by and through which man argues and experiences possible models of reality.(28)

The point is also physical. Winston is tortured into seeing five fingers instead of four and there "was no deformity" (p. 207). The individual is hounded and denied even the space occupied by his body. ["Space is nothing but the form of all appearances of outer sense. It is the subjective condition of sensibility under which alone outer intuition is possible for us."(29)

Though denying reality at an external level, the Party recognizes the importance of the human mind and concentrates all its efforts to conquer it — through language, media, torture, and isolation, and through destroying the concepts of time and privacy. Nowhere is it assumed that the human mind is passive, for "what knowledge have we of anything, save through our own minds" (pp. 222-223). People rebel both consciously and unconsciously and retreat further and further into inner recesses. Both rebellion and suppression of rebellion have importance only if the mind is presumed to be an active agent.(30)

Winston's attempts, however, to withstand the external pressures give way until the area of freedom exists only in the Chestnut Tree Cafe and game of chess.(31) Nineteen Eighty-Four is a continued debate about the theory of knowledge and the nature of the human mind. O'Brien and the Party present one set of arguments while Winston presents the other; there is also a third point of view existing in the world of the rebel. There is an essential affinity between the structure of the mind and the cosmos, and if external reality can be controlled, the mind can also be controlled. The premise is Kantian to begin with:

> There can be no doubt that all our knowledge begins with
> experience . . . .
>   But though all our knowledge begins with experience, it
> does not follow that all arises out of experience. For it
> may well be that even our empirical knowledge is made up of
> what we receive through impressions and of what our own fac-
> ulty of knowledge supplies from itself.(32)

This premise, however, assumes the freedom both of experience and of re-flection. Suppose, Orwell asks, that this freedom is denied and that the structure of the world available to man is drastically changed; what, then, is the nature of knowledge and how does it affect the human mind? In this connection the title Orwell at one stage had considered a likely one for Nineteen Eighty-Four, "The Last Man in Europe," is indicative of the side he is on. Winston refuses to believe that the kind of society envisaged by the Party can actually come into being; lacking vitality, it would "disintegrate" or "commit suicide" (p. 216).(33)

A few years earlier Orwell was involved in a controversy regarding his views on pacifism in the pages of Partisan Review. At that time he wrote:

> I have never attacked "the intellectuals" or "the intel-
> ligentsia" en bloc. I have used a lot of ink and done myself
> a lot of harm by attacking the successive literary cliques
> which have infested this country not because they were intel-
> lectuals but precisely because they were not what I mean by
> true intellectuals.(34)

And what he meant by "true intellectuals" he defined on a number of occa-sions in both positive and negative terms. Negatively, his comments on the left-wing writers(35) as well as on the liberals(36) define what a true intellectual is not. One can also sense his disapproval of with-drawal in "Inside the Whale" when he writes of Miller, who performed "the essential Jonah act."(37) In positive terms Orwell's view of the role of the intellectual emerges in his emphasis on the need for freedom, in his view of the creative act,(38) of his view of art and the purpose of art,(39) in the responsibility he feels that the writer owes society,(40) and the commitment he should have to his own integrity:

> The first thing we ask of a writer is that he shall not
> tell lies, that he shall say what he really thinks, what he
> really feels. The worst thing we can say about a work of art
> is that it is insincere.(41)

Sincerity is possible only in a world of freedom, where one is not frightened of committing a heresy. And the writer/intellectual has to be a "free" intelligence not committed to any party ideology or privileged minority. Orwell's concept of the "unattached" intellectual is in some measure a development of the ideas of Julien Benda, who disapproved of any political engagement on the part of writers, for he felt that it downgraded them from their position as disinterested moral guides, espe-cially when they brought their sensibility and powers of persuasion to bear upon this interest in politics, when they allowed it to "colour the essence of their work and to mark all its productions."(42)

Orwell goes further than Benda, for his attitude is a questioning of
the Marxian thesis that people are products of their environment. The
logical conclusion would be on the lines of the behaviorist approach toward language and society, which in his opinion fails to exhaust the full
reality of human beings: at least as it is at present. This is the main
theme of Nineteen Eighty-Four whereby the theory of mind is predominantly
Kantian in its inclination. Both commitment and alienation isolate and
impose artificial patterns of reality: hence the belief in the "unattached" intelligentsia.

NOTES

1.   George Orwell, "Charles Dickens" (1940) in The Collected Essays, Journalism and Letters of George Orwell, ed. by Sonia Orwell and
Ian Angus, 4 vols. (London: Secker and Warburg, 1968), I: 460. In all
future references the title CEJL will be used.

2.   George Woodcock, "George Orwell, 19th century Liberal," Politics (December 1946): 384-388. George Orwell: The Critical Heritage,
ed. Jeffrey Meyers (London: Routledge and Kegan Paul, 1975), p. 246.

3.   D. S. Savage, "The Fatalism of George Orwell," The Present, New
Pelican Guide to English Literature, vol. 8, ed. Boris Ford (Harmondsworth: Penguin, 1983), pp. 129-146.

4.   Ben Knight, The Idea of the Clerisy in the Nineteenth Century
(London: Cambridge University Press, 1978), p. 2

5.   Matthew Arnold, Culture and Anarchy (1869) (London: Cambridge
University Press, 1971), pp. 95-96.

6.   This may not have been so in Russia. See Hugh Seton-Watson,
"The Russian Intellectual," Encounter (September 1955. Also see "The Up-
rooted Intellectual," an extract from Dostoevsky's The Diary of a Writer,
and Nicholas Berdyaev's essay "The People versus the Intellectual." All
three essays are included in the anthology The Intellectuals: A Controversial Portrait, ed George B. de Huszar (New York: The Free Press,
1960).

7.   Most of the young writers of the period felt alienated not only
from their class and position but also from their family backgrounds and
moved toward commitment. Among these were Louis MacNeice, Stephen Spender, and W. H. Auden. Alongside could be ranged men such as Christopher
Caudwell. Noel Annan comments briefly on this in the essay on Mill in
The English Mind, ed. Hugh Sykes Davies and George Watson (London: Cambridge University Press, 1964), p. 238.

8.   "It is clear that the special position of the English intellectuals during the past ten years, as purely negative creatures, mere anti-
Blimps, was a by-product of ruling class stupidity" ("England Your England," CEJL, II: 74).

9.   Victory or Vested Interest, comp. John Parker (London: Labour
Book Service, 1942), pp. 84-86. See also pp. 81-83.

10.   The world of the tramp also happens to be an equal one — the
nearest one could come to equality. See The Road to Wigan Pier (1937)
(Harmondsworth: Penguin, 1962), p. 136. (hereafter RWP).

11.   CEJL, I: 521-525.

12.   Orwell was critical of imposing it on the lower classes, although he conceded the value of education. See RWP, pp. 103–104.

13.   George Orwell, "Such, Such Were the Joys" (New York: Harcourt, Brace & Company, 1953). The essay was first published in Partisan Review in 1952. There is internal evidence that the essay may have been written in the early forties (see p. 58).

14.   Ibid., pp. 160–18, 36.

15   Ibid., pp. 14–17.

16.   Ibid., p. 15: "You had to proclaim your offence with your own lips."

17.   Ibid., p. 29, 51.

18.   Ibid., p. 39.

19.   Ibid., p. 51.

20.   The diary form was important to Orwell. See "Why I Write," in CEJL, I: 2. During the war Orwell also kept a diary.

21.   When Winston Smith thinks of the Proles, he realizes that it is both a mystical truth and a palpable absurdity; in the human beings it became "an act of faith." See Nineteen Eighty-Four (1949) (Harmondsworth: Penguin, 1962), p. 72 (hereafter NEF).

22.   Immanuel Kant, Critique of Pure Reason, trans. Norman Kemp Smith (London: Macmillan, 1953), p. 52.

23.   Ibid., Orwell also discusses this in NEF. While Winston feels the need to believe in continuity and external reality, O'Brien tells him that the Party was capable of controlling reality, even of producing a dual system of astronomy (p. 213).

24.   Kant, Critique of Pure Reason, p. 55.

25.   Orwell's concern with language pervades almost all his work and is an important part of his theory of the mind. "Politics and the English Language" (1946) was written as a protest against the idea of political quietism and Stuart Chase's book The Tyranny of Words (1939).

26.   Kant, Critque of Pure Reason, p. 75.

27.   Ibid., p. 79.

28.   Steiner, "Linguistics and Poetics," in Extraterritorial (Harmondsworth: Penguin, 1971), p. 144.

29.   Kant, Critique of Pure Reason, p. 71.

30.   Winston attempts to keep the inner heart inviolate (NEF, p. 225).

31.   Orwell, Nineteen Eighty-Four, pp. 47, 231, 235. Also see George Steiner's essay "A Death of Kings," in Extraterritorial, pp. 58–60.

32.   Kant, Critique of Pure Reason, pp. 41–42.

33.   The ending of the novel is ambiguous. It does not state that Winston's cognition has failed: he wills himself toward a state where he can die. He is never really defeated or conquered: he is aware of the dichotomy right to the very end.

34.   CEJL, II: 229.

35.   See specifically, "Culture and Democracy," pp. 82-84.

36.   See particularly his review of Russell's Power: A New Social Analysis in CEJL, I: 375.

37.   CEJL, I: 521.

38.   "The Prevention of Literature," in CEJL, IV: 71.

39.   Ibid., p. 65.

40.   CEJL, III: 229.

41.   "Literature and Totalitarianism," in CEJL, II: 134-135.

42.   Julien Benda, "The Treason of the Intellectuals," trans. Richard Aldington, in The Intellectuals: A Controversial Portrait, (New York: Free Press), p. 221.

7.
Nineteen Eighty-Four and the Spirit of Schweik
MICHAEL ORANGE

For many readers the most frightening moment in <u>Nineteen Eighty-Four</u> occurs when O'Brien has Winston Smith at his mercy in Room 101 and the rat mask begins to close on the victim's face. The scene is a set-piece, carefully prepared for and introduced only when the victim is properly rested so that he can appreciate it. There is a sort of logic to its position in the novel, explicated by the torturer as the difference between pain and "the unendurable."(1) Winston has been given electric torture until he is deemed to have made satisfactory intellectual progress, but his emotional development remains unsatisfactory. He hates Big Brother still. Now that he is to confront "the worst thing in the world" (p. 403), however, he will capitulate in his feelings too as the threat of the rats does its work effectively.

In Orwell's writing of the scene there is a curious disjunction between the two modes of torture, one all electricity and dials, the other bestial and direct. Clearly the levels correspond to intellect and feeling. However, there is a less obvious disparity in tone as well, announced when O'Brien brings the mask close enough to Winston's face to block out all other vision. Winston is now eyeball-to-eyeball with the preprandial rodents. And O'Brien remarks, "as didactically as ever," that what Winston is about to suffer "was a common punishment in Imperial China" (p. 406). It is a startling touch and perhaps only funny on a second reading, when it sounds laughably inappropriate. The comment does preserve the sense of O'Brien's detachment from any fellow-feeling, but it may also tilt the scene, at an unfortunate moment as one of the novel's climaxes approaches, toward a world of devilish torturers and their helpless victims who a few years later would be attempting much the same thing at the expense of James Bond.

The introduction to this scene indicates the novel's fictional referents more clearly:

> At each stage of his imprisonment he had known, or seemed to know, whereabouts he was in the windowless building. Possibly there were slight differences in the air pressure. The cells where the guards had beaten him were below ground level. The room where he had been interrogated by O'Brien was high up near the roof. This place was many metres underground, as deep down as it was possible to go. (p. 403)

It is clear where Room 101 is sited. Orwell has taken us to the Gothic wing of the house of fiction and to a dungeon adjacent to the one in which Charles Maturin's Lorenzo Moncada has been placed. The latter's torturers, the Superior and his four assistant monks, clearly stand in an ancestral relationship to O'Brien:

> I said, "I am in your power, -- I am guilty in your eyes, -- accomplish your purpose, but do not keep me long in pain." The Superior, without heeding, or perhaps hearing me, said, "Now you are in the posture that becomes you." At hearing these words, which sounded less dreadful than I had feared, I prostrated myself to the ground. A few moments before I would have thought this a degradation, but fear is very debasing.(2)

And Room 101's location recalls the cell to which poor Lorenzo is led:

> They crossed the aisle; there was a dark passage near it which I had never observed before. We entered it. A low door at the end presented a frightful perspective. . . . They hurried me down the steps to this door, which was considerably below the level of the passage. It was a long time before they could open it; many keys were tried; perhaps they might have felt some agitation at the thoughts of the violence they were going to commit. But this delay increased my terrors beyond expression; I imagined this terrible vault had never been unclosed before; that I was to be the first victim inhumed within it; and that their determination was, I should never quit it alive. (pp. 143-144)

Even more striking perhaps is the affinity displayed between the two writers in terms of psychological detail. Lorenzo begs for light in his cell:

> I petitioned for this with as much earnestness as I could have done for my liberty. Thus it is that misery always breaks down the mind into petty details. We have not strength to comprehend the whole of our calamity. We feel not the mountain which is heaped on us, but the nearest grains press on and grind us. (p. 144)

Orwell develops the technique and the insight as O'Brien forces Winston to concentrate on the number of fingers he holds out before his face.

It is worth dwelling on the Gothic aspect of Nineteen Eighty-Four and in particular on the way that it recalls the Inquisition because Orwell refers to the latter explicitly in a review of N. de Basily's Russia under Soviet Rule:

> The terrifying thing about the modern dictatorships is that they are something entirely unprecedented. Their end cannot be foreseen. In the past every tyranny was sooner or later overthrown, or at least resisted, because of "human nature," which as a matter of course desired liberty. But we cannot be at all certain that "human nature" is constant. It may be just as possible to produce a breed of men who do not wish for liberty as to produce a breed of hornless cows. The Inquisition failed, but then the Inquisition had not the resources of the modern state. The radio, press-censorship, standardized education and the secret police have altered everything.(3)

In light of this comment, it looks as though Nineteen Eighty-Four will make a point about the modernized inquisitions of the totalitarian state, and sure enough, when Orwell came to write the novel he emphasized the modern appurtenances of electricity and dials in Winston's torture, and made O'Brien refer to the shortcomings of the Inquisition (pp. 377-378). That is why there seems such a disjunction when Winston is suddenly marched backward in time, and through the history of the novel, to the rat cage. There is a disturbing element in this because the fictional child appears no longer to acknowledge its parent. The rat cage is not explicitly presented as a valuable, cruder instrument from history, smoothly assimilated into the modern bureaucracy's panoply of power. There is no hint of self-awareness or irony. Instead, Orwell rewrites Gothic quite straight here, exploiting sensationalism and fear as does Maturin. (It is worth noting that Maturin is celebrated these days not for his views on Catholicism but for whatever talents he possesses as a novelist.) It is not surprising, therefore, that in the Imperial China remark Orwell sounds unintentionally funny. The humor springs from the perhaps unwitting use of an unassimilated literary mode:

> "The worst thing in the world," said O'Brien, "varies from individual to individual. It may be burial alive, or death by fire, or by drowning, or by impalement, or fifty other deaths. There are cases where it is some quite trivial thing, not even fatal." (p. 403)

Everyone has private fears, no doubt. However, "the worst thing in the world" has overtones of a comic book, of a schoolboyish fantasy about power to which the evocation of Imperial China a little later is precisely appropriate: "the worst thing in the world" needs a touch of Oriental devilry to set it off.(4) To place convincing perceptions about inner vulnerability in such a light also indicates a dark complicity in sado-masochistic fantasy, present elsewhere in the novel -- for example, when Julia and Winston go to O'Brien's flat and the latter begins his "catechism":

> "You are prepared to cheat, to forge, to blackmail, to corrupt the minds of children, to distribute habit-forming drugs, to encourage prostitution, to disseminate venereal diseases -- to do anything which is likely to cause demoralization and weaken the power of the Party?"
> "Yes."
> "If, for example, it would somehow serve our interests to throw sulphuric acid in a child's face -- are you prepared to do that?"
> "Yes." (p. 305)

The gratuitous violence of the last question emerges in its qualifications: "If, for example, it would somehow serve our interests." Although this is part of O'Brien's testing of them and is thereby intended for shock value, these qualifications indicate Orwell's complicity, in that he seeks to do to his readers what O'Brien does to the rebels. The same process is observable when Winston is degraded after his tortures:

> "Even your hair is coming out in handfuls. Look!" He plucked at Winston's head and brought away a tuft of hair. . . . He seized one of Winston's remaining front teeth between his powerful thumb and forefinger. A twinge of pain shot through Winston's jaw. O'Brien had wrenched the loose tooth out by its roots. He tossed it across the cell. (p. 394)

It is an assault on the reader quite as much as on Winston. And the reader has been carefully prepared for the rat phobia, too, earlier in the novel (pp. 280-281). This prolepsis is orchestrated so that it functions as part of the novel's creation of the technological inquisition because it represents a frightening instance of the new sophistication of surveillance techniques. In Room 101 it seems inevitable that Winston's private phobia has been known all along to the authorities.

Nevertheless the "worst thing in the world" should not be accorded great solemnity of response. On rational reflection it may seem quite unlikely that such a simple key to the unlocking of psychological defenses will succeed so spectacularly. Is the pain of electric shock torture really less likely to produce final capitulation than a custom-made refinement such as the rats? The novel allows for no such perspective in its sensationalist exploitation of private fears. Only O'Brien's ritualistic incantation of "the worst thing in the world" and the reversion to late eighteenth-century Gothic idiom represented by the rat cage indicate that Orwell may be attempting to overpersuade.

A different aspect of Gothic is evident in Orwell's very effective use of fairy tale in the novel: "It was a bright cold day in April, and the clocks were striking thirteen" (p. 157). This will be an adult version of those tales for children which are claimed to have benign developmental results. Big Brother as the Big Bad Wolf, the Thought Police as the embodiment of childlike guilt projections, and even a political orator as Rumpelstiltskin (pp. 312-313) contribute effectively to a sense of childhood nightmare reified. The technique does not exclude bathos, though. The bells of St. Clement's Dane, which evoke a world of children's games so different from Airstrip One, are used to characterize the apparently private retreat at Mr. Charrington's. But they -- or the lines that evoke them -- reappear inopportunely when Winston and Julia are betrayed, giving a slightly ludicrous touch to an otherwise frightening scene:

> "The house is surrounded," said Winston.
> "The house is surrounded," said the voice.
> He heard Julia snap her teeth together. "I suppose we may as well say good-bye," she said.
> "You may as well say good-bye," said the voice. And then another quite different voice, a thin, cultivated voice which Winston had the impression of having heard before, struck in: "And by the way, while we are on the subject, 'Here comes a candle to light you to bed, here comes a chopper to chop off your head!'" (p. 349)

Certainly this signals the cruel inverson of Winston's and Julia's own fairy tale world, as it is now revealed to have been, but it is crudely interpolated here in the context of black uniforms, ironshod boots, and truncheons. Nevertheless it suggests that the deployment of fairy tale throughout may be curiously reassuring in terms of the novel's own status: that Nineteen Eighty-Four is itself paradigmatically a fairy tale, a politically healthy "use of enchantment."(5)

Elsewhere Nineteen Eighty-Four develops the technological leap forward in Gothic fiction found in Mary Shelley's Frankenstein, or The Modern Prometheus (1818), which was such an effective sophistication of horror fiction, particularly in the way it foregrounded the modern scientist conducting his experiments with "the principle of life."(6) Frankenstein is another of O'Brien's fictive ancestors, and at the novel's end Winston seems no less monstrous than Mary Shelley's creature (although O'Brien and the Inner Party, as may be inferred from Daphne Patai,(7) are not shown to understand fully the symbiotic relationship between the social monster they have produced and their own needs for domination). But Gothic permeates the Inner Party in terms of social organization as well. The link here is Dickens, for whom Orwell had such admiration. In Little

Dorrit Dickens bathed not only Mrs. Clennam's residence but the entire
bureaucracy in a flickering Gothic light, which Orwell makes use of (as
did Kafka before him) in dramatizing the coercive effect of social institutions. The Circumlocution Office, as Daniel Doyce testifies, is both
all-powerful and death to creative enterprise, and Dickens consistently
presents the bureaucracy in terms of indifferent torturers and their victims. Without going to the extremes of Orwell's picture, he also shows
the Barnacles and their colleagues and relations securely and perpetually
in command.
     However, there is a vital distinction between _Little Dorrit_ and
Nineteen Eighty-Four. Dickens's narrator's tone still contrives to retain some sanity, partly because it refuses to forfeit its own ironies
and amusement whatever the provocation of labyrinthine and irresponsible
administration, as deadly in its own fashion as Maturin's Inquisition,
and partly because Dickens is still determined on indignant resistance.
The sardonic humor of Young Barnacle's portrayal is a weapon of political
offense: that Orwell deliberately exterminates any such resistance in
Nineteen Eighty-Four measures the degree of transformation involved in
the Circumlocution Office's conversion into the Inner Party.
     Despite this a question remains concerning efficiency. Orwell was
issuing a warning about the possible effects of totalitarian political
systems on concepts of humanity, and the logic of the warning demands the
imagining of utterly effective political instruments. He posits a version of human perfectibility, a small section of the populace so flaw-
lessly in control of themselves that they will remain powerful in perpe-
tuity. It is an audacious literary strategy, that even risks comparisons
between one of the novel's leading figures and God or Antichrist:

     He watched the heavy yet graceful form strolling to and
     fro, in and out of the range of his vision. O'Brien was a
     being in all ways larger than himself. There was no idea
     that he had ever had, or could have, that O'Brien had not
     long ago known, examined and rejected. His mind contained
     Winston's mind. (p. 380)

The description extends the concept of totalitarianism unironically and
completely: a political system whose leaders are drawn from less than
fifteen percent of the total population finds apotheosis here.
     Such a vision is eloquent on the totalitarian danger. But it is
also, by omission, a statement about the remainder of the populace -- or,
rather, about Orwell's attitude toward them, particularly the Proles. By
this stage in the novel Winston's hope of the Proles is being remorse-
lessly extinguished, but criticism of the novel should not necessarily
follow him. Instead, it may be important to reiterate that a quite unusual concept of perfectibility informs the presentation of the Inner
Party and that this perfectibility rests on total efficiency in the exe-
cution of Party philosophy. This is where Orwell parts company utterly
with _Little Dorrit_: to have conceived of the Barnacles in this way would
have been one of Dickens's greatest pieces of sarcasm. The greatest defense against totalitarianism may yet be perceived as a saving human inefficiency.
     Nineteen Eighty-Four's pessimism excludes completely (and no doubt
deliberately) any such resistant forces as Daniel Doyce or _Little Dor-
rit_'s narrator. It excludes also any such figure as twentieth-century
European literature's great symbol of dogged inefficiency, of proletarian
resistance to all forms of tyranny, the "good soldier" Schweik. One of
the latter's anecdotes crystalizes the loss:

     Years ago the station master at Svitava was a Mr.
     Wagner. He was a devil to his subordinates and gave them

hell whenever he could, but the chap he was most down on was
the points-man Jungwirt. Finally in despair the wretched man
went and drowned himself in the river. But before doing so,
he wrote a letter to the station master saying that he'd come
and haunt him in the night. And to tell you the honest
truth, that was exactly what he did. In the night the good
station master was sitting at his telegraph receiver when the
bell rang and he received the following telegram: "How are
you, you old bastard? Jungwirt." This lasted a whole week
and the station master began to send official telegrams a-
cross all the lines to answer the ghost: "Forgive me, Jungwirt." And in the night the receiver knocked out the following reply: "Go and hang yourself on the signals at the
bridge. Jungwirt." And the station master obeyed. Afterwards they gaoled the telegraphist from the station before
Svitava.(8)

The snaring of the oppressor by using up-to-date technology in the
guise of supernatural force provides a pleasant counterpoint to the world
of Nineteen Eighty-Four, but the inconsequential innocence of the story
indicates that from the perspective of the latter Schweik will remain for
ever a harmless prole. At least, this might be the sole implication were
it not that a compatriot of Hasek's, Milan Kundera, revived the spirit of
Schweik within a modern political system often compared to Nineteen
Eighty-Four's in his 1967 novel The Joke. For much of the latter, the
period in which it is set is the same as for Orwell's novel -- if the
latter is to be taken as set in or near 1948 (Bernard Crick is the most
recent of commentators who insist on this).(9) Thus The Joke presents an
insider's experience of a political reality that Orwell essentially spec-
ulated about from the outside. The difference in tone is about as great
as it could be, as Kundera's title intimates, although in his preface to
the 1982 edition he states that he began writing The Joke in 1962. Today, Kundera states,

the dissolution of Stalinism in Central Europe [has become]
difficult to explain. Russian Communism (no other has existed in Czechoslovakia) was so completely foreign to Central
European (Polish, Hungarian, Czech) traditions that the large
majority of people spontaneously rejected it. Behind the
Communist facade a gradual liberalization process took place,
a process that saw the creation (in spite of the official
ideology, which no one could question but no one took seriously) of many outstanding films, plays, and works of literature.(10)

The pre-1968 liberalization may in part explain Kundera's freedom of tone
in his novel, and his historical perspective clearly gives him some advantages denied Orwell. Nevertheless episodes such as Ludvik Jahn's discovery of Lucie Sebetka during his service in the penal battalion when he
works in the mines, or the humour of his schoolmate Kovalik's "welcomings
of citizens to new life" ceremonies illuminate by their wry amusement the
unremitting intensity of Orwell's masterpiece. Parsons in Nineteen
Eighty-Four is perhaps the equivalent of Kovalik in The Joke. But however satisfying the revenge on the former (betrayed by his children), Orwell's evident hatred of the figure helps to lock Nineteen Eighty-Four
into a vision of repressive boarding school for life.(11)

To foreground tales of school revenge, Gothic horrors, fairy-tale
motifs, not to mention Winston's diary and Goldstein's testament, reveals
the intertextual density of Nineteen Eighty-Four's texture. It may also
assist in decoding a work of formidable enclosing power, reminding us

that it functions as a fictional text rather than an ideological instrument -- perhaps a necessary reminder when that text is so often used as a kind of political bludgeon by parties Orwell might well have anathematized.

NOTES

1.   George Orwell, Nineteen Eighty-Four, ed. Bernard Crick (Oxford: Clarendon, 1984), p. 404. Subsequent references are to this edition.

2.   Charles Robert Maturin, Melmoth the Wanderer: A Tale, ed. Douglas Grant (London: Oxford University Press), p. 142. Subsequent references are to this edition.

3.   New English Weekly, 12 January 1939, in The Collected Essays, Journalism and Letters of George Orwell, ed. Sonia Orwell and Ian Angus, 4 vols. (London: Secker & Warburg, 1968), I: An Age Like This : 1920 -- 1940, pp. 380-381.

4.   See Crick's comments, Nineteen Eighty-Four, pp. 442-443.

5.   The term is Bruno Bettelheim's: The Uses of Enchantment: The Meaning and Importance of Fairy Tales (London: Thames and Hudson, 1976).

6.   James Kinsely and M. K. Joseph, eds., The World's Classics (Oxford: Oxford University Press, 1980), p. 51.

7.   "Gamesmanship and Androcentrism in Orwell's 1984," PMLA 97 (1982): 856-870.

8.   Jaroslav Hasek, The Good Soldier Schweik and His Fortunes in the World War, trans. Cecil Parrott (Harmondsworth: Penguin, 1974), p. 227.

9.   Nineteen Eighty-Four, pp. 20-24.

10.   Milan Kundera, The Joke, trans M. H. Heim (Harmondsworth: Penguin, 1984), p. vi.

11.   Anthony West's point, although made reductively. See Principles and Persuasions (London: Eyre & Spottiswoode, 1958), pp. 157-159. Bernard Crick's overreaction tries to obscure how effectively the schoolboy sense of deprivation, injustice, hunger, and isolation is made to work in the novel. See George Orwell: A Life, rev. ed. (Harmondsworth: Penguin, 1982), pp. 525-526, 593-594).

8.
Orwell, Self-Taught Student of English History

R. L. PATTERSON

Orwell's and Samuel Johnson's names are not commonly yoked. Yet the Great Cham would appreciate The Lion and the Unicorn's opening. The prospect of being bombed in a moment, like that of being hanged in a fortnight, concentrates the mind.

Events other than the Blitz led Orwell to write this little book. He needed money, as usual; Inside the Whale had brought him an advance of all of 20.(1) The summer of 1940 found him almost unemployed. The army rejected him; the Home Guard made a poor substitute; he looked in vain for civilian war work. Into the void came the project for a series of "Searchlight Books" which he limned with T. R. Fyvel and Frederick Warburg. Today the general title looks banal; then it invoked the nightly contrast of blackout with antiaircraft defenses. The books would, the three men hoped, set out the need and means for a planned renewal of Britain and the Commonwealth; their prospectus used the latter word, not "Empire." Bernard Crick has concisely explained the men's vision and the venture's publishing history. He has praised and simply summarized Lion while damning some readers for not appreciating it.(2) The most popular American anthology of Orwell's essays reprinted only the first chapter.(3) Commentators Crick does not name have ignored it;(4) another misread it as propaganda composed for the Ministry of Information.(5) True, Lion belongs to the genre of books promoting the war effort -- but only on the editors' terms.

The text poses exegetical problems. Its subtitle, "Socialism and the English Genius," anticipates a better world after the war. Details parallel parts of Orwell's diary for the autumn of 1940 and the "London Letters" he was beginning for Partisan Review. Some passages anticipate what he later said in The English People. Some echo themes from The Road to Wigan Pier and Homage to Catalonia. At first glance it seems right to call Lion an epitome of Orwell's matured ideas. Yet from different starting points William J. West and Arthur Eckstein have challenged this line of thinking. They identify Orwell's truest ideas as pessimistic; these they trace to concrete experience during the war.(6) Simply following these scholars, however, one misses the extent of Orwell's disillusionment. One can also overlook -- as this essay must overlook -- the problem of interpreting what he let be published in The English People.

Orwell has, of course, no standing as "historian." He lived outside the academic milieu, had few friends within it, and so (for example) lost touch with his sometime friend Steven Runciman after they left Eton.(7) The Orwell whom people study in schools and universities was, in American slang, a dropout. Yet he taught himself literary criticism to the point where Q. D. Leavis deigned to praise Inside the Whale.(8) Peter Stansky and William Abrahams lament that he never studied at Eton works by men

such as Charles Booth and Seebohm Rowntree.(9)   Yet detail about houses
and budgets in Wigan Pier surely derives from models such as their work.
One may infer that Orwell taught himself sociology.   So he had to do with
history.
     Eric Blair learned at St. Cyprian's to hate the subject.   Flip, the
Headmaster's wife, taught him that lesson.   She did so by drilling the
boys with mnemonics, lists of dates, and empty phrases.   Accidentally or_
on purpose he misquoted one such cliche in "Such, Such Were the Joys . .
." by calling Canning Pitt.(10)   He also failed to tell that her cramming
helped (or made?) him win the Harrow History Prize, a fact Cyril Connolly
had already published in Enemies of Promise.(11)   Eton failed to improve
his distaste.   When he took the entrance examination for the Burmese police, his mark in history was far lower than in any other written paper.(12)   His later brief service as a teacher reinforced his dislike of
the subject.(13)   Yet Orwell needed history.   Too much of what passes for
it consists of trivia, cant, or self-serving falsehood.   His vision of a
better world therefore demanded understanding of his and his readers'
true situation.
     Lion presents a variation on the common version of English history,
known by the label "Whig."   Not all students or writers accept that version.   The journalist Henry Fairlie blames its "lie" for justifying the
rise and power of "the Establishment."   He also has admitted framing his
first use of the epithet while working daily with bright young Roman
Catholics.(14)   Orwell despised such people.   He called Christian orthodoxy "a lie, semi-conscious desire for keeping the rich rich and the poor
poor."(15)   He upheld a wholly secular view of history, as of morals and
politics.   Yet doing so does not impose a "Whig" version.   Orwell also
rejected the revolutionary futurist paradigm.   At Barcelona in 1936 he
had, for a few days, felt its appeal.   Doing so does some credit to his
imagination.   The euphoria did not last, and its going away gave his
writings about Spain much of their sadness, much of their urgency.
     Orwell's secular, down-to-earth approach to English history amounted
to more than a hypothetical via media.   It had an empiricist foundation
in respect for facts and a reporter's eye for gathering them.   It had
walls such as his conscious Englishness.   Inside the structure one could
decorate, furnish, and (where need be) rebuild.   Socialism as taught by
Marxist doctrine and the Labour Party had never "really touched the heart
of the English people."(16)   To work in England it required a basis in
"the English genius"; hence Lion's subtitle.   Orwell's subject matter and
taste came together to make him begin the work with vivid, sensual images.   First, he itemized things; bitterer beer, heavier coins, greener
grass.   The last example may echo Blake's Jerusalem; it certainly does
many travelers' response -- for instance, Macaulay's.(17)   From things
Orwell passed to look at ordinary people.   A group of soft adjectives
such as "gentle" almost makes the picture condescending; but Orwell
brings readers up short by observing the frequency of "bad teeth."   In
context this one shaft says more about the ideals of the later National
Health Service than a dozen blue books or Fabian tracts.   Then Orwell
turned to social relations.   Examples such as gardening, pub life, and
tea drinking served as a metonymy for values of home, voluntary sociabil-
ity, and privacy.(18)
     Orwell returned to these motifs in writing after Lion.   The title of
his column in Tribune, "As I Please," put the matter bluntly.   He let imagination go in a fancy about an ideal pub, "The Moon under Water."(19)
With fine irony in 1946 he itemized a "paradise" where people were never
alone and always in earshot of broadcast music.(20)   He opened himself to
scorn by those who do not share his discrete tastes or general English-
ness.   Yet on balance the identification of self with nation worked.   It
had a factual, measurable basis, since so many shared his values.   More
important, it cut across lines of class, education, and affected style.

Dons and miners shared (and still share) the culture of pubs even though they commonly go to different locals.

So Orwell prepared readers for grand generalization. He had hinted at it near his beginning, when he applied "gentle" to the behavior of common people. England, he said, was a single family. He used the metaphor twice in Lion. The second time he qualified it by noting "wrong members in control."(21) Some, for instance, hibernated through the thirties, refusing to see Hitler's menace. Earlier he had invoked the old image of a "hanging judge." But at least the judge represented law and incorruptibility;(22) his role also symbolized civilian values; there had never been a "naval dictatorship."(23) English people lacked the continental habit of glorifying soldiers and uniforms; they went almost too far the other way. The army's drill had no goose step; here Orwell used a symbol he became fond of, later potent in Nineteen Eighty-Four.(24) Hence, he predicted, England would never have a Gestapo.(25)

Why the dislike for the military? In later years Orwell suggested common revulsion at Oliver Cromwell.(26) In Lion he found more recent root. The family had so far left wrong people in power. "At any normal time the ruling class will rob, mismanage, . . . lead us into the muck"; and yet there was a check to its destructiveness. "Let them get a tug from below that they cannot avoid feeling, and it is difficult for them not to respond."(27) Naked power, vertically imposed, had no positive tradition in England. Orwell's insight anticipated others by two socialist professional historians. Eric Hobsbawm identified — in the late 1960s, of all times — "the fundamental political fact . . . , that this country could not and cannot be run in flat defiance of its working-class majority."(28) Edward Thompson, in the peroration of his Whigs and Hunters, hammered home the theme of law in the eighteenth-century. "The rulers were, . . . whether willingly or unwillingly, the prisoners of their own rhetoric; they played the games of power according to rules which suited them, but they could not break the rules or the whole game would be thrown away."(29)

The argument looks circular. England is nonmilitary. Thompson clearly has been the problem; he solved it, at least as of twelve years ago, by stating that people became the "prisoners of their own rhetoric." Orwell anticipated Thompson's judgment. Britain's rulers "believe in the letter of the law."(30) Orwell had no illusions about the law's historic base, summed up later in Brough Macpherson's label, "possessive individualism."(31) Near the war's end proprietors of some squares in London began putting up new fences, to replace iron railings taken out earlier for scrap. Orwell complained in Tribune. A correspondent took him to task, calling use of these squares by the public a kind of stealing. Nonsense, replied Orwell. Many proprietors of English land "simply seized it by force, afterwards hiring lawyers to provide them with title-deeds . . . upon no sort of pretext except that they had the power to do so."(32) So, in origin, much of law was sham. Yet appeal to it worked. A few months after this exchange he lamented that during the war the law never suppressed, and in the end protected, pacifists.(33)

Regard for law and tradition did not rest perfectly with reactionaries. Nor did it with "the English left-wing intelligentsia." According to Orwell, they "worship Stalin because they have lost their patriotism and their religious belief without losing the need for a god and a fatherland," and so could efficiently "transfer their allegiance to Hitler if Germany won."(34) Persons on both political extremes lacked, to use a favorite word of Orwell's, patriotism. The key argument of Lion's first chapter distinguished it from its parody, militarism. Patriotism can, for instance, appeal to all kinds of people; "not even the rich are uninfluenced by it."(35) The "English genius" taught "gentle" habits, where ordinary persons mimicked and outperformed their supposed betters; such manners worked reciprocally with private interest such as pleasures taken without unwanted musical background.

From here Orwell made a breathtaking leap. One does not expect an agnostic to celebrate "a deep tinge of Christian feeling." Granted that when compared to patriotism both "Christianity and international Social-ism are as weak as straw."(36) Christianity underlay "the English ge-nius." "The whole English-speaking world is haunted" [he must have en-joyed echoing Marx] "by the idea of human equality. . . . The _idea_ is there," derived from "the 'Jewish' . . . idea, . . . that Hitler came in-to the world to destroy."(37) Hence he could look forward with optimism as 1940 ended. "The fact that we are at war has tuned Socialism from a textbook word into realisable policy."(38) Again, "if we alter our structure from below we shall get the government we need."(39)

Orwell simply assumed in 1940 the permanence of gentle manners, of hatred for militarism, of respect for vaguely Christian values and the rule of law. He did so because he thought he knew English history. En-glishmen could "from below" by simple means reaffirm their basic charac-ter and remove "wrong members." They would sidestep totalitarianism. No wonder that some careless readers can imagine _Lion_ written for the Minis-try of Information. One must therefore ask a "whiggish" question: What went wrong with his vision?

Orwell misread the direness of conditions in 1940. He said that a winning war effort would demand drastic changes at home and in the em-pire. Overseas, for instance, there must be dominion status for India as a groundwork for later independence, and a war council with nonwhite mem-bers. In Britain land and banks must be nationalized, public schools op-ened to a great number of ordinary boys, and so forth.(40) None of these changes happened, except the painful separation of India after the war. Orwell misread because he underestimated, of all things, patriotism. The rich did not sell out to Hilter. Coal miners and hop pickers, George Bowlings and Gordon Comstocks — all believed too much in their English culture, including the "Whig" doctrines that explained the culture.

Far from least, he also extrapolated too much from his own frustra-tion. Perversely, the war seemed to vindicate the system. Politicans whom Orwell despised such as Eden and Halifax remained in office until the Labour victory in 1945.(41) Indeed, as William J. West has sug-gested, the war promoted ugly rather than ideal aspects of socialism, such as manipulation of truth.(42)

The boy Eric Blair grew up hearing much nonsense. A great deal of the pain in _The Road to Wigan Pier_, "A Hanging," "Shooting an Elephant," "Such, Such were the Joys . . . ," and many other of his writings comes from their confessional quality. Orwell remembered the falsehoods and his effort to get rid of them. Experiences in Spain put the problem in hard focus. He learned the crucial importance of facts and of lies mas-querading as facts. He found lying postures of the "left-wing intelli-gentsia" and their so-called opponents — such as _Tribune_'s correspondent who said that Orwell sanctioned theft -- alike. The cheerful, patriotic Orwell of 1941 believed, perhaps naively, that facts were facts and truth would prevail. He had learned, by himself and for himself; hence others could do likewise. He would not keep any party line or draw one for oth-ers. Thus he ended by not drawing any for himself. There lies much of his worth and appeal; there too lies much of his pathos.

I thank Arthur Eckstein and William J. West for suggestions about substantive content; Keith Jennison and Marilyn Patterson for editorial advice; and (far from least) Mary Giordano, Jodi Hover, and Lisa Doyle for their typing.

NOTES

1.   George Orwell to Geoffrey Gorer, April 3, 1940, in Collected Essays, Journalism and Letters of George Orwell, ed. Sonia Orwell and Ian Angus, 4 vols (London: Secker and Warburg, 1968) [Hereafter CEJL], I: 528. Copyright 1968 by Harcourt Brace Jovanovich, Inc. reprinted by permission.

2.   Bernard Crick, George Orwell, a Life (Boston, 1980), pp. 273-278.

3.   The anonymously edited A Collection of Essays (Garden City, N.Y.: Doubleday Anchor Books, 1957; reissued New York: Harcourt Brace Jovanovich, Inc., n.d.).

4.   Alex Zwerding, Orwell and the Left (New Haven, 1974); Miriam Gross, ed., The World of Geroge Orwell (London, 1971).

5.   Christopher Small, The Road to Miniluv (London, 1975), pp. 103, 219.

6.   William J. West in discussion with Howard Fink and others, George Orwell International Conference, Hofstra University, Hempstead, New York, October 11, 1984; Arthur Eckstein, "Nineteen Eighty-Four and George Orwell's Other View of Capitalism," presented at same, October 12, 1984.

7.   Orwell's only letter to him in CEJL was written in 1920 (I: 11-12).

8.   Q. D. Leavis, review of Inside the Whale, Scrutiny (September 1940): 173-176.

9.   Peter Stansky and William Abrahams, The Unknown Orwell (New York, 1972), p. 139.

10.   Orwell, "Such, Such Were the Joys . . . ," CEJL IV: 337.

11.   Cyril Connolly, Enemies of Promise and Other Essays (Garden City, N.Y.: Doubleday Anchor Books, 1960), p. 170.

12   Stansky and Abrahams, The Unknown Orwell, p. 155.

13.   Orwell, "As I Please," Tribune, March 14, 1947; CEJL, IV: 306-307.

14.   Henry Fairlie, "Evolution of a Term," The New Yorker, October 19, 1968, p. 184.

15.   Orwell, review of Malcolm Muggeridge, The Thirties, Time and Tide, April 6, 1940; CEJL, II: 15.

16.   Orwell, The Lion and The Unicorn [Hereafter Lion], in ibid., II: 101.

17.   G. O. Trevelyan, The Life and Letters of Lord Macaulay (New York, 1875), II: 335.

18.   Lion, CEJL, II: 57.

19.   Orwell, "The Moon under Water," Evening Standard, February 9, 1946, in ibid., III: 44-47

20.   Orwell, "Pleasure Spots," Tribune, January 11, 1946, in ibid., IV: 79-80.

21.   Lion, II: 84; cf. ibid., II: 68.   Compare "Kipling," in ibid, II: 186.

22.   Ibid., II: 62.

23.   Ibid., II: p. 61.

24.   Ibid., II: p. 62. Compare O. "Raffles and Mrs. Blandish," in ibid., III: 218.

25.   Ibid., II: 59. Compare "London Letter to Partisan Review," April 1941; in ibid., II: 120.

26.   Ibid., "Notes on Nationalism," III: 369.

27.   Ibid., II: 74.

28.   E. J. Hobsbawm, Industry and Empire, (Harmondsworth: Penguin, 1969), p. 17.

29.   E. P. Thompson, Whigs and Hunters (New York, 1975), p. 263. Copyright 1975 by E. P. Thompson; reprinted by permission of Pantheon Books, a division of Random House, Inc.

30.   Orwell, "London Letter to Partisan Review," April 1941, in CEJL, II: 119.

31.   C. B. Macpherson, The Political Theory of Possessive Individualism (Oxford, 1962).

32.   Orwell, "As I Please," Tribune, August 18, 1944, in CEJL, III: 207.

33.   "London Letter to Partisan Review," June 5, 1945, in ibid., III: 384.

34.   Ibid., May 1943 in CEJL, II: 286.

35.   Lion, in ibid., II 66.

36.   Ibid., p. 56.

37.   Ibid., p. 106.

38.   Ibid., p. 94.

39.   Ibid., p. 86.

40.   Ibid., p. 96.

41.   Ibid., p. 69.

42.   See note 6.

9.
"A Monument to the Obvious": George Orwell and Poetry

ROSALY DeMAIOS ROFFMAN

Because of his versatilty and brilliance, no one took seriously Orwell's confession in "Why I Write" that above all he wanted to be a poet. Surprisingly he wrote poems all his life in addition to reviews and essays on the subject -- even though he decided not to seek its publication. When I attended a Nineteen Eighty-Four conference sponsored by the University of Akron, I asked Orwell's biographer, Bernard Crick, about Orwell's abandonment of this genre. He suggested that I look at Orwell's "poem" file in the London archives, the existence of which came as a shock. In the meantime I discovered that although scholars had written extensively on the language and metaphor in this writer's work, no one had ever done anything with his poems (albeit a slim output). In those archives I saw, too, a few youthful and lesser-known verses that did get published in his lifetime.

These poems provide a key to his own views on poetry and meaning. Clearly he had definite ideas about what poetry should be: literature that serves the greatest number of people. Therefore since he believed that "poetry takes us off the earth," he worried that "it sometimes succeeds for the wrong reasons." He was to insist that logic and poetry, in spite of being odd siblings, must coexist in the same household; and he never believed that they lived comfortably under the same roof of contemporaries whose priorities Orwell would argue were askew. Orwell's attitude toward literature is reflected in his poetry and consistent with his idea that all writing had to be a force in the world for good -- and to do that it had to be moral and above all accessible. In his journal (1919) one can see the playful persona that was to stay with him throughout his works -- here is the unpublished verse "Suggested by a Tooth Paste Advertisement" -- which shows that Orwell quite early discerned the power of poetry in advertising, and he understood its widespread appeal no matter how trivial the subject.

Suggested by a Tooth Paste Adertisement.

(Long ago, I used to chant this sometimes as I washed my teeth, but that is a practice I have abandoned for two years or more. My self respect and my last tooth brush both wore out soon after I got here.)

Brush your teeth up and down, brother,
Oh, brush them up and down!
All the folks in London Town
Brush their teeth right up and down,
Oh! How they shine!

> Aren't they bloody fine?
> Night and morning, my brother,
> Oh brush them up and down!

In "Politics vs. Literature" Orwell praises Swift as a good writer but calls him "insane," for "if one is capable of intellectual detachment one can perceive merit in a writer whom one deeply disagrees with but enjoyment is a different matter."(1)   Although he valued writing primarily as a "free and sincere expression of a human truth,"(2) he wanted his audience to enjoy his verse and above all he wanted his poems to be understood.   In his reviews and essays on poetry he divides poets into two respective camps: those he could recite after two readings who express popular sentiments, and "the others" he denounces as the elitist and "fascist" promoters of obscurity, those Orwell accused of corrupting our language.

Although Orwell did not think himself a poet, his first publication was poetry, but he abandoned the aspiration to become a poet as it became clear that his tastes, which ran to music hall verse, doggerel, hymns, and marching songs, were at odds with his contemporaries. But he often wrote about poetry, and occasionally a poem of his would appear in print. Most of the time, however, he simply tucked them into an "unpublished" poems file or into his novels, journals, and essays.

What kind of poetry did he write? The poem he appends to his 1943 essay "Looking Back on the Spanish War" is probably Orwell at his best. The poem addresses an unnamed Italian soldier who, like Orwell, had volthe unteered to fight in Spain in 1936. Orwell claims for this soldier an identity — this often-quoted finale (which provided George Woodcock with title for this well-known study of Orwell):

> But that thing that I saw in your face
> No power can disinherit
> No bomb that ever burst
> Shatters the crystal spirit.(3)

"No bomb that ever burst/Shatters the crystal spirit" is a typical Orwell line. It could stand as epigraph or slogan, though he was skeptical of slogans. Orwell, however, respected the popular sentiments of slogans and voiced disdain for lack of clarity in the sloganless poetry written by his peers.

Orwell's own poetry, less celebratory than political, addresses the prose themes of his life. A favorite theme was the oppression of the defenseless. He is their spokesman, and his poems, even on personal subjects, often border on propaganda. The sentiments expressed are bare — Orwell's young soldier, the archetypal vicitm of war, "was born knowing what [Orwell] had learned/Out of books and slowly." The voice in his poems is the same voice full of self-blame that we hear in the protagonists of his novels and the "I" of his essays who watches a hanging and shoots an elephant. His poems always articulate a position on the dramatic conflict he creates in these verse stories.

In most Orwell poems there is no problem identifying the drama between the speaker and the addressee or occasion. The death of the young Italian soldier whose hand Orwell shook before the young man's tragic death becomes the occasion for the elegy. The sadness and distaste of the speaker for war, "the lie that slew you is buried/under a deeper lie," mounts until the poem's finale, when the soldier's spirit, even in death, transcends the powers that disregard "his battered face/Purer than any woman's."

Orwell's first published poem was also about war. But Orwell the man never returned to the same sentiments he expressed as an eleven-year-old boy. This poem, entitled "Awake Young Men of England," was accepted immediately upon submission to the <u>Henley and South Oxfordshire Standard</u> and was awarded a prize. It implores young men to enlist by the thousands;

> Oh! give me the strength of the Lion
>   The wisdom of Reynard the Fox
> And then I'll hurl troops at the Germans
>   And give them the hardest of knocks.(4)

Like all his poems, this one has a definite and conventional rhyme scheme. The meter of this poem owes a debt to the popular poet Robert Service with language that is "subKipling at his wartime worst."(5) Orwell was convinced quite early that poetry had to rhyme and that no matter how hostile the average man "is to poetry he is not strongly hostile to verse."(6)

What Orwell did in the poems he wrote as a child (and he recalls his earliest poem at the age of five about a tiger with chairlike teeth in "Why I Write") he did in his later verses as well. The movement is from an "I" to a "We"; the narrator is always isolated, seeks camaraderie, and has a deep distrust of intellectual solutions to problems. That is why Orwell preferred the vulgarity of the music hall and the marching song with a direct-line approach to human emotions. For Orwell popular songs are never embarrassing simply because they are obvious. The doggerel and music hall sentiments of Blair go along with the slogans and social messages of George Orwell — the boy is always with the man.

Unlike his contemporaries, he never abandoned strict and singable rhythms in favor of free verse. Two years later the same newspaper published the poem Orwell wrote for an assignment in school on the occasion of the death of Kitchener. Orwell's three-stanzaed elegy concludes:

> Who follows in his steps no danger shuns
>   Nor stoops to conquer by shameful deed
> An honest and unselfish race he runs,
>   From fear and malice freed.(7)

Orwell eventually labels these unabashed sentiments the stuff of "good bad poetry," which in his Kipling essay he characterizes as a faint sign of "emotional overlap" between the intellectual and the ordinary man. Good bad poems belabor the obvious; they work through "bare sentiment." Orwell believed that poetry was disliked by most people and set himself the task of doing something to alter that opinion. He even made the daring suggestion that poetry be read on the radio as an aid to understanding.(8)

Orwell, who had a classical bias and education, expresses an early love for Shakespeare and Milton, an admiration for Housman, Hopkins, and Lawrence, and a constant ambivalence about Kipling's verse, whose rhythms have a way of intruding on Orwell's poetry. He was convinced that enthusiasm for poetry could be generated only if the poetry appeared in disguised form — in folk poetry, doggerel, nonsense verse, and songs that soldiers made up, "including some of the words that go with the bugle calls." As far as he was concerned, these were the authentic forms for poetry — and Richard Blair, his adopted son, recalls how his father would entertain him with his own versions of childhood songs and nursery rhymes.(9) On a page of the journals he kept at Jura he wrote:

> Swing child Elizabeth under the apple tree
> Few shall escape the jaws of the crocodile
> As you are, so were we, as we are, you must be.
> Swing, swing, swing.

Whenever he could Orwell incorporated hymns, doggerel, and verse into his novels and essays. Minimus composes a stirring hymn in Animal Farm, and the washerwoman blues song and nursery rhymes are constant motifs in Nineteen Eighty-Four. Gordon Comstock, second-rate poet and protagonist in Keep the Aspidistra Flying, struggles with the composition of a single poem throughout this novel and gives up poetry writing altogether at the end of this work.(10)

A favorite sentiment in Orwell's poetry may be described as nostalgia. Even at the age of seventeen he submitted an ode to College Days which expresses the same reverence for country life later to be savored by such characters as Gordon. The longing for and idealization of the past recurs in a number of places as a reminder frequently of better days.

> Hills we have climbed and bogs that we have sat in
> Pools where we have drenched our feet in mid-December,
> Trains we have packed, woods we have lost our hat in
> When you are past and gone, we will remember.(11)

Orwell did not publish again for twelve years; though in 1918 he sent a sympathetic poem to his close childhood friend, Jacintha Buddicom, with whom he used to play a game called "set piece poetry." Buddicom says Orwell became quite good at it in her book, Eric and Us, especially in the coining of "undictionary" words. In a poem entitled "Pagan" Orwell tries to fuse the romantic and the ordinary, which clearly became the unresolved challenge of his aesthetic capabilities in poetry.

> So here are you and here am I,
>   Where we may think our gods to be;
> Above the earth beneath the sky,
>   Naked souls alive and free.
>
> The Autumn wind goes rustling by
>   And stirs the stubble at our feet
> Out of the West it whispering blows,
>   Stops to caress and onward goes.(12)

Orwell could write poems like "Pagan," but he could entertain his classmates with satirical portraits of their teachers. In the file is a poem written in 1919:

> Then up waddled Wog and he squeaked in Greek:
> 'I've grown another hair on my cheek,'
> Crace replied in Latin with his toadlike smile
> And I hope you've grown a lovely new pile.
> With a loud deep fart from the bottom of my heart
> How'd you like Venetian art?(13)

The caricature is a plea for sanity and the rhythm is reminiscent of the chorus-girl's verse he was later to admire so much in Inside the Whale.

Tucked into the poem file are two pieces Orwell wrote after he had resigned his post in Burma in 1925. Written at about the same time, their subject is an encounter with a prostitute. They are curious poems that differ considerably in tone -- in neither is the prostitute made to be the victim.

The first, "The Lesser Evil," centers on the speaker's choice between attending a brothel or a church on Sunday. "Once more devout old maids were bawling/Their ugly rhymes of death and pain." The speaker resentfully chooses the hardly attractive but definitely lesser of two evils; perhaps he does so regretfully.

The woman waited for me there
        As down the little street I trod
And musing on her oily hair,
        I turned into the house of God.(14)

The rhythm calls to mind the minor character Ampleforth, who appears
in Nineteen Eighty-Four and is punished for Thoughtcrime. But his real
crime is being a rhyming poet!   When he can think only of "God" as a
rhyme for "sod" he becomes instantly suspect to the party.
    The second poem, "Romance," is more humorously cynical and centers
less on the brothel than on the venal maiden by whom (in three brief
stanzas) the "I" of the poem is attracted. The speaker becomes more aggressive as the maiden's shrewdness surfaces. Orwell's sense of play and
amusement at being "taken in" accounts for the tone of romance. The poem
demonstrates Orwell's kinship both to Housman, a poet he admired for his
themes of "disappointed hedonism," and to Kipling, whose "rhythms" and
"mysterious East" sentiments were well known to him.

When I was young and had no sense
        In far-off Mandalay
I lost my heart to a Burmese girl
        As lovely as the day.

But the finale in Orwell's poems is a surprise exercise in "bravado" --
as the girl holds out for more money.

She looked at me, so pure, so sad,
        The loveliest thing alive,
And in her lisping virgin voice
        Stood out for twenty-five
The gentleman in the poem actually offered her only
twenty.(15)

In notes made for Burmese Days, Orwell composed an epitaph that he
later decided to delete. Perhaps this poem best characterizes the Burmese experience for Orwell. The epitaph was for John Flory, -- so full
of self-loathing that he leaves this message in verse and then commits
suicide.

O stranger, as you voyage here
And read this welcome, shed no tear;
But take this single gift I give,
And learn from me how not to live.(16)

Soon after the Burmese poems three pieces by Orwell were published
in Adelphi. The first, entitled "Poem," returns us to an earlier theme
of autumnal melancholy -- it is frequently autumn in Orwell's poems, the
spur for his nostalgia.
    In "Poem" a strong alienated figure sadly muses on his future. Un-
like earlier generations who were nurtured not by a belief in personal
immortality but by faith that "their way of life would continue," modern
man, Orwell laments, has a dubious connection to past and future:

And I see the people thronging the streets
The death-marked people, they and I
Goalless, rootless, like leaves drifting,
Blind to the earth and to the sky --

The poem is set in autumn and is almost devoid of metaphors and imagery, but its heavy-handed pronouncements are clear. It is effective

because of a strong rhythm and clear message. Yet what we have here are
borderline if not full-fledged cliches — sere elms "brooding in the
mist," "a stream of precious life that flows within us," and "hours burn-
ing clear and brave/Like candle flames in windless air." The unhappy
speaker in this poem urges the audience to speak out regardless of the
consequences.

> So shall we in the rout of life
> Some thought, some faith, some meaning save,
> And speak it once before we go
> In silence to the silent grave.(17)

In 1933 Orwell also was reading Lawrence and wrote admiringly about
his having seized on an "aspect of things that no one else would have
noticed." He saw in Lawrence "a movement away from our mechanized civilization, which is not going to happen, and which he knows is not going
to happen." In October Orwell's new poem, perhaps reflecting Lawrence's
influence, was published in Adelphi (one of the three places that published Orwell's poetry while he was alive). This haunting allegorical
gem tells the story of two men who barter clothes against a meal, each
man thinking he has improved his lot.

> Bargaining for a deal,
> Naked skin for empty skin
> Clothes against a meal

The two men face each other pitifully at the end of this poem, hope-
lessly gulled by false panaceas. The poem ends as it began with one man
hungry, one man cold:

> A dressed man and a naked man
> Stood by the kip-house fire.(18)

A third poem published in Adelphi that year with the curious title
"On a Ruined Farm Near the His Master's Voice Gramophone Factory" is a
meditation on the dissolution of the traditional decencies of England
closely linked to the countryside (already an important theme in The Road
To Wigan Pier, Coming up for Air, and The Lion and the Unicorn). The
speaker stands at the "lichened gate/With warring worlds on either hand";
he sees the factory towers and remembers the ruined countryside. Orwell
asks why his world, his home is yet,

> So alien still? For I can neither
> Dwell in that world, nor turn again
> To scythe and spade, but only loiter
> Among the trees the smoke has slain.

The speaker is left standing (as is typical in almost all of these poems)
in the final verse, "moveless still between the water and the corn."(19)
In the essay "Why I Write" Orwell considers his own dilemma as a
writer forced to become a pamphleteer. In a little poem that he wrote
about this predicament Orwell clarifies his moral commitment and laments
its cost to him as a writer, again wistfully conjuring up a more idealized past. It begins, "A happy vicar I might have been/Two hundred years
ago." But as the poem develops he charges himself instead with the role
of truthmonger.

> But girl's bellies and apricots,
> Roach in shaded stream,

> Horses, ducks in a flight at dawn,
> All these are a dream.

The rude awakening appears in the final stanza:

> I dreamed I dwelt in marble halls,
> And woke to find it true;
> I wasn't born for an age like this:
> Was Smith? Was Jones? Were you?(20)

Again we have the speaker as the collective voice and the familiar stance of alienated man.

After the Spanish Civil War Orwell never wavered again, even in his poetry. He promised that everything he wrote would be in the service of socialism, and stated that it was clearly "nonsense in our period to think that one can avoid writing of such subjects." It was in this regard that he felt the least enthusiasm for his fellow poets, such as Pound, who in their "pessimistic conservatism" "plumped for fascism."(21)

The last draft of an unfinished poem appears in a hospital notebook in which Orwell was also working on a revision of Nineteen Eighty-Four. In these last fragments his commitment to the clear moral purposes of the poet is reiterated. That Orwell decided to write a poem and not an essay about his childhood sexual encounter with a plumber's daughter is significant. It is obviously a moment he recalls with great pain and from the perspective of a mature man. Orwell regrets not the sexual encounter but the rejection of the little girl because she was "common." This is what he is thinking about on his death-bed, and even at this difficult time Orwell carries the responsibility and emotional effect of this incident unabashedly with him into the poem. The seven year-old plumber's daughter "shows me all she's got":

> How long did that idyll last?
> Not even as long as spring
> I think that May was still in bloom
> When I did the deathly thing.(22)

The "deathly thing" in question has to do with class snobbery and personal rejection. Orwell tells us that he has paid a price since that day: "I have never loved/Save those who loved me not." Though unfinished, this is one of the most moving of Orwell's poems. He uses his personal experience to project a simple truth or prescribe a basic tenet for living an uncorrupted life. His alienated speaker is meant to be everyman -- and the songs he sings are simple ones.

No matter how politely he dissociated himself from the writing of verse, Orwell's poems deserve examination. Twelve were published in his lifetime and about eleven more drafts and pieces were tucked into the files; it is not clear what, if anything, Orwell intended to do with them. But his poems provide another dimension of his aesthetic sensibilities -- in his poems we see his definition of poetry. Hugh Kenner, the American literary critic, remarked recently that Orwell elected not to be a poet because he believed that poets were not as concerned with the "trustworthiness"(23) of words as is the journalist or novelist. Thus Orwell, who was to write poetry reviews and verse all his life, doubted that modern poetry could do anyone much good and externalized his experiences in much the way that greeting card versifiers do; his personal emotions were less important than communicating with his public. Still, it is obvious that writing poetry meant enough for him to continue to do it throughout his life.

Orwell was a precursor of the poets who today express their political views in personal poetry that is meant to reach a wide audience. It

is a kind of poetry that celebrates the common man and woman, their ori-
dinary aspirations and their extraordinary pain. I think we are seeing
an echo of Orwell's concerns in a poem about torture in El Salvador by C.
Forche, about prison fights by E. Knight, about women's anger by A. Rich,
about ecology by R. Bly. The good bad poems he himself wrote were "monuments to the obvious," but Orwell spoke out for a viable connection between subject matter and expression, and struggled with that problem and
reponsibility his entire life. I think about how he might enjoy the efforts today to capture the poetry of preliterate people as well as the
folk who are natural poets without any theory at all. I think he would
have endorsed the poetry of a woman named M. Mahnkey from the Ozarks
whose poems, like her "To a Melancholy Lady" do what Orwell says poems
should do.

> Raise some guineas
> Raise some gourds
> Make a little gesture towards
> A richer life in service passed
> To leave some imprint at the last
> If not great deeds
> Or golden words
> The raise some guineas
> Raise some gourds.(24)

Or the soldier who wrote home from Vietnam before he died:

> Take what they have left
> and what they have taught you
> with their dying
> and keep it with your own . . .
> And in that time when men decide and feel safe
> to call the war insane,
> take one moment to embrace
> those gentle heroes
> you left behind . . .(25)

Both of these poems, like the poems written by Orwell, are monuments to
the obvious. We are richer for them.

NOTES

   References to material in The Collected Essays, Journalism and Letters of George Orwell edited by Sonia Orwell and Ian Angus, four volumes
(New York: Harcourt Brace Jovanovich, 1968) will be referred to as CEJL.
Material in the Orwell Collection in the Manuscripts and Rare Books Department of University College, London, is referred to as "Orwell Archive." Reference numbers are not given as the materials are still being
processed. But the cited works are accessible since the Archives were
opened in May 1984.

   1.   CEJL, IV, "Politics vs. Literature," p. 221.

   2.   Wayne Warncke, "George Orwell's Critical Approach to Literature," Southern Humanities Review, II: 486-487.

   3.   "Looking Back on the Spanish War" (written in 1942), in CEJL,
II: 249.

   4.   Published on October 2, 1914.

5.   Bernard Crick, George Orwell, (London: Penguin, 1980), p. 85.

6.   "Rudyard Kipling," in Orwell Reader (New York: Harcourt Brace Jovanovich, 1956), p. 281.

7.   Published on July 21, 1916.

8.   CEJL, II: 194-195.

9.   July 9, 1984, Penguin Bookstore, Covent Garden, reception to honor George Orwell Summer School. Richard Blair shared this bit of information and memory with me.

10.   The archives do not include poems found in novels and journals in the "published" and "unpublished" file(s) of Orwell's poems. These poems may be added to the number and are mentioned in this paper.

11.   Orwell Archive, "Ode to Field Days," Printer's Proof, A. 143, 920.
12.   Orwell Archive, "The Pagan," Ps., 4pgs., S.3283. 1918.

13.   Bernard Crick cites Denys King-Farlow speaking in "George Orwell: A Programme of Recorded Reminiscences," arranged and narrated by Rayner Heppenstall, recorded on August 20, 1960, and first broadcast on November 2, 1960 (BBC Archives, Ref. No. TLO 24177). Cope in Orwell Archive. See "College Days with George Orwell."

14.   This and the poem in note 15 are in the "unpublished" poems file in the Orwell Archives, S. 3295, 1928-1929.

15.   Ibid.

16.   CEJL, I: 516-518.

17.   Adelphi, March 1933 or CEJL, p. 119.

18.   CEJL, I: 516-518.

19.   This is one of Orwell's best-known poems. Its cynicism and futility make the brief drama into a balanced drama -- reminiscent of ballad casualness. CEJL, I: 4-5. This poem first appeared in Adelphi in December 1936.

20.   CEJL, I: 5.

21.   In an entire essay, originally published as "Dickens, Dali and Others" in 1946 (CEJL, III: 273-276), Orwell despairs over the large numbers (best writers) of his time whom he calls "reactionary" — Yeats is the primary example. He writes that "although fascism doesn't offer any real reaction to the past, those who yearn for the past will accept fascism sooner than its probable alternatives."

22.   Crick cites a "hospital notebook" in which he jotted down this unfinished poem. It is the same notebook that he used in 1948 to make some final notes toward the revision of Nineteen Eighty-Four. In George Orwell, pp. 44-45.

23.   Conference on George Orwell and Nineteen Eighty-Four held in Rosemont College, Pennsylvania April 1984. Kenner spoke on Orwell's documentary style and believability.

24.   <u>Ozarks Lyrics</u>, (Point Lookout, MO: School of the Ozark, Point Lookout, 1980), p. 61.

25.   <u>New York Times</u>, September 30, 1984, p. 1, col. 4.

10.
George Orwell and the Problematics of Nonfiction
HOWARD WOLF

George Orwell is one of a small (dare I say select?) group of writers in England and America whose influence is so pervasive that we may feel it is not even necessary for us to read him: an author who has written a book so embedded in our lives, Nineteen Eighty-Four, that we may not be able even to remember if we have read it or not. This is also the case with Robinson Crusoe, Gulliver's Travels, Oliver Twist, and Huck Finn, to name a few.

This curious fate of Nineteen Eighty-Four would please Orwell, if one can imagine catching him off-guard taking pleasure in anything after Burma, after 1936, two of the irreversible lines of demarcation in his career. It might please him to know that he had disappeared as the author of his most important book. This disappearance would mark a further step in the erasure of personality and class origins he tried so hard to achieve.

Having effaced his personality as Eric Blair to become George Orwell, he may have succeeded finally in washing the slate clean of George Orwell as well. This positive elimination of the self, if I may call it that, is a curious accomplice of the eradication of old identity and then the manufacture of new consciousness in Nineteen Eighty-Four.

Orwell might be pleased that his flight from biological origin, socio-economic background, and literary recognition was complete. He would have succeeded at last in making a complete riches to rags story out of his life; he would have succeeded in becoming common and plain (Protestant and Democratic, terms he loved, if we can impute love to him as a dominant emotion). He would have escaped at last from the tyranny, as he felt it, of being special, different, of having even a small place in the "lower upper-middle class" (Wigan Pier).

He might be able to say at last about himself what he says about the "working class" in "The Art of Donald McGill":

> And this reflects, on a comic level, the working-class out-
> look which takes it as a matter of course that youth and ad-
> venture — almost, indeed, [individual life] — end . . .
> with marriage.(1)

If Nineteen Eighty-Four presents a somewhat accurate representation of advanced totalitarian technologies at work in the conditioning of the individual, Orwell himself, on the other side of the coin, shows us his moral and even poignant attempt as a modern man to level himself and become a common, ordinary, defeated, and Mass man because these terms became, for Orwell, for better or worse (and it was both), the inescapable terms of common humanity in the twentieth-century.

Even as Orwell struggled in his life and in his writing to surrender personality to the "essentially public, non-individual activities that the age forces on all of us," it is equally true and ironic that most of his work bears the clear stamp of authorial presence and autobiography.(2) For all of Orwell's attempts to escape the "perqs," of the "pre-1914 age, a moment of personal and cultural privilege to which he returns somewhat obsessively in his writing, he could not escape the need, habit, or usefulness of autobiography as a genre."(3) Even if Eric Blair gave way to the identity of George Orwell, someone (figure or fiction), as it were, had to bear witness to the political and historical forces impinging upon his self.

Driven by the necessity to bear witness where others would choose silence or distortion, the persona, if not the person, of George Orwell speaks in the first person about "his" experience of Burma in "Shooting an Elephant" and "A Hanging"; about the experience of boarding school in "Such, Such Were the Joys . . ."; about the slops and kitchens of Paris in "Down and Out in Paris and London"; and about the experiences of Spain, that crucial 1936 event, in "Looking Back upon the Spanish War" and Homage to Catalonia.

It is as if the struggle between authorhsip and anonymity, between autobiography and impersonality were for Orwell a struggle itself between, on the one hand, the accrued weight of the nineteenth-century with its claims about self and character (see, e.g., Orwell's mixed feelings about Dickens and Kipling) and, on the other, the thrust of the twentieth-century toward the surrender of the self to Socialist theory;(4) between the privileges of pre-1914 humanism and the annihilation of self in the cogs of the totalitarian machines of the modern period (see Chaplin's film Modern Times).

For all of Eric Blair's efforts to become George Orwell and for George Orwell, as author, to suppress the presence of the author, for all of Orwell's efforts to become at one with his subjects in, say, The Road to Wigan Pier, there remains the need, passion, and perversion for him to be an "I," however constructed.

The full meaning or implication this doubleness for Orwell or for us is not clear, but we do Orwell, man and creator, a disservice, if we approach him in our naivete and need as though he were a guileless and artless writer. If we do this we rob him of his necessary struggles, of the terrible conflicts that the twentieth-century imposes on us to sort out somehow the claims of the self from the impingement of mass movements, technology, and all those tendencies that have assaulted and weakened the concept of the self.(5)

Where I once admired the directness and honesty of Orwell and admired Trilling's essay, "George Orwell and the Politics of Truth" (see The Opposing Self), as I admired Irving Howe's essay, "As the Bones Know" (see Decline of the New), I now see a more difficult struggle in Orwell between the claims of nonfiction and its relationship to history and the inescapable presence of the author;(6) between the claims of creative or constructed writing and what we called confidently "journalism" from about 1660 to 1960 (a three hundred-year grace period when it seemed clear, despite the emergence of modernism, that we knew the important distinctions between truth and falsehood, fiction and facts, self and narrator, history and imagination).

Just as it would be a disservice to Orwell to accept his or any critic's claim about his being only "a good man"(7) or a "virtuous man,"(8) so would it be a reduction and evasion of Orwell's complexity as a man and writer to accept at face value his own claims about the possibilities of writing transparent prose, a prose that could give us just history. We do him a disservice if we agree completely with him that "good prose is like a window pane."(9) We do him a disservice if we see only the values of what Howe calls "a stripped speech."(10)

We must remember that in the same essay, "Why I Write," Orwell also says without much elaboration, "Above the level of a railway guide, no book is quite free from esthetic considerations." Just as Orwell could not quite free himself from the legacy of personality and the relationship of that personality to the mood and ambience of his own somewhat privileged background in the social history of pre-1914 England, so he could not quite liberate himself from a set of attitudes about language that complicates, if it not negates, the claims for transparency.

We are likely to remember the sentence about the windowpane, with its clarity and deceptive disclaimer of metaphor even as it invokes one, and not remember that he says in the same crucial essay:

> I give all this background information because I do not think
> one can assess a writer's motives without knowing something
> of his early development. His subject matter will be deter-
> mined by the age he lives in -- at least this is true in tum-
> ultuous, revolutionary ages like our own -- but before he
> ever begins to write he will have acquired an emotional atti-
> tude from which he will never completely escape.(11)

Just as the "I" asserts itself in Orwell against the effacements of the self, so does his late nineteenth and early twentieth-century "development" assert itself against the claims of twentieth-century ideology. The "I" which Orwell associates with the humanism of character of the pre-1914 period asserts itself against the faceless totalitarianisms of the twentieth-century. In a similar way the pastoral associations of the pre-1914 period are opposed to the technologies and technological fantasies of totalitariansim in the modern period.

These positive associations with the nineteenth-century assert themselves in Orwell against, and despite, his preference for socialism and advanced industrialism. In a sense Orwell would have wanted -- ideally -- a fusion of democratic socialism in a pastoral environment, a synthesis he imagines in Wigan Pier.

One cannot separate in this way Orwell's sense of his language from the emotional attitude of his childhood about reading. Language can never be transparent for Orwell because language leads to literature for him in both subtle and obvious ways. Orwell is always poignant (a rare quality for him) when he remembers the literature of his childhood, the literature of the "pre-1914 age" toward which he has such divided feelings; the literature that embodies for him both the terms of imperialism, Etonian pride, and snobbery, and the class cruelty of "bullies" against "new boys," as much as it embodies a feeling of relaxation, tranquility, of being "out for a walk," with all the attendant boyhood associations of freedom and exploration:

> No One can look back on his schooldays and say with truth
> that they were altogether unhappy.
>   I have good memories of Crossgates, among a horde of bad
> ones. Sometimes on summer afternoons there were wonderful
> expeditions across the Downs, or to Beachy Head, where one
> bathed dangerously among the chalk boulders and came home
> covered with cuts. And there were still more wonderful mid-
> summer evenings when, as a special treat, we were not driven
> off to bed as usual but allowed to wander about the grounds
> in the long twilight, ending up with a plunge into the swim-
> ming bath at about nine o'clock. There was the joy of waking
> early on summer mornings and getting an hour's undisturbed
> reading (Ian Hay, Thackeray, Kipling and H. G. Wells were the
> favourite authors of my boyhood) in the sunlit, sleeping dor-
> mitory. There was also cricket, which I was no good at but

with which I conducted a sort of hopeless love affair up to
the age of about eighteen. And there was the caterpillars --
the silky green and purple puss-moth, the ghostly green pop-
lar-hawk, the privet hawk, large as one's third finger, spec-
imens of which could be illicitly purchased for sixpence at a
shop in the town -- and, when one could escape long enough
from the master who was "taking the walk," there was the excitement of dredging the dew-ponds on the Downs for enormous
newts with orange-coloured bellies. This business of being
out for a walk, coming across something of fascinating interest and then being dragged away from it by a yell from the
master, like a dog jerked onwards by the leash, is an important feature of school life.(12)

Nowhere is this bonding of language and experience, literature and
experience, clearer than in Orwell's "How the Poor Die." If the essay
moves us because of its accurate charting of the debasements of the poor
and sick in Hospital X in 1920, if the account of Hospital X becomes a
blueprint and metaphor for the dehumanizing effects of institutions in
the twentieth-century, it is also, we can see now, a made story of memory, a story of recall, a story of making associations that connect experience and literature through the memory and remembering of childhood.
    Orwell says at the beginning of the essay/story, "When we got into
the ward I was aware of a strange feeling of familiarity whose origin I
did not succeed in pinning down till later in the night."(13) By the end
of the long, dark night of the dehumanized body and soul, Orwell says,
"what the scene reminded me of, of course, was the reeking, pain-filled
hospitals of the Nineteenth Century," an "unearthing from memory" of
Tennyson's "The Children's Hospital," which I had not thought about for
twenty years," a poem Orwell had shuddered over (not without pleasure,
one imagines) with a sick-nurse in childhood.(14)
    Elsewhere in this essay/story, one of the masterpieces of the pre-
1936 period, Orwell mentions War and Peace, Melville's Whitejacket, among
other books, and, of course, Dickens and Kipling -- those prototypical
writers, for Orwell, of the oppressed and the oppressors as it was depicted in the nineteenth-century. If it is clear that Orwell's own
thinking is closer to Dickens's thinking than to Kipling's, it is also
true that he is sympathetic to Kipling, as his essay on Kipling makes
clear and as we would have understood anyway all along.
    For all of Orwell's objection to the inhumanities of Raj imperial-
ism, to what he called the "pre-chloroform" era, he could not get around
a certain kind of cozy feeling for Kipling -- the feeling, inevitably, of
childhood that he associates with the Victorian period.
    Whatever else is true, Orwell was always looking for home even as he
repudiated his middle-class civil servant origins. This is one facet of
the psychological and social mystery of his life. In this respect there
is a crucial passage in The Road to Wigan Pier, a book infused with autobiography and theory, as well as social investigation, where Orwell finds
a pocket of bourgeois comfort in the midst of the working class he has
come to defend:

        I should say that a manual worker, if he is in steady
    work and drawing good wages -- an "if" which gets bigger and
    bigger -- has a better chance of being happy than an "edu-
    cated" man. His home life seems to fall more naturally into
    sane and comely shape. I have often been struck by the pecu-
    liar easy completeness, the perfect symmetry as it were, of a
    working-class interior at its best. Especially on winter eve-
    nings after tea, when the fire glows in the open range and
    dances mirrored in the steel fender, when Father, in shirt-

sleeves sits in the rocking chair at one side of the fire
reading the racing finals, and Mother sits on the other with
her sewing, and the children are happy with a pennorth of
mint humbugs, and the dog lolls roasting himself on the rag
mat -- it is a good place to be in, provided that you can be
not only in it but sufficiently _of_ it to be taken for
granted.(15)

This Henry Moore version of the working-class family interior, as it
were, seems to get at the very heart of a double-search in Orwell for the
completeness of "home life" and the rejection of those middle-class values as embodied in English culture. If that culture made a virtue of the
"home," it also made an ethic out of keeping "good wages" low.
    This contradiction between acceptance and rejection of the nine-
teenth-century values lies at the heart of Orwell as it lies in the center "How the Poor Die." In the long night of personal suffering and em-
pathetic sorrow for his fellow sufferers, Orwell takes comfort in the
very literature that itself, to some extent, _justified_ the suffering in
the first place -- through sublimation (Tennyson) or moral heroics
(Kipling).
    What is clear, in any case, is that there is nothing "transparent"
about Orwell's use of language in "How the Poor Die." The "transparent"
gives way to the personally recollected as, in another context, the quest
for anonymous and impersonal history gave way to the intervention of author, personality, persona of self, the "I" of autobiographical writings.
    Orwell's interest in the shaping and reshaping powers of language
achieves full expression in _Nineteen Eighty-Four_ (a work that shows Orwell's preoccupation with the connection of language to experience),
though it is read usually for its political and apocalyptic images rather
than for its intelligence about the connection between language and consciousness.
    Whatever else it might be, _Nineteen Eighty-Four_ is a book about lan-
guage. From start to finish the book is about the "erasure" of personality through the manipulation of language. Writing in one's own voice
with one's own hand is the book's decisive and subversive act: "To mark
the paper was the decisive act.   In small clumsy letters he wrote:
April 4th, 1984."(16) When people mention _Nineteen Eighty-Four_, they
usually mean, I think, to invoke an image of anonymity created through
the authoritarian uses of technology. They usually mention Big Brother
as an equivalent for the Boss, of the school, or now the computer and
word processor, and there may be elements of truth in these associations.
However, but it is preeminently and predominantly a book about language
and the power of language to shape a new self -- something Orwell could
understand because he had done it to himself, in a way, in a variety of
ways.
    When people mention _Nineteen Eighty-Four_, having read it or not,
they usually also mean to bring a terminal date to mind. The book and
date are intended to suggest an end of humanism, the culmination of modern history leading to the annihilation of character as we understood it
from Wordsworth through Freud, and there _is_ an uncanny way in which the
book (text? document? -- one hesitates to call it merely a novel), does
feel terminal.
    But the book, in fact, begins in _Nineteen Eighty-Four._ The pro-
cesses and tendencies leading to the obliteration of the "19th Century
Self" are far from complete. Although "no book written before approxi-
mately 1960 could be translated as a whole, various writers, such as
Shakespeare, Milton, Swift, Byron, and Dickens and some others, were
therefore in [_process_] of translation."(17)

With wisdom, perhaps charity or illusion, Orwell sets the date for the final erasure of the humanistic and literary past (they are inseparable for him) in 2050.

> It was chiefly in order to allow time for the preliminary work of translation that the final adoption of Newspeak had been fixed for so late a date as 2050.(18)

The novel, as most people invoke and feel it, should be called 2050.

Where we thought we had sailed through a projected future to a culmination, where we have been waiting since the book's publication in 1949 to discover if the awesome projection would turn out to be terrible truths, we now find that we have only arrived at the beginning of Orwell's scenario for our eventual demise as individual and conscious human beings.

This is the future we must now contemplate -- or have the ratios of technology and inhumanity changed? Will the old values of privacy and friendship be eradicated in quite the same way toward the same ends that Orwell envisioned? If we cannot predict the shape the future, we can certainly see that available technology -- in particular the combining of the computer with video elements -- makes Orwell's forecast all the more possible, if not probable.

If Orwell leaves us a profound legacy, it may not be so much in terms of the actual political history we are likely to know as in his seeing how powerful connections between media and history can shape consciousness and make a new kind of man and woman possible.

Darwin had seen adaptation to environment as the dominant principle in life; Freud and Marx had seen "conflict" (from the related, if different, perspectives of "ambivalence" and "dialectic") as the significant force in human history. Where these major thinkers had staked their claims in these ways, Orwell left us with no less profound a set of questions about the relationships of technology and language, language as technology, to consciousness.

Because Orwell had intervened in his own life by inventing "George Orwell" and because he had seen the role of literature and language in shaping his own destiny, so he could imagine a future in which the means of producing signs and significations and distributing language (and symbols) might be used to create a new man and make a new history.

Despite the fact that Orwell does not leave us so much with a version of history that is compatible with the actual events of our global history, he does point us in the direction of seeing in what terms, among others, this history must be understood: that is, the connection between television and community; the shift from a culture of literature to one of information; and, most subtly, a surrender of consciousness to neurological and retinal stimulations.

As Nineteen Eighty-Four alerts us to the dangers of state control of information, it also dramatizes honestly and creatively the psychological and aesthetic appeal of surrendering the self in a period of pervasive anxiety. As Winston's surrender marks "negatively" an end to humanity, Eric Blair's "positive" surrender to George Orwell and Orwell's disappearance into his greatest work, his contemporary myth, marks a problematic triumph of the imagination in his fiction and nonfiction.

By looking, then, at the problematic of nonfiction in Orwell, we may come to see the double possibilities of language, symbolic systems, and the distribution of these systems of signs and symbols by advanced technological societies. We may come to see both the constructive and destructive possibilities of transforming the self through language.

NOTES

1.   George Orwell, "The Art of Donald McGill," in The Collected Essays, Journalism and Letters of George Orwell. vol. II, My Country Right or Left 1940–1943, eds. Sonia Orwell and Ian Angus (Harmondsworth: Penguin, 1970), p. 189. All references to this edition will be cited as CEJL.

2.   "Why I Write," in CEJL, I, An Age Like This 1920–1940, p. 28.

3.   "Such, Such Were the Joys," in CEJL, IV, In Front of Your Nose, 1945–1950, p. 407.

4.   "Charles Dickens," in CEJL, I: 454–504; "Rudyard Kipling," in CEJL, II: 215–229.

5.   Milan Kundera, "Man Thinks, God Laughs," The New York Review of Books, June 13, 1985, pp. 11–12.

6.   Lionel Trilling, The Opposing Self (New York, 1969); Irving Howe, Decline of the New (New York, 1970).

7.   Howe, Decline of the New, pp. 274–275.

8.   Trilling, The Opposing Self, p. 154.

9.   "Why I Write," CEJL, I: 30.

10.   Howe, Decline of The New, p. 274.

11.   "Why I Write," p. 25.

12.   "Such, Such Were the Joys," p. 394.

13.   George Orwell, "How the Poor Die," in The Orwell Reader (Fiction, Essays, and Reportage by George Orwell), intro. Richard H. Rovere (New York, 1956), p. 86.

14.   The Orwell Reader, pp. 94–95.

15.   George Orwell, The Road to Wigan Pier (New York: Harcourt Brace Jovanovich, 1958), p. 117.

16.   George Orwell, Nineteen Eighty-Four, "Afterword" by Erich Fromm (New York, 1961), p. 10.

17.   Ibid., p. 256.

18.   Ibid.

Part II

The Political Man

11.
Nineteen Eighty-Four
and *Gravity's Rainbow*:
Two Anti-Utopias Compared
J. BAKKER

George Orwell's <u>Nineteen Eighty-Four</u> appeared in 1949. The novel describes the future in the year of the book's title, not as it will be but as it could be, provided certain trends in the political, social, and economic foundations of the world situation in the 1940s assert themselves.

In this future the world consists of three monster slave states, all engaged in war or continuously preparing for war and therefore under permanent dictatorial rule. The world in 1984 is a totalitarian world. In one of these monster states, Oceania, the ruling power elite, the Inner Party, wields absolute power through an omnipotent secret police, called Thought Police, and a specially designed language, called Newspeak, developed for the purpose of controlling people's minds and thus controlling "truth."

In trying to maintain his individuality, Winston Smith, a minor Party member employed in the Ministry of Truth, gets involved in a struggle against the Party's ruthless despotism. It is a struggle in which he is destined to be defeated, what with the omnipotence of those in power and some of his own particular weaknesses. There is, however, nothing to reconcile the reader to his defeat. Unlike the heroes of old, he gains nothing by it, no halo of heroism, no honor, no admiration, no pity. Even death is denied him. At the end of the novel Winston Smith is no longer the man he was but in love with what he once hated: Big Brother.

Although <u>Nineteen Eighty-Four</u> deals with the future, fantasy does not play a prominent part in the book. The external world remains largely recognizable, and this also applies to Orwell's treatment of his unusual subject matter: plot and characterization are approached from the traditional novelistic angle and lack the experimental. What makes this traditional treatment remarkable, though, is the intensity with which Orwell dramatizes some of his obsessions, such as the ease with which the individual ceases to be an end in himself and becomes a means toward someone else's ends; the ease with which objective truth disappears the moment it proves harmful to whatever cause man pursues, whether with the noblest or the basest intentions.

Thomas Pynchon's novel <u>Gravity's Rainbow</u> appeared in 1973. The book deals, strictly speaking, with the past -- with Europe toward the end of World War II and just after. In a more profound sense, however, it is, like <u>Nineteen Eighty-Four,</u> a novel about the future. What it foresees is the emergence of a new order from the postwar ruins of the old bourgeois order of a Europe that has in the novel ceased to exist. As Tchitcherine, one of the innumerable characters in the novel, realizes: "Oh, a state begins to take form in the stateless German night, a state that spans oceans and surface politics, so sovereign as the International or the Church of Rome, and the Rocket is its soul."(1)

Spanning the earth like a deadly rainbow, the rocket's trajectory curves through the sky. Whenever it will be launched, the Rocket is destined to crash to the earth under the pull of gravity: Gravity's Rainbow. It thus enables the ruling power elites to keep mankind under the constant threat of extinction. The Rocket, the most advanced product of human technology to date, forces man to take a road that leads in one direction only: toward the creation of a totalitarian world.

Pynchon's novel, huge and complex like a modern rocket, fantastic and experimental where Nineteen Eighty-Four remains largely traditional and naturalistic, contains a great number of plots that all in one way or another touch or interlock through the presence of the Rocket, here the German V-2, which therefore not only becomes one of the book's main characters but its chief metaphor as well.

It is, however, the story of Tyrone Slothrop, a graduate of Harvard and now an American Army Lieutenant working for achtung (one of Pynchon's suggestive acronyms, standing here for Allied Clearing House Technical Units, Northern Germany), which is central and exemplary of the novel's larger significance. At the same time it shows a remarkable resemblance to Winston Smith's story in Nineteen Eighty-Four. What unites the two stories in terms of subject matter and apocalyptic mood is already noticeable in the similarity of locale. Although the scene of Orwell's novel is the monster slave state of Oceania in 1984 and that of Pynchon's book Europe at the end of World War II and just after, we should not be deluded. The place where Winston Smith lives and works may be the capital of Oceania, but its description clearly fits wartime London when the city was being attacked by German V-1's and V-2's. Whole sections have been destroyed by the rocketbombs, which still fall daily on the city. In the streets there are houses with grimy battered doorways; windows are broken and boarded up; the pavements littered with rubble; and plaster and rat-infested holes gape where once stood houses. The grimy, shabby, and desolate cityscape Orwell evokes belongs to the wastelands of World War II rather than the future.

Pynchon's novel, too, opens with a description of London under attack by the V-2's, and the same image of a city ravaged and laid waste by war emerges. When the scene of action moves to the continent, the "Zone" where the mopping-up operations of the Allied forces are carried out and the various Intelligence Services are busily engaged in playing their dark, secret games, this picture of a war-ravaged world is only intensified.

This Zone acquires special significance in Gravity's Rainbow, but to understand this we must first take a close look at the kind of world that emerges from Pynchon's novel. It is a world controlled by a force referred to as "They" or "The Firm," which in concrete terms appears to be a worldwide organization of huge corporations and cartels such as General Electric, Shell, or I. G. Farben — multinationals, in fact. It can therefore ignore geographical and political boundaries and conduct its activities without fear of external censure or control.

These activities consist primarily in "buying and selling." Even war thus becomes "a celebration of markets," and everything and everyone, friend or foe, is used to achieve this "celebration." What The Firm represents is the System, which only takes from the world — a closed ecological entity — but never gives back anything. It demands the constant increase of "productivity" and "earnings" and thus removes from the world "these vast quantities of energy to keep its own tiny desperate fraction showing a profit: and not only of humanity — [but] most of the world, animal, vegetable and mineral is laid waste in the process" (p. 412).

The System is, in fact, dedicated to annihilating the organic world, transforming it into a dead world. Its soul is the Rocket, a mechanical thing, the product of a relentless application of the cause-and-effect principle, which everything and everyone in the realm of human activities is made to obey. The result is a rigidly patterned world, a vast bureaucratization of human institutions, a totalitarian world where the concepts of freedom and individuality have become illusory.

Both Nineteen Eighty-Four and Gravity's Rainbow, then, describe the world of the future, a totalitarian world in which the ruling elite wields absolute power -- in Orwell's novel called the Inner Party; in Pynchon's, The Firm. It is also here, however, that the first fundamental difference between the two novels emerges.

When considering the matter of totalitarianism, one may want to know what the forces are that work toward this phenomenon. Why do people want absolute power? Is it ideology that motivates them, or personal ambition, or both? Orwell does not give a satisfactory answer to this question, but there is the implication that what he ultimately believes is that people want power for the sake of power, for the love of power. As O'Brien replies to Winston Smith when the latter asks him why they want absolute control: "If you want a picture of the future, imagine a boot stamping on a human face — forever."(2) So what in the final analysis will effect in Nineteen Eighty-Four mankind's totalitarian future lies in the realm of "conventional" psychology.

In Gravity's Rainbow the force that works toward a totalitarian future is the process of nature itself, in which, in accordance with the theory of thermodynamics, closed systems -- and the earth is a closed system -- will decline into entropy. In the human world this force works through the system that "sooner or later must crash to its death when its addiction to energy has become more than the rest of the world can supply." (p. 412). This addiction can be satisfied only if inside the system everything is fixed and patterned, for only then are the conditions created under which maximum production is guaranteed. One paradigmatic product of such a consorted effort in rigid cause-and-effect thinking and planning is the Rocket, which therefore becomes "an entire sytem won away from the feminine darkness, held against the entropies of lovable but scatterbrained Mother Nature" (p. 324). But although the Rocket may be immune to entropy, what it represents is an order not of life but of death: it is not only incapable of renewing itself when it disintegrates — in contrast to Mother Nature -- but it also functions as a permanent threat to mankind.

Whereas Orwell still places the origin of totalitarianism in human nature (there are those who love power and will go to any lengths to assert it and continue asserting it), Pynchon locates it in the second law of thermodynamics, which works in the external as well as in the human world. Once this process has been acknowledged the rest follows with iron logic: the rigid organization of life and work; the bureaucratization of human institutions, involving the loss of individual autonomy, a development clinched by the production of highly sophisticated technological hardware that escapes ordinary human comprehension and that consequently becomes to those in power an additional means of effecting absolute control.

If Orwell's apocalyptic view of the future originates from such an "old-fashioned" vice as human frailty, Pynchon's finds its origin in what he has come to look upon as a worldwide conspiracy in which nature is the prime plotter, a conspiracy set up to use everyone and everything for one purpose only: to tranform the organic world into a world of dead objects, a process that in the human world must ultimately lead to totalitarianism.

Those invested with powers in <u>Nineteen Eighty-Four</u> (the Inner Party) and <u>Gravity's Rainbow</u> (The Firm) assume a human face in the characters of O'Brien and Dr. Pointsman, respectively. What O'Brien, a high and dedicated member of the Inner Party, fears in Winston Smith, Pointsman, a Pavlovian behaviorist, fears in Tyrone Slothrop: loss of total control. O'Brien's love of absolute power cannot tolerate anyone questioning the Party line, as Winston Smith does. Pointsman, the scientist who can deal with the world only from the vantage point of logic, cannot tolerate anyone defying cause-and-effect thinking, as Slothrop does when he shows that he possesses the uncanny power of predicting the fall of the V-2's. Smith and Slothrop must therefore be eliminated, and this is what happens. At the end of the two novels both Smith and Slothrop have dissolved, ceased to exist as autonomous individuals.

There is, however, again a fundamental difference to be discerned in the way in which this loss of individuality is effected. In <u>Nineteen Eighty-Four</u> O'Brien succeeds in destroying Winston Smith by exploiting two of the latter's fatal weaknesses. Smith's rebellion against the Party is based on typical Christian-humanist views. The trouble is that he is hardly in a position to make his stand on the strength of these beliefs. All he can rely on are a number of nostalgic memories and feelings of physical and mental discomfort. What they really amount to becomes apparent when he promises O'Brien that he is prepared to throw sulphuric acid in a child's face if that would weaken the power of the Party. By making such a promise he proves himself to be no better than the people he has sworn to fight, as O'Brien is quick to point out, thus brutally destroying Smith's claim to moral superiority.

Smith's second weakness, of a psychological nature, is his mortal fear of rats. Although he has withstood months of brainwashing and torture, he courageously refuses to give up his love for Julia, feeling that as long as he is able to do this he has retained his basic humanity. When, however, he is exposed to two enormous half-starved rats which are about to devour his head, he breaks down and, screaming like an animal, transfers the punishment to Julia. By betraying Julia he destroys his essential self, becomes an empty shell to be filled with whatever the Party thinks fit. At the end of the novel Winston Smith loves Big Brother and despises Julia.

At first glance Tyrone Slothrop's loss of individuality in <u>Gravity's Rainbow</u> seems to show some similarity with Winston Smith's. What starts his disintegration is also a shattering sense of betrayal when he realizes that the woman he loves, Katje, is an agent of The Firm sent by Pointsman and instructed to keep Slothrop under close surveillance. However, this is not the real cause of his final dissolution.

Pointman's machinations are mainly responsible for Slothrop's growing suspicion that he is being used, that there is a "peculiar structure" to his life. But the real nature of this peculiar structure does not become clear to Slothrop until he learns that as a baby he was subjected to an experiment conducted by a certain Laszlo Jamf, a famous chemist, who worked for I. G. Farben. The after effects of this experiment are in fact responsible for Slothrop's ability to predict the location of the V-2's falling on London. It convinces him that there is a close relationship between him and the Rocket, a conviction corroborated by his discovery that the chemical substance used by Jamf in his experiment is also a vital element in the Rocket's system. The Rocket thus becomes his grail, which he must find if he is to escape the control of "Them" and recover his individual autonomy.

That this search is taking place in the Zone is no accident. In contrast to the System, the Zone is a vacuum, where nothing is fixed — even The Firm cannot wield power here — and where there are no patterns. It is an area of "the new Uncertainty," where everyone and everything is adrift, where the principle of indeterminacy reigns, offering people like Slothrop an opportunity to elude the games played by Pointsman, his helpers, the Allies, the Russians, the black market-eers.

In a metaphoric sense the System and the Zone can therefore be said to represent two states of mind: a state of paranoia and a state of anti-paranoia.(3) The paranoia induced by the system is the idea that "everything is connected, everything in the Creation" (p. 703). The nature of this all-embracing connection is the subservience of everyone and everything to the System's overriding goal: to transform everything that is alive and feeling into dead, unfeeling objects, a transformation culminating in the Rocket and the debris around it.

Anti-paranoia is that state of mind "where nothing is connected to anything," a condition prevailing in the Zone. But as Slothrop himself experiences on his wanderings north in search of the Rocket, it is a condition which "not many of us can bear for long" (p. 434). Escape from a completely patterned and deterministic world, the System's world, may give momentary relief, but it is impossible to live permanently out-side any meaningful pattern. What those living outside the System will be doomed to go on doing is "kicking endlessly among the plastic trivia . . . , trying . . . to make sense out of, to find the meanest sharp sliver of truth in so much replication, so much waste" (p. 590).

The effect it has on Slothrop is a growing numbness, a loss of emo-tion and feeling. Becoming convinced that both outside and within the separateness of the self there is nothing, a void, Slothrop starts dis-solving, and the suggestion that even to this belief he is conditioned as part of "their" determination to control the individual is in keeping with the general "conspiracy" theory that permeates the novel from be-ginning to end: " — what if They're using it [the void] on you? . . . What if it's in Their interest to have you believing that?" (p. 697).

Slothrop's predicament is insoluble. He may think that he has es-caped The Firm's control by going to the Zone, but once there he cannot prevent chaos from engulfing him. Instead of being present "at his own assembly," he witnesses his "disassembling." Conditioned to function only within the System, he lacks the means to make sense of his exis-tence in the Zone, the world of indeterminacy. Belief in indeterminacy, implying the possibility of free will, might have saved Slothrop, but this belief is outside the reach of a man conditioned by cause and ef-fect. Paranoia, cause-and-effect thinking in its pathological form, could still have supported him — it made him flee to the Zone in escap-ing from "Them." But when Slothrop fails to find the Rocket, his "grail," he ceases to know who he is and thus ceases to be paranoid.

Slothrop's position, then, is even more desperate than Winston Smith's. Smith's defiance of the Inner Party might have succeeded but for his paralyzing fear of rats, a fear originating neither from socio-political nor existential conditions. His defeat does not irrevocably mean the death of the human spirit, even if its chances of survival re-main minimal. Slothrop's defiance of The Firm, however, is forever doomed to fail. Spending one night on top of Jamf's grave in the Ger-man mountains, Slothrop dreams that he is Jamf. The suggestion is obvi-ous: he is not only the product but even the creator of the system from which he wants to escape.

We are thus faced with two alternatives in Gravity's Rainbow: one lives either in a rigidly structured world (a paranoid, totalitarian world) or in an unmeaning, structureless, blank world (an anti-paranoid world), and both are equally fatal to the survival of the human spirit.

Does Pynchon leave us without any hope, then? Not quite. If there is any, it lies in those who live among the trivia and waste, in "the preterite," as Pynchon calls them: the people for whom the System has no use, the "passed over," the abandoned, the rejected. It is, of course, no accident that one of Slothrop's ancestors wrote a book called

On Preterition in which he argued that the neglected and the despised
are as important as the elect — those who are in a position to use and
manipulate others. For only among them, among the preterite, could the
will be born to quit the games that have preempted reality (politics,
religion, philosophy, the arts, which have trapped reality in fixed patterns). Only among them could a Counterforce, opposing the trend toward
totalitarianism, come into existence. It is even believed by some that
there is already a counterforce in the Zone. But Roger Mexico, one of
the few characters who understands the necessity of abandoning the games
that people are playing if man's spirit is to be set free, is realistic
enough to acknowledge that the chances of the preterite being roused to
action are very small indeed. What is likely to prevent them from asserting themselves is their basic lack of concern, their spiritual tor-
por, induced and sustained by the massive presence of what The Firm has
to offer them in terms of material satisfaction, primarily money.

There is again a remarkable parallel here to Nineteen Eighty-Four,
if we replace "the preterite" both "the proles." Winston Smith, too,
thinks that if there is hope it lies in the proles, because

> only there, in those swarming disregarded masses, eighty-five
> percent of the population of Oceania, could the force to
> destroy the Party ever be generated. Its enemies, if it had
> any enemies, had no way of coming together or even of
> identifying one another. Even if the legendary Brotherhood
> existed, as just possibly it might, it was inconceivable that
> its members could ever assemble in larger numbers than twos
> and threes. But the proles, if only they could somehow
> become conscious of their own strength, would have no need to
> conspire. They needed only to rise up and shake themselves
> like a horse shaking off flies. If they chose they could
> blow the Party to pieces tomorrow morning. Surely sooner or
> later it must occur to them to do it. And yet — ! (p. 60)

"And yet — !" Like Roger Mexico, Winston Smith realizes that the proles
could never be forged into an organization, a political or military
force, because they were without general ideas. They were concerned only
with their own petty grievances, unaware of the "larger evils." This is
why one of the Party's slogans could be "Proles and animals are free" (p.
62). The world of the proles can therefore be compared with that of the
Zone in Gravity's Rainbow. Like the Zone it is a fluid, unstructured
world permitting a certain measure of freedom, which, however, is basically ineffectual because it lacks a specific goal from which it could
derive direction and strength. Besides, the moment the proles decide to
organize themselves, they would cease to be proles and would become another System.

The hope for a counterforce set against totalitarianism is present
in both novels, but it is not very strong, and whether it will ever be
fulfilled remains extremely doubtful.

Between 1949, when Nineteen Eighty-Four was published, and 1973, the
year of publication of Gravity's Rainbow, lie twenty-four years, a time
span in which the world has changed, in some respects greatly, and in
others hardly. The feeling of apocalypse engendered by the atom bomb is
still with us — has, in fact, increased, as also Pynchon's novel proves.
In comparison with the vastness and range of Gravity's Rainbow, Nineteen
Eighty-Four seems almost naive in its exploration of this feeling.
Orwell's method now strikes us as reductive in that he imposes a fixed
pattern upon the world, taking as his starting point the view that man
loves power for the sake of power and that objective truth can be made to
disappear, assumptions that may or may not be true. Pynchon refuses to

fall for the temptation of reduction. The patterns he sees are constantly checked or refuted, dropped or woven into different ones. He
thus makes it impossible for the reader to reduce the kaleidoscopic complexity of the world mirrored in the novel to one meaning. The very pattern of the novel's narration, consisting of a bewildering variety of all
types of discourse where Orwell uses only one, the naturalistic-realistic
mode, already precludes such a reading.

To give an example: even Slothrop's disintegration remains ambiguous and defies one conclusive reading. When he is about to vanish from
the pages of the novel, he sees a rainbow -- a real one -- "a stout rainbow cock driven down out of the cubic clouds into Earth, green wet-val-
leyed Earth, and his chest fills and he stands crying, not a thing in his
head, just feeling natural." (p. 626). What this extraordinary image
seems to suggest is a vision in which the death-giving Rocket is offset
by the regenerative, life-giving power of the Earth.

Later there is a story about Slothrop that he "is being broken down
. . . and scattered" (p. 738), but there is also the rumor that he may be
"among the gray and preterite souls" (p. 742), to participate, for all
one knows, in the Counterforce.

When the novel closes, the Rocket, falling a mile per second,
reaches the last delta-t, which may either remain "an unmeasurable gap"
or become the infinitesimal fraction of a second before "this old the-
atre" -- Western civilization, or what is left of it -- will be destroyed. The end seems inevitable, but there may be something in man that
refuses to accept cause-and-effect logic as the sole determinant of his
destiny. Pynchon's fascination with probability and indeterminacy theories seems to indicate routes of escape.

Yet there is little doubt that the prevailing tone of Gravity's
Rainbow is even more darkly pessimistic than that of Nineteen Eighty-
Four. What distinguishes Pynchon from Orwell is that he remains suspicious of all the games played by man, including the cause-and-effect
game, the one Orwell plays so brilliantly but perhaps too compulsively.
Pynchon does not seem to rule out the possibility that there is more going on in the world than our Pointsmen are able to acknowledge, and even
if Pynchon's book shows precious little love or religion to back up this
claim, for the sake of our peace of mind we should not ignore it.

NOTES

1.   Thomas Pynchon, Gravity's Rainbow (London: Jonathan Cape,
1973), p. 566. All further page references are to this edition.

2.   George Orwell, Nineteen Eighty-Four (1949; reprint Signet Classic, 1981), p. 220. All further page references are to this edition.

3.   I am indebted for this idea to Tony Tanner. See his Thomas
Pynchon (London: Methuen, 1982), pp. 80-81.

12.
Nineteen Eighty-Four
and George Orwell's
Other View of Capitalism

A. M. ECKSTEIN

To the end of his life George Orwell remained a socialist. And regarding
Nineteen Eighty-Four specifically, he wrote to Francis Henson: "My recent novel is not intended as an attack on Socialism or on the British
Labour Party, of which I am a supporter."(1) Yet if Orwell remained in
his own mind a man of the Left, something of a paradox appears if we survey the references to the capitalist "past" in Nineteen Eighty-Four.
This capitalist "past," of course, is to a great extent Orwell's present.
And seen from the world of Ingsoc, the capitalist "past" has much to recommend it -- indeed, just about everything to recommend it.

First, material life for the average person had been far better in
the "past" than under Ingsoc. Examples are numerous: the wide avail-
ability in the "past" of real coffee, real sugar, real chocolate, good
beer, wine, fruit, solidly built furniture, elevators that worked.(2)
Second, and more important, in the "past" there had existed real individual freedom: freedom of thought, human rights, even freedom of speech.
The total suppression of human rights under Ingsoc is, of course, the
main theme of Nineeten Eighty-Four and needs no detailing here. But that
such freedom had once existed Orwell is careful in the to make clear in
the novel: we are not dealing here with mere theoretical human possibility. In the "past," then, it had been usual for people to read well-
made books in the cozy privacy of their own homes -- without fear of the
Thought Police.(3)   In the "past" people had kept diaries to record
events and thoughts for themselves: this had been taken for granted.(4)
In the "past" human relationships had existed naturally, without constant
state interference.(5)   In the "past" there had been no imprisonment
without trial; no public executions; no torture to extract confes-
sions.(6)   In the "past" orators espousing all sorts of political opinions had even had their free public say in Hyde Park.(7)

And from Goldstein's Book Orwell's hero Winston Smith learns that
this "past" had not been a mere accident. Relative plenty had resulted
from the increasing use of industrial machines in the late nineteenth and
early twentieth-centuries, which in turn had led to wide distribution of
goods and greatly increased standards of living.(8)   Relative individual
freedom had prevailed because

> the heirs of the French, English and American revolutions had
> partly believed their own phrases about the rights of man,
> freedom of speech, equality before the law . . . and had even
> allowed their conduct to be influenced by them to some ex-
> tent.(9)

Capitalism, according to the Party, had meant poverty and slavery.(10) In the course of the first part of Nineteen Eighty-Four Winston Smith's historical researches reveal that this is a lie. The capitalist "past" had not been perfect: prosperity and freedom had been only partial.(11) But obviously the previous capitalist civilization had been preferable beyond measure to the current Ingsoc State. Conversely, Winston comes to see that it is Ingsoc itself that is responsible for the current conditions of poverty and slavery.(12)

Since Orwell was a socialist, this basically positive depiction of "past" capitalist society in Nineteen Eighty-Four represents a problem. And the problem is compounded by a closer examination of the Henson Letter. Orwell explains that Nineteen Eighty-Four is not intended as an attack on socialism; yet in the very next phrase he also says that the book is intended as "a show-up of the perversions to which a centralized economy is liable."(13) Thus we have a convinced socialist who has written a book in which the effects of a centralized, planned economy are socially disastrous, and in which capitalist society appears quite attractive -- especially (but not solely) by contrast. The first element here can probably be explained as the outgrowth of Orwell's ongoing conflict with the authoritarian Left — the Communists and their hangers-on. But the second element is even more intriguing since, strictly speaking, it is unnecessary to the theme of the novel. That is, there was simply no need for Orwell to portray the "past" capitalist world so attractively in order to condemn the brutal totalitarianism of the Ingsoc State. We are dealing here at least partly with an ambivalence -- even a contradiction — in Orwell's attitude toward capitalism, or so I will argue. Basically Orwell despised capitalism; but especially in his most pessimistic moods he was willing to concede it a crucial virtue.

In Orwell's original forebodings about the destruction of civilization (1933), the engine of destruction would be Huxley's "Fordification": capitalism and consumerism. People would become docile wage-slaves, their lives utterly in the hands of "the bankers."(14) Under the impact of the cataclysmic events of the 1930s, however -- the coming of Hitler, the Soviet purge trials, the Spanish Civil War — a different vision eventually began to impose itself. By 1938 Orwell was coming to fear that civilization would be destroyed by the worldwide triumph of state dictatorship.(15)

The first detailed exposition of this dark vision occurs in Orwell's essay on Henry Miller: "Inside the Whale" (written in the summer and fall of 1939). In seeking to explain the political quietism of Miller's writing Orwell argues that an inevitable historical process is leading to the destruction of "Western civilization" — which he defines as laissez-faire capitalism plus liberal-Christian culture.(16) What is coming is the centralized state; the new world war will only hasten its arrival. But the implications of this have not been fully understood, Orwell says, because people have falsely imagined that socialism would be a better form of liberalism. Instead, "almost certainly we are moving into an age of totalitarian dictatorships" — an age in which both freedom of thought and the autonomous individual are going to be stamped out. But this in turn means that "literature, in the form we have known it, must suffer at least a temporary death" -- for literature had depended upon the existence of the autonomous individual writer.(17) In the present a writer may well choose to aid the coming of the new age, but he cannot contribute to this political process as a writer, "for as a writer he is liberal, and what is happening is the destruction of liberalism."(18) Hence Henry Miller's political quietism. As a writer — as a liberal -- the only honest subject left to him in this age of violent transformation is personal life (sex).

In this essay Orwell emphasizes that literature as we have known it depends upon individual freedom of thought and that both depend upon the

existence of a "Liberal-Christian culture." No direct link is made between literature and the existence of capitalism as an economic system —
although there are some hints in that direction. Nor is Orwell against
socialism: the centralized state may be grim, but it may also be a grim
necessity. This is why Orwell allows writers to join the struggle to
bring about the new world (although not as writers). And Orwell does not
completely abandon hope that this new world might eventually produce its
own great literature (of a new sort, it is true). Thus he ends the essay
with the assertion that Miller's political quietism proves the impossibility of any major literature "until the world has shaken itself into
its new shape."(19)

Still, Orwell's publisher, Victor Gollancz, a man of strong left-
wing views, wrote Orwell that he was being too pessimistic about the future. Orwell replied (January 4, 1940):

> You are perhaps right in thinking I am over-pessimistic. It
> is quite possible that freedom of thought etc may survive in
> an economically totalitarian society. We can't tell until a
> collectivised economy has been tried out in a western coun-
> try.(20)

But at the moment, Orwell continues, he is more worried about intellectuals stupidly equating British democracy with fascism or despotism:
given the current threat from Germany, he hopes that the common people
will have more sense. For us there are two points to note in this important letter. First, Orwell here is not fully pessimistic about the effects of a collectivized economy upon intellectual freedom. Yet we can
see his unease with the idea that a society might be both "economicaly
totalitarian" and intellectually free: it is possible, but somehow for
him not logical. Second, Orwell brings Gollancz back from theory to
reality, firmly asserting the value of the freedoms currently existing in
Britian: bourgeois Britian is not a fascist despotism and deserves defending by everyone.

If in the Gollancz letter Orwell is uncertain about the fate of intellectual freedom in a collectivized economy, nine months later he is
definitely optimistic. In "The Lion and the Unicorn: Socialism and the
English Genius" (written in the fall of 1940) Orwell proposed a revolutionary program, including nationalization of industry and equalization
of incomes through punitive taxation.(21) But, he asserts, his socialist
regime will not degenerate into tryanny and will respect human rights because it will be solidly grounded in the prevailing gentleness of English
culture.(22) This idea seems an amplification of Orwell's remarks to
Gollancz about the possibility of humane -- Western -- economic collectivism, combined with Orwell's new patriotic approval of the basic forms
of English life.(23)

And it is probably no accident that Orwell, hopeful of an English
and democratic socialism, now is explicitly disdainful of economic liberty per se. In modern England

> the liberty of the individual is still believed in, almost as
> in the nineteenth century. But this has nothing to do with
> economic liberty, the right to exploit others for profit.(24)

Even in "The Lion and the Unicorn," though, Orwell's criticisms of
British capitalist society are quite restrained. Basically it is econom-
ically too inefficient to cope with the current military crisis, and it
produces an upper class too stupid to win the war.(25) But it has also
spread prosperity much farther down the social scale than was previously
thought possible.(26) And with all its faults, the claim of British society to be democratic is not a complete sham — nor is its claim to

respect human rights. This is because the prevailing belief in justice
and liberty tends to influence actual social conduct.(27)   This, of
course, is precisely the picture of the capitalist "past" drawn by Goldstein in Nineteen Eighty-Four.(28)

Orwell's confident mood of autumn 1940 — the odd euphoria of the
Battle of Britain — did not last long, however: he soon relapsed into
pessimism. Even before "The Lion and the Unicorn" came out in print, his
hopes for an immediate democratic socialist revolution had already
faded.(29) Moreover Britain was still fighting practically alone against
Nazi Germany, and in the spring of 1941 the war news was genuinely terrible. England now seemed to Orwell to be on the verge of losing the war;
at the very least a long grim struggle was in the offing, with untold
negative effects on English society. Thus we find him writing in his
diary on May 18, 1941: "Within two years we shall either be conquered or
we shall be a socialist republic fighting for its life, with a secret
police force and half the population starving."(30)

Britian defeated (or even occupied), Britian a starving socialist
police state: this had not been the vision of 1940. Deep fears about
the future now led Orwell to an even sharper appreciation of the virtues
of the present than he had expressed in "The Lion and the Unicorn." The
result: two essays, in April and May 1941, which are of significance in
the development of Orwell's thought but which have not received the attention they deserve. For reasons of space, and because in it his "other" view of capitalism is most clear (and because it is far more accessible to American students of Orwell), I will concentrate on the second of
these essys, "Literature and Totalitarianism."(31)   But some of Orwell's
ideas here are foreshadowed a month earlier in the startlingly titled
"Will Freedom Die with Capitalism?"(32)

"Literature and Totalitarianism" originated as a talk for the BBC
Overseas Service and was then published in The Listener. The lecture was
broacast on May 21, 1941 — just about the time Orwell was filling his
diary with the darkest forebodings about the English future. In fact
"Literature and Totalitarianism" is only the second full-scale exposition
of Orwell's nightmare vision of worldwide tyranny (the first being "Inside the Whale").

Orwell begins by explaining that European literature over the past
400 years has been the product of the autonomous individual, concerned
only to write with honest and emotional authenticity. But in "the age of
the totalitarian state," which is likely to be a world wide phenomenon,
the individual is not going to be allowed any freedom whatever. And the
origin of the totalitarian state, Orwell now says, is basically economic:
the end of "free capitalism" and its replacement by "a centralized economy."(33) The result:

> the economic liberty of the individual, and to a great extent
> his liberty to do what he likes . . . comes to a end. Now,
> till recently the implications of this were not foreseen. It
> was never fully realised that the disappearance of economic
> liberty would have any effect on intellectual liberty. So-
> cialism was usually thought of as a sort of moralised liber-
> alism. The state would take charge of your economic life,
> and set you free from the fear of poverty . . . but it would
> have no need to interfere with your private intellectual
> life. . . . Now, on the existing evidence, one must admit
> that these ideas have been falsified. Totalitarianism has
> abolished freedom of thought to an extent unheard of in any
> previous age. . . . Can literature survive in such an atmo-
> sphere? . . . It cannot. If totalitarianism becomes world-
> wide and permanent, what we have known as literature must
> come to an end. And it will not do — as may appear plaus-

ible at first -- to say that what will come to an end is
merely the literature of post-Renaissance Europe.(34)

Frankly this is an astonishing passage. The linking of economic
liberty with other liberties represents a complete reversal from Orwell's
position in "The Lion and the Unicorn" (see earlier). The explicit connecting of economic liberty with intellectual liberty, the explicit connecting of centralized control over the economy with centralized control
over the private intellect -- this is an analysis worthy of Norman Pod-
horetz.

Much of "Literature and Totalitarianism" obviously is based on ideas
we first encountered in "Inside the Whale." But there are at least two
significant changes. First, the existence of the honest, autonomous
writer, and thus of literature as we know it, is now attributed precisely
to the existence of economic liberty itself. Second, a centralized economy, once it becomes totalitarian, will mean not just the death of "bourgeois literature" (as in "Inside the Whale") but of literature, period.

Orwell does try to sound a hopeful note at the end, but the attempt
only reveals his current despair. Literature's survival, he says, depends on those countries where liberalism has sunk its deepest roots:

> Though a collectivised economy is bound to come, those coun-
> tries [may] know how to evolve a form of Socialism which is
> not totalitarian, in which freedom of thought can survive the
> disappearance of economic liberty.(35)

But this idea -- which lay at the very heart of "The Lion and the Unicorn" -- is now called a mere "pious hope."(36) Even gentle Britian was
not immune from socialist totalitarianism, as Orwell had already written.
That, of course, is one of the points of Nineteen Eighty-Four.

Now, after "Literature and Totalitarianism," Orwell never returned
to an explicit, full-scale discussion of the connection between economic
liberty and intellectual freedom. This is at first sight odd, for Orwell
was a writer capable of repeating an idea ad nauseam. The reason for his
reticence here seems obvious, however: the implication of this view of
the social impact of capitalist economics versus socialist economics made
Orwell the socialist very uncomfortable, challenging his most cherished
ideals about how a "just" society should look. Those ideals he never
gave up. But the ideas evolved in the spring of 1941 did have an enduring influence upon his life and work. The simplest evidence comes from
the Henson letter: Nineteen Eighty-Four is "a show-up of the perversions
to which a centralised economy is liable."(37) The emphasis here on the
economic origins of Big Brother points directly back to "Literature and
Totalitarianism."

It is also striking that after 1941 Orwell occasionally wrote passages extolling nineteenth-century capitalist society as a society characterized, above all, by freedom: the most noticeable example is in
"Riding Down to Bangor" (1946).(38) But this is not to suggest that Orwell's view of capitalism ever became basically positive. On the contrary. Whatever his occasionally idealized view of a stage of capitalism
in the past, Orwell feared and loathed what he saw as the giant "monopoly" capitalism of the present. As powerful and as impersonal as the
State, it was just as capable of crushing the individual.(39)

Yet as I hope I have shown, by the early 1940s Orwell had also become deeply suspicious of economic collectivism per se because the power
it gave the State seemed to threaten individual intellectual freedom to
an unheard-of extent. As the Henson letter shows, this suspicion never
faded. And it was clearly difficult to reconcile these attitudes with
fervent advocacy of socialism, since socialism inevitably involves some
form of economic collectivism, as well as an expansion of government con-

trol over society. Orwell understood this conflict perfectly.(40)   His
difficulty here may help account for the general "paleness" of Orwell's
pro-socialist writing after 1941 and his sharply changed focus of social
concern: the concentration of his literary energies on the defense of
civil liberties and intellectual freedom.(41)   He had come to see how
fragile these things actually were and from how many directions they were
threatened.

Orwell's friend T. R. Fyvel now tells us that when the postwar
Labour government began nationalization of industry and punitive taxation
of income — two of the measures Orwell had proposed in "The Lion and the
Unicorn" -- Orwell "was not against these measures (!) . . . only he had
become profoundly suspicious of any extension of state power."(42)   How
deeply Orwell had changed since the euphoria of 1940.   Fyvel believes
that Orwell always remained a socialist -- and then at the last moment he
introduces a crucial qualification: "he was formally a socialist."(43)

If Orwell was "formally a socialist," what was he really? Obviously
a complicated and sometimes self-contradictory human being. Fyvel concludes that more than anything else, Orwell was a pessimist; and this is
in line with the judgment of another of Orwell's friends, Herbert
Read.(44)   But I would suggest that besides the polarity of pessimism/so-
cialism there was another polarity in Orwell's thoughts. As a political
person he considered himself a socialist, but as a writer he was a liberal.   I mean the term in the specific way Orwell himself used it, the way
he felt was vital to a writer: "liberty-loving," especially regarding
freedom of speech.(45)   Thus as a writer -- as a liberal -- Orwell in-
tensely valued liberal and tolerant surroundings, valued the relatively
liberal and tolerant surroundings provided by bourgeois Britain, and
feared that economic collectivism would lead to the destruction of liberalism and toleration because of the concurrent growth it would give to
ever-greedy state power. I think that this fear, which Orwell felt as a
writer, eventually came to balance the ideals of "social justice" and
economic equality which Orwell upheld as a (democratic) socialist.   This
goes a long way toward explaining the social emphasis in Nineteen Eighty-
Four on the destruction of autonomous thought by the Party and, conversely, the novel's depiction of prerevolutionary capitalist society as in
many ways benign.

But, of course, writer and socialist were one man. And Orwell himself was well aware of the fundamental ambivalence into which he had fal-
len. Witness this passage:

> If one thinks of the artist as . . . an autonomous individual
> who owes nothing to society, then the golden age of the art-
> ist was the age of capitalism. He had then escaped from the
> patron and had not yet been captured by the bureaucrat. . . .
> Yet it remains true that capitalism, which in many ways was
> kind to the artist and the intellectual generally, is doomed
> and is not worth saving anyway. So you arrive at these two
> antithetical facts: (1) Society cannot be arranged for the
> benefit of artists; (2)   without artists civilisation per-
> ishes. I have not yet seen this dilemma solved (there must
> be a solution), and it is not often that it is honestly dis-
> cussed.(46)

"There must be a solution": Orwell offers none here, and one may
wonder whether he ever found one. The best he seems to have been able to
come up with actually was advocacy of a human "change of heart" -- an argument of desperation.(47)   But at least Orwell honestly discussed the
problem (as he saw it) of the potentially profound conflict between intellectual freedom and economic centralization. This dilemma, I think,
lies at the origin of Orwell's "other" view of capitalism.

NOTES

1.   George Orwell, The Collected Essays, Journalism and Letters of George Orwell, ed. Sonia Orwell and Ian Angus, 4 vols. (New York: Harcourt, Brace & World, 1968), (Hereafter referred to as CEJL), IV: 502 (June 16, 1949).

2.   Orwell, Nineteen Eighty-Four (New York: Harcourt Brace Jovanovich, 1949; Signet Classic), p. 5; p. 21 with pp. 118-119; p. 70; p. 76; p. 101; p. 120; pp. 121-122; p. 141.

3.   Ibid., pp. 92 and 164-165.

4.   Ibid., pp. 80; cf. pp. 9-11.

5.   This is why the life of intimacy and honesty lived by Winston Smith and Julia above the old junk shop is explicitly called a relic of an earlier age: Ibid., p. 124.

6.   Ibid., p. 169.

7.   Ibid., p. 77.

8.   Ibid., p. 168.

9.   Ibid.

10.   Ibid., pp. 61-63; 83.

11.   Ibid., p. 157.

12.   Ibid., pp. 152-164 (Goldstein's Book).

13.   CEJL, IV: 502.

14.   Ibid., I: 120-121 (June ? 1933).

15.   Ibid., I: 330 (May ? 1938).

16.   Ibid., I: 525.

17.   Ibid.

18.   Ibid., I: 526.

19.   Ibid., I: 527 (my italics).

20.   Ibid., I: 409.

21.   Ibid., II.

22.   Ibid., II: 101-102.

23.   Ibid., for Orwell's "conversion" to British patriotism in August.

24.   Ibid., II: 59.

25.   Ibid., II: 69-73, 103.

26.   Ibid., II: 76.

27.   Ibid., II: 63.

28.   Ibid., Nineteen Eighty-Four, p. 168.

29.   Ibid., CEJL, II: 49-50 (January 3, 1941).

30.   Ibid., II: 401.

31.   Ibid., II: 134-137.

32.   "Will Freedom Die with Capitalism?" The Left News (April 1941): 1682-1685 (not in CEJL and very difficult to obtain in the United States). Neither this essay nor "Literature and Totalitarianism" receives more than a bare mention in any scholarly study of Orwell.

33.   CEJL, II: 134-135.

34.   Ibid., my italics.

35.   Ibid., II: 137.

36.   Ibid.

37.   Ibid., IV: 502.

38.   Ibid., IV: 246-247.

39.   See especially CEJL, III: 117-118 (Orwell's bitter remarks at the beginning of his tandem, review of F. A. Hayek, The Road to Serfdom, and K. Zilliacus, The Mirror of the Past).

40.   Ibid., IV: 18; also see III: 1441.

41.   On the change of focus in Orwell's social concerns see Raymond Williams, George Orwell (New York: Columbia University Press, 1971), pp. 63-68.

42.   T. R. Fyvel, George Orwell: A Personal Memoir (New York: Macmillan, 1982), p. 208.

43.   Orwell as a socialist: ibid., pp. 114 and 208. The qualification: Fyvel, George Orwell, p. 208.

44.   Ibid., Herbert Read, in his review of Nineteen Eighty-Four, in George Orwell: The Critical Heritage, ed.   Jeffrey Meyers (London and Boston: Routledge & Kegan Paul, 1975), p. 285. For an excellent general discussion of Orwell's pessimism and its conflict with his socialism, see also Alan Zwerdling, Orwell and the Left (New Haven and London: Yale University Press, 1974), pp. 96-113.

45.   See especially CEJL, IV: 159.

46.   Ibid., III: 229-230 (my italics).

47.   Ibid., IV: 18; also see II: 15-18.

13.
Orwell versus Koestler:
Nineteen Eighty-Four
as Optimistic Satire
HOWARD FINK

The intellectual relations between Orwell and his friend Arthur Koestler were complex and ambiguous. The two writers, both veterans of the Spanish Civil War and political rebels, were drawn together when Koestler came to Britain in 1940. Orwell was already familiar with Koestler's writings; he admiringly reviewed Koestler's Spanish Testament in 1938. In a 1943 review of Koestler's fictional autobiography, Arrival And Departure, Orwell claims that "for the past dozen years we in England have received our political education chiefly from foreigners; . . . none, except perhaps Silone, cried more effectively than Arthur Koestler." And in discussing Koestler's The Yogi and the Commissar in "What Is Socialism?" (1946), Orwell calls this book simply the best discussion of the problems of twentieth-century socialism.(1) In their novels as in their essays, Koestler and Orwell deal with many of the same concerns, especially the conflict between personal and political vision. Orwell much admires Koestler's solutions to the aesthetic problems of political content in fiction.

Yet despite the personal, political, and literary sympathy between the two writers, Orwell clearly has irreconcileable differences with Koestler and objects to the ultimate philosophical implications in Koestler's later novels. In his 1944 essay, "Arthur Koestler" Orwell attacks Koestler's political perfectionism, his utopianism, because, he feels, the failure of Koestler's political dreams have led him to a dangerous political quietism.(2) Orwell sees a root problem in Koestler's loss of faith in the common man, the backbone and hope of the Marxist revolution, and in Koestler's related failure of hope in the political intellectual, whose basic motivation Koestler believes to be, inevitably, individual neurosis.

All of these themes find their way into Nineteen Eighty-Four, where they have special importance in our understanding of the hero and of the final message. Orwell's attitude toward Koestler's political limitations clarifies the distance between the failure of Winston Smith's political rebellion and Orwell's own relatively optimistic position. Winston's fate must not be confused with Orwell's ultimate vision. Winston is a figure patterned after Koestler's ficitional heroes: political intellectuals whose failures illustrate the limitations of contemporary political attitudes. Orwell clearly identifies the influence of Koestler on Nineteen Eighty-Four by a number of echoes and parodies of themes and images from Koestler's works, especially Darkness at Noon. Before looking more closely at Nineteen Eighty-Four, however, let us see what Orwell's essays on Koestler reveal of these connections.

One of the themes that draws Orwell to Koestler's writings is the latter's treatment of the concept of power in revolutions. But although

Orwell accepts much of Koestler's analysis, he cannot agree with Koestler's negative conclusions on this subject. In his "Koestler" essay Orwell argues that "Koestler's published work really centres about the Moscow trials. His main theme is the decadence of revolutions owing to the corrupting effect of power." (III: 235) In elaborating on the presence of this theme in Koestler's Darkness at Noon, Orwell goes on to reveal the quarrel he has on this subject:

> If one writes about the Moscow trials one must answer the question, "Why did the accused confess?" and which answer one makes is a political decision. Koestler answers, in effect, "Because these people had been rotted by the Revolution which they served," and in doing so he comes near to claiming that revolutions are of their nature bad. . . . Revolution, Koestler seems to say, is a corrupting process. . . . It is not merely that "power corrupts": so also do the ways of attaining power. (III: 240)

Orwell makes a more optimistic political deduction from these trials:

> If one assumes that the accused in the Moscow trials were made to confess by means of some kind of terrorism, one is only saying that one particular set of revolutionary leaders has gone astray. Individuals, and not the situation, are to blame. (III: 240)

In a 1945 essay entitled "Catastrophic Gradualism"(3) Orwell discusses Koestler's attempt in The Yogi and the Commissar to deal constructively with this problem of power in revolutions:

> Throughout history, one revolution after another has simply led to a change of masters, because no serious effort has been made to eliminate the power instinct. . . . Koestler calls for a "new fraternity in a new spiritual climate, whose leaders are tied by a vow of poverty to share the life of the masses, and debarred by the laws of fraternity from attaining unchecked power." (IV: 18-19)

Orwell is skeptical, however, of how closely Koestler's own convictions correspond to his new ideal:

> Koestler is generally assumed to have come down on the side of the Yogi. Actually . . . Koestler is somewhat nearer to the Commissar's end. He believes in action, in violence where necessary, and consequently in the shifts and compromises that are inseparable from government. (IV: 17)

Orwell suggests in his "Koestler" essay several specific sources for Koestler's pessimism about the possibility of successful revolution. These sources are Koestler's lack of faith in the masses, his belief that revolutionary political action issues from individual neurosis, and his overidealism or perfectionism. Orwell has, of course, already discussed the intellectual's lack of admiration for the common man in The Road to Wigan Pier.(4) In that book he speaks mainly to the English middle classes in an attempt to get their support for an alliance with the working classes, which he sees as the only way to carry out a successful revolution. The greatest obstacle to this alliance, Orwell argues is bourgeois prejudice and lack of information about the proletariat. In the "Koestler" essay, Orwell identifies exactly this prejudice in Koestler; he refers to Koestler's confession in Scum of the Earth that "he had never made contact with real proletarians, only with the educated minority," and he goes on to quote what he calls Koestler's "pessimistic conclusion: 'Without education of the masses, no social progress; without social progress, no education of the masses.'   In Scum of the Earth Koestler ceases to idealize the common people." (III: 241) This position of Koestler is far from the traditional Marxist idealization of the masses, a necessary corollary of the belief that they will inherit the earth.

A related attack in the "Koestler" essay is Orwell's criticism of Koestler's cynicism concerning the psychological limitations of the political idealist.   Orwell defines Arrival and Departure(5) as "a tract purporting to show that revolutionary creeds are rationalizations of neurotic impulses." (III: 242) What Orwell objects to in this autobiographical novel is the pessimistic conclusion that Koestler arrives at by imposing, on a Marxist utopian political vision, the Freudian view of man as determined by his unconscious: the title of Orwell's 1943 review of Arrival and Departure is, as we have seen, "Freud or Marx?"   In this novel Koestler describes the protagonist as a "clinical, textbook case" of neurotic guilt. As Orwell points out in his "Koestler" essay "the psycho-analyst drags out of [Slavek] him the fact that his revolutionary enthusiasm is not founded on any real belief in historical necessity, but on a morbid guilt complex. . . . By the time that he gets an opportunity of serving the Allies he has lost all reason for wanting to do so." (III: 242)   Despite Orwell's agreement with Koestler that "it may be true in all cases that revolutionary activity is the result of personal maladjustment," (III: 242) Orwell finds Peter Slavek's final irrational urge to action as unsatisfactory from a philosophical or political point of view as his earlier neurotic motivations. Orwell comes to the more optimistic conclusion that despite personal flaws the ideals of socialism are objectively valid motivations: "With such a history as [Slavek] has behind him, he would be able to see that certain things have to be done. . . .   History has to move in a certain direction, even if it has to be pushed that way by neurotics." (III: 243) For Orwell the fact of individual neurotic motivation to political action, however universal, can never be allowed to gainsay the moral vision leading to political action.

The final charge that Orwell brings in his "Koestler" essay is that Koestler's pessimism stems in an essential way from his idealism, which is unrealistic and "hedonistic." Koestler's ultimate objective, as Orwell points out, is a pure utopian ideal: it is "the Earthly paradise, the Sun State," of which Koestler writes so clearly in his Spartacus. As a result of the inevitable failure of this unrealistic utopian ideal, Orwell charges that Koestler has retreated to the opposite extreme, to "short-term pessimism, . . . the quasi-mystical belief that for the present there is no remedy, all political action is useless, but that somehow, somewhere in space and time, human life will cease to be the miserable brutish thing it now is." (III: 243) This pessimism of Koestler's is tantamount to the paralysis of all political action, and Orwell objects in a central passage, which indeed is the polemic conclusion to his "Koestler" essay:

At the basis of this [pessimism] lies his hedonism, which leads him to think of the Earthly Paradise as desirable. Perhaps, however, whether desirable or not, it is impossible. Perhaps some degree of suffering is ineradicable from human life, perhaps the choice before man is always a choice of evils, perhaps even the aim of Socialism is not to make the world perfect but to make it better. All revolutions are failures, but they are not all the same failure. It is his unwillingness to admit this that has led Koestler's mind temporarily into a blind alley. (III: 244)

Orwell rejects the practical — psychological, class, political — objections of Koestler to the possibility of revolution. And Orwell goes beyond, to a more positive belief in the possibility of revolution, based on an ultimately spiritual solution to the problem: a new, normative spiritual vision to replace Koestler's extreme Yogi idealism, its corollary, hedonism and Koestler's ultimate pessimistic reaction. These themes are central to Orwell's intentions in Nineteen Eighty-Four; the evidence is the many echoes and parodies found there of Koestler's beliefs and his fictional strategies.

Nineteen Eighty-Four(6) reflects the world created by Koestler in his novels, especially Darkness at Noon:(7) life in a totalitarian country in general, and in particular the scene, atmosphere, and processes of political arrest, torture, confession, and liquidation. The number of echoes of Koestler's work in Nineteen Eighty-Four, including frequent verbal equivalents, precludes mere coincidence. At the head of the Party in Darkness at Noon stands the figure of Stalin, the high priest celebrating the mass of his cult. The portrait of Stalin "hung over every bed or side-board in the country and stared at people with frozen eyes." This image is faithfully parodied in Nineteen Eighty-Four; everywhere in Oceania, on the signboards, on the landings of every building "the poster with the enormous face gazed from the wall. . . . BIG BROTHER IS WATCHING YOU, the caption said, while the dark eyes looked deep into Winston's own" (Nineteen Eighty-Four, pp. 5-6).

The political religions of both Koestler's Russia and Orwell's Oceania have been simplifed to absolute good and evil. Rubashov writes in his diary, "What is presented as right must shine like gold; what is presented as wrong must be as black as pitch" (DN, p. 224). Orwell echoes this archetypal opposition:

> White always mates, he thought with a sort of cloudy mysticism. Always, without exception, it is so arranged. In no chess problem since the beginning of the world has black ever won. Did it not symbolize the eternal, unvarying triumph of Good over Evil? (Nineteen Eighty-Four, p. 25)

There is further opportunity for parody in the infallible correctness of the party line in Darkness at Noon, which is controlled by a periodic updating of written materials. Such a revision takes place while Rubashov is head of the trade delegation:

> The classics of social science appeared with new footnotes and commentaries, the old histories were replaced by new histories, the old memoires of dead revolutionary leaders were replaced by new memoires of the same defunct. Rubashov remarked jokingly to Arlova that the only thing left to be done was to publish a new and revised edition of the back numbers of all newspapers. (DN, p. 117)

Orwell takes up this obvious challenge to his parodic gifts; Rubashov's joke becomes a reality in the world of Nineteen Eighty-Four. Winston Smith himself is one of the hundreds of people in the Ministry of Truth who are necessary for the task of transforming the printed documents of Oceania; it is clearer now why his specific task is to update the back numbers of the Times. Orwell goes even further, from parody to satiric exaggeration:

> This process of continuous alteration was applied not only to
> newspapers, but to books, periodicals, pamphlets, posters,
> leaflets, films, sound-tracks, cartoons, photographs — to
> every kind of literature or documentation which might con-
> ceivably hold any political or ideological significance. Day
> by day and almost minute by minute the past was brought up to
> date. (Nineteen Eighty-Four, p. 43)

The form and function of this effective satire of information control,
exaggeration to the point of self-ridicule, is as obvious as the kernel
of the parody in Darkness at Noon.

The impossibility of unorthodoxy in Russia is described in Darkness
at Noon. It is not only the conscious rebel who is destroyed by the Soviet party; anyone who is aware enough to be able consciously to articulate the party's philosophy is theoretically dangerous, no matter how
loyal. When Ivanov, Rubashov's old friend and his first inquisitor, is
himself liquidated, Rubashov speculates on the reason: "perhaps because
he was mentally superior and too witty, and because his loyalty to No. 1
was based on logical considerations and not on blind faith. He was too
clever" (DN, p. 178). Orwell creates an icy echo of Rubashov's speculation in Winston's thoughts about Syme:

> One of these days, thought Winston with sudden deep convic-
> tion, Syme will be vaporized. He is too intelligent. He
> sees too clearly and speaks too plainly. . . . Unquestionably
> Syme will be vaporized, Winston thought again. . . . There
> was something he lacked: discretion, aloofness, a sort of
> saving stupidity. . . . Orthodoxy was unconsciousness.
> (Nineteen Eighty-Four, pp. 56-58)

When Winston is finally arrested, the prison atmosphere is very much like
that described in Darkness at Noon: the complete impersonality of Rubashov's captors, the destruction of time, the unending surveillance, the
threat of certain death, and especially the constant artificial light in
the prison where Rubashov finds himself. This light is the central philosophical symbol of Koestler's novel and, appropriately, the ironic symbol of its title, Darkness at Noon. It is echoed in Nineteen Eighty-Four
by the phrase "the place of no darkness." At first this image is a positive symbol of Winston's utopian ideal; after his arrest it becomes an
ironically reversed comment on that ideal: the constant light in the
Ministry of Love where he is held prisoner. "In this place, he knew instinctively, the lights would never be turned out. It was the place with
no darkness" (Nineteen Eighty-Four, p. 235).

The cycle through which Rubashov passes is a well-worn Soviet 1930s
ritual of arrest, torture, interrogation, confession, release, employment
in a useless sinecure, rearrest, a second confession, repentance, conversion to orthodoxy, and death. This pattern, the fruit of Koestler's own
experience, is closely followed by Orwell in the fates both of the trio
of Jones, Aaronson, and Rutherford and later of Winston himself. During
the ritual each ruling party insists on controlling its victims' minds as
well as their bodies; Rubashov writes, "We persecuted the seeds of evil
not only in men's deeds but in their thoughts. We admitted no private
sphere, not even inside a man's skull" (DN, p. 101). In Nineteen Eighty-
Four Winston's faith before his arrest that you control at least "the few
cubic centimeters inside your skull" is proved false; he must surrender
to O'Brien especially his conscious internal reality.

At the end of this ritual of purification in Koestler's novel is the
bullet in the back of Rubashov's neck which he accepts as the inevitable
fate of the rebel (DN, pp. 21, 254). In Nineteen Eighty-Four from the
moment Winston Smith admits his rebellion, even privately in his diary,

he also knows that his is the same fate: "theyll shoot me i dont care theyll shoot me in the back of the neck i dont care down with big brother they always shoot you in the back of the neck" (Nineteen Eighty-Four, p. 23). Winston's fate is an echo of Koestler's pessimistic political vision. If it is asked how Winston knows he will receive a bullet precisely in the back of the neck, or how he knows that the lights will never be turned out in the Minstry of Love, the answer is that his creator is making a precise, ironic reference to the world of Darkness at Noon. By Winston's final failure Orwell emphasizes the inevitable failure of the utopian vision and the methods of the political intelligentsia described by Koestler.

It is on this point that Orwell's novel diverges from Koestler's. For in Nineteen Eighty-Four Orwell does not cancel the possibility of freedom and equality or the perfectibility of society. To understand this, however, it is necessary for the reader to recognize Orwell's attitude toward his protagonist and to withdraw from Winston. For, despite Winston's intense desire for escape from the rigid constructs of Oceania, he rejects the ultimate value of the individual in favor of a substitute orthodoxy demanding, like the party's, a ruthless exploitation of individuals for the sake of the group. Winston has no faith in the Proles, ability for revolution. Furthermore Winston's political faith is seen to be an excessive and unrealistic idealism. Finally, like the hero of Arrival and Departure, Winston's primary motive for political action is a neurotic trauma from his childhood, though he understands this only after his Freudian dreams in the secret bedroom with Julia.

To begin with Winston's compulsive orthodoxy: though rebelling against the party hierarchy and its symbols, Winston is not satisfied with his recreation of the past in isolation with Julia. Like the correct political intellectual that he is, he must find a new mass faith and a new political power base with which to identify. When Winston contacts the Brotherhood (as he believes) through O'Brien, he willingly accepts a new political religion, with the same antihuman moral flaws as that of the party he has rejected.

The Marxist faith in the ability of the masses to carry out the revolution, which Orwell says Koestler lost before Arrival and Departure, is impossible for Winston to believe or act on. Koestler's pessimistic epigram (attacked by Orwell in his "Koestler" essay), "Without education of the masses, no social progress; without social progress, no education of the masses," (III: 241) is closely echoed by Winston's pessimistic belief that "until they become conscious they will never rebel, and until after they have rebelled they cannot become conscious" (Nineteen Eighty-Four, p. 74). Perhaps the most bitterly ironic attack on Winston's lack of faith in the Proles is the early scene in which Winston acts out the role of a political intellectual in confrontation with the old Prole in the pub. Winston questions him in an attempt to discover whether the history books tell the truth about the past. But the two of them speak at cross-purposes, although this is not immediately apparent because the confrontation is reported from Winston's point of view. Studied closely, however, the scene turns out to mean exactly the reverse of Winston's reported impression. His questions are on a completely theoretical, "historical" level, while the Prole offers in answer a series of authentic personal reminiscences, which function as quite satisfactory replies to Winston's questions. Winston cannot understand these replies, first because they contradict the accepted versions of the Brotherhood orthodoxy, but more seriously because he cannot accept the authority of the Prole's, real memories, because of his class prejudice against him (Nineteen Eighty-Four, pp. 92-96). It is clear even at this point that Winston's position is not to be confused with that of Orwell, who has condemned the class prejudice of his fellow left-intellectuals as early as Wigan Pier.

It will take a long apprenticeship with Julia, and the resurrection of his repressed memories of his family, to enable Winston to replace his abstract, intellectual approach and his middle-class prejudice by an appreciation of the human value of the Proles, near the end he can say

> the people of only two generations ago . . . were governed by
> private loyalties which they did not question. What mattered
> were individual relationships and a completely helpless ges-
> ture, an embrace, a tear . . . could have value in itself.
> The Proles, it suddenly occurred to him, had remained in this
> condition. . . . For the first time in his life he did not
> despise the Proles. . . . The Proles had stayed human.
> (Nineteen Eighty-Four, pp. 169-170)

A new faith in validity of the ordinary people leads both Rubashov and Winston Smith in their respective novels to a new social vision, a mystical utopian vision of the individual-as-unique and at the same time identified with mankind as a whole. In Darkness at Noon this vision is seen by Rubashov as a mysterious spiritual revelation of what is significantly called the "oceanic sense" (DN, p. 244). From his "oceanic sense" grows Rubashov's social vision of the future:

> Perhaps later . . . the new movement would arise. . . . Per-
> haps the members of the new party will . . . [achieve] the
> joining of a million individuals to form a new entity which,
> no longer an amorphous mass, will develop a consciousness and
> an individuality of its own, with an oceanic feeling in-
> creased a millionfold. (DN, p. 244)

In Nineteen Eighty-Four Winston has a similar vision just before his arrest. The Prole grandmother-washerwoman which he and Julia contemplate from their secret room becomes the symbol of the vitality and indestructibility of mankind and its potential in the future:

> The mysterious reverence he felt for her was somehow mixed up
> with the aspect of the pale, cloudless sky, stretching away
> behind the chimney pots into interminable distance. It was
> curious to think that the sky was the same for everybody. .
> . . And the people under the sky were also very much the
> same -- everywhere, all over the world, hundreds of thousands
> of millions of people just like this . . . who were storing
> up in their hearts and bellies and muscles the power that
> would one day overturn the world. . . . Sooner or later it
> would happen, strength would change into consciousness.
> (Nineteen Eighty Four, p. 226)

The new vision of the future articulated by the figure of the washerwoman is further symbolized here by Orwell through the image of the sky; this pale blue sky is precisely Koestler's own symbol for his "oceanic sense":

> Over the machine-gun tower one could see a patch of blue. It
> was pale, and reminded him of that particular blue which he
> had seen overhead when as a boy he lay on the grass. . . .
> Apparently even a patch of blue sky was enough to cause the
> "oceanic state." (DN, p. 245)

For Rubashov, as for Winston, the human vision results from the reestablishment of contact with one's childhood roots. But beyond this optimistic vision, both protagonists fall into the short-term pessimism for which, Orwell has criticized Koestler in his essays. As Rubashov says,

"Perhaps later, much later, the new movement would arise;" and further, "History had a slow pulse; man counted in years, history in generations. Perhaps it was still only the second day of creation" (DN, pp. 248-249). As for Winston, his faith in the Proles cannot overcome his conviction that Utopia can be conceived only in the far future: "Our only true life is in the future. . . . But how far away that future may be there is no knowing. It may be a thousand years" (Nineteen Eighty-Four p. 181). And Again:

> The proles were immortal. . . . In the end their awakening would come. And until that happened, though it might be a thousand years, they would stay alive." (Nineteen Eighty-Four, p. 226)

It should be clear by now that Orwell separates Winston from our sympathy at this point. As we have seen, he has criticized Koestler's vision of a long-delayed future utopia as political quietism. Indeed, he parodies Koestler's visionary "oceanic state" of mind most cruelly in Nineteen Eighty-Four by calling the despotic political state -- which has swallowed up England and which victimizes Winston Smith -- by the very name of Koestler's ideal (mental) state: "Oceania." Winston, by echoing Rubashov's long-term optimism but short-term pessimism, is being distanced from the reader. The future, Orwell argues, will no longer belong to the Rubashovs and Winstons; not to the Koestlers but to a newer, more conscious and saner generation, which resides in the fertile loins of the proletariat:

> And could he be sure that when their time came the world they constructed would not be just as alien to him, Winston Smith, as the world of the Party? Yes, because at least it would be a world of sanity." (Nineteen Eighty-Four, p. 226)

Orwell here unmistakably separates the dehumanized and neurotic political intellectual from the human hope of the future, and from the new society mankind will surely create.(8)

This is the clearest indication that the final ritual and failure of Winston Smith, so much like Rubashov's and Koestler's own experience, is not to be generalized to the final message of the novel itself, or to be confused with Orwell's own position. Nineteen Eighty-Four is best understood as a satiric parody of Darkness at Noon, its pessimism and overidealism. The novel, concludes then, with Orwell's rejection of Marxist communal and state utopianism, in favor of his positive belief in the possibility of a more reasonable program of melioration of society, based on a more human and rational ideal, once the errors of the bourgeois intellectual are left behind. And this is just how Orwell concludes his "Koestler" essay: "Perhaps some degree of suffering is ineradicable from human life, perhaps . . . even the aim of Socialism is not to make the world perfect but to make it better."

The writings of Arthur Koestler provide Orwell with details of totalitarian methods and life in an oligarchical regime, which Orwell projects into the imagined Britain of Nineteen Eighty-Four. More important for Orwell, Koestler provides a model for the hero of Nineteen Eighty-Four: Rubashov is an epitome of the political intellectual with his rationalization of cruel methods, his political religion (or "Nationalism" as Orwell terms it), his neurosis, and his final "short-term" despair of social revolution; and Winston Smith is patterned after Koestler's hero. Orwell's attitude toward the material he uses from, Koestler is indicated in Nineteen Eighty-Four through ironic reversal, exaggeration, and other forms of parody. By these techniques Orwell communicates his criticism of the overidealism and materialism of contemporary political ideology.

The parody quality of Winston Smith and of the events of the novel pre-
clude accepting literally the pessimism suggested by Winston's fate. The
reversal of all hope is part of the parody-exaggeration itself; and the
final message is an optimistic vision of a strong and sane mankind.(9)

NOTES
    1.   George Orwell's review of Spanish Testament appeared in Time
and Tide, February 5, 1938; in Collected Essays, Journalism and Letters
of George Orwell, ed. Sonia Orwell and Ian Angus 4 vols. (London: Secker
and Warburg. 1968), I: 295-296; cited subsequently as CEJL. Orwell's review of Arrival and Departure, "Freud or Marx?" appeared in Manchester
Evening News, December 9, 1943. His article "What Is Socialism?" appeared in Manchester Evening News January 31, 1946.

    2.   George Orwell, "Arthur Koestler," written in 1944 and first
published in Critical Essays 1946, CEJL, III: 234-244.

    3.   George Orwell, "Catastrophic Gradualism," Common Wealth Review,
November 1945; CEJL, IV: 15-19.

    4.   George Orwell, The Road to Wigan Pier (London: Gollancz,
1937).

    5.   Arthur Koestler, Arrival and Departure (London: Cape, 1943);
cited subsequently in the text as AD.

    6.   George Orwell, Nineteen Eighty-Four (London: Secker and War-
burg, 1949).

    7.   Arthur Kostler, Darkness at Noon, trans. D Hardy (London: Cape,
1940); cited subsequently in the text as DN.

    8.   Kostler's theme of the political activist's neurosis and its
effects on his political decisions is cearly reflected in the pardoy of
Winston Smith's childhood traumas and his "sexual" cure through his relation with Julia, as well as his rat-induced neurosis at the climax of
Nineteen Eighty-Four. The subject is to extensive for ths paper, but it
is clear that Koestler's Freudian pessimism is one of the main objects of
Orwell's criticism.

    9.   There is clear evidence in Nineteen Eighty-Four for this opti-
mistic interpretation, especially the whole tenor the "Appendix Newspeak"; see my article, "Newspeak: The Epitome of Parody Technique in
Nineteen Eighty-Four," Critical Survey V, no. 2 (Summer 1971).

14.
Nineteen Eighty-Four
and the Massaging of the Media
W. RUSSEL GRAY

George Orwell's Nineteen Eighty-Four has become a rarity among novels --
a distinguished literary work and an immensely popular thriller. With
Huxley's Brave New World and Zamyatin's We it ranks among the century's
most respected dystopian novels. As to its popularity, thirty-five years
after initial publication tens of millions are estimated to have read it
in sixty-two languages, and more than 150,000 hardcover and ten million
paperbacks have been printed.(1) Entering calendar 1984, paperback sales
averaged 62,000 monthly at the sixty-sixth printing. Much of this popularity derives from Nineteen Eighty-Four's increasing relevance, a prominent example of which is Orwell's chilling sense of how susceptible our
mass media are to manipulation.

In one of the novel's satirical incidents Winston Smith escapes the
boredom of revising history by inventing a nonexistent party hero. "Comrade Ogilvy" is too good to be true. As a youngster he wanted only military toys. At age six he joined Big Brother's organization of young in-
formers. At eleven he denounced his uncle. At twenty-three he died preventing important dispatches from falling into enemy hands.

The fictitious Ogilvy, of course, was a stereotyped hero. So much
so that Winston probably could have succeeded as a contemporary television writer. In a recent behind-the-scenes critique of prime-time television, Tod Gitlin stressed that in today's programming the cardinal virtue is to play it safe.(2) Like Comrade Ogilvy, many action series
heroes are simple and predictable -- their television life spans one continuous melodrama.

Straws in the wind indicate that television may be abdicating some
of its traditional social responsibility in informational programming as
well. Consider the blurring of the information/entertainment distinction
and the increasingly popular "Happy News" format in which attractive news
team members fool around with each other and the weatherperson. In mid-
1982 a broadcasting official sanguinely acknowledged the trend by coining
the term "infortainment." Big Brother could not have unsaid it better!
Indeed, in the quest for ratings, manner -- not matter -- and image identification have become cardinal: a Los Angeles TV station fired two an-
chormen after measuring galvanic skin responses of sample audience members; and there was talk in the industry that sweat glands were being
measured in Seattle, Chicago, Minneapolis, Denver, and St. Louis.(3)

Have the print media been faring any better? Two of the Vietnam
war's biggest stories nearly got buried: My Lai and the Tonkin Gulf mystery. Fortunately the persistence of two maverick investigative journalists broke the stories despite Orwellian obstacles.

Seymour Hersh might have missed his My Lai story had he relied only
on the less-than-100-word Associated Press account from Fort Benning when

one Lieutenant Calley was charged. The release did not mention how many murders and gave practically no background. It was as if Big Brother's Ministry of Truth had rewritten, simplified, and sanitized history.

It later amazed British journalist Phillip Knightley that not one newspaper or broadcasting station had called AP for further details. Tipped by a source, Hersh dug up the omitted details, only to have his future Pulitzer Prize story rejected by Life and Look. Undaunted, he syndicated the story through a little-known news agency run by an acquaintance.(4)

The Hersh story received less attention in some papers than a space mission and a coincidental attack on the liberal press by Vice President Spiro Agnew (now a nonperson).(5) But a stunning coincidence in Cleveland gave new momentum to Hersh's second story on the massacre. The Plain Dealer printed pictures of the victims taken by an Army photographer. Strangely, however, many of the readers who reacted by telephone during the first twenty-four hours disapproved not of the event depicted but of the publication of the evidence.(6) One is chillingly reminded of the irrational loyalty of Big Brother's populace -- particularly their insensitivity to atrocities by their military. We recall that early in Nineteen Eighty-Four Winston Smith seems strangely inured to the bombing and machine-gunning of civilians in a newsreel he mentions in his forbidden diary. Perhaps a kind of doublethink had been occurring in Vietnam. After Hersh's stories sank in, many reporters began remembering horrifying incidents that initally had seemed unremarkable.(7)

Joseph Goulden, another reporter, probably thought that he already was in Orwell's Nineteen Eighty-Four when he tried to piece together the government's untold side of alleged attacks on two destroyers in Tonkin Gulf in August 1964. It later appeared that government selectivity in releasing details influenced Time, Life, and, later, Newsweek to report in a flurry of patriotism.(8) Such reporting would seem more appropriate to Big Brother's Truth Ministry. Lest we forget, in an overheated patriotic atmosphere Congress enacted a war powers resolution that effectively delegated its war-making prerogative to the president.

Philadelphia Inquirer reporter Goulden was taken aback by a development at the Senate's 1968 Tonkin Gulf hearings. Under close questioning by Senators Fulbright, Morse, and McCarthy, Defense Secretary MacNamara seemed to contradict some of his 1964 Tonkin statements. In the story he sent to Philadelphia, Goulden highlighted this development. However, his editors revised the story, and the reporter had a lesson in the mutability of the present. The published lead flatly contradicted what Goulden thought he heard the day before, for it stated emphatically that the United States had not provoked the Tonkin incidents.(9)

Goulden left the Inquirer and as a freelance investigative writer sought out crewmen and others involved in the Tonkin affair. The detailed findings he reported in his book about the matter cast considerable doubt on the government's 1964 and 1968 versions of the alleged North Vietnamese attacks.(10)

Many Orwellian developments surfaced during Goulden's research. A mysteriously sanitized transcript of the 1964 hearings, released two years later by the Pentagon and State Department, did not mention a connection Senator Morse had noted. Just before U.S. destroyers drew allegedly unprovoked fire there had been South Vietnamese naval raids and concurrent U.S. patrol activity. Also, the Fulbright Committee had to prepare for its 1967 and 1968 hearings without knowing of a crucial cable in which the captain of the Maddox had expressed doubt that the second provocation (August 4, 1964) involved hostile North Vietnamese actions. Furthermore by February 1969, when the committee was questioning MacNamara, it did not know of Sonarman Patrick Park. During the alleged attack of August 4 Park risked court-martial by balking at a direct order to fire at a "big target" in the Tonkin overcast. The target that the Maddox was about to blow out of the water was not an attacking torpedo boat but the Maddox's patrol companion, the Turner Joy! Given the overcast, it is not inconceivable that the August 4 "attack" may have been a mis-perception of one of our own ships. Strangely, Sonarman Park's name was missing from the list of destroyer crewman the Pentagon gave Goulden as late as July 1968. Apparently Park had become a nonperson to the Penta-gon. Also, when Goulden finally got to read the biographical sketch of Maddox skipper Herrick in the Internal Regulations Division of the Navy Office of Information, there was no mention of the second attack, which government witnesses claimed took place. The point is crucial because the second attack became the proximate cause of our retaliatory air strike. Finally a commander who had read cable traffic about the August 4 incident leaked helpful hints to Fulbright. After confessing his actions to his superior, the commander was subjected to a psychiatric ex-amination. He passed but was given another, which also found him fit.(11)

Implausible as they now seem, all of these events occurred. The moral? In time of war truth is the first casualty. Even a solid consti-tution can be circumvented when strong-willed officials exploit the age-old behavioral principles that make the best of us susceptible to mind-molding.

One such principle is the willingness to accept a polarization of reasonable differences into good guy/bad guy conflicts. Card-stacking is one means to that end. The Senate, news media, and Fulbright Committee got only the side of the Tonkin story that would arouse patriotic hostil-ity. Similarly, in Nineteen Eighty-Four citizens hear only negative views of sex, capitalism, and designated international enemies. Name-calling was another polarizing ploy in the Tonkin episode. In a rela-tively subtle application the Navy subjected a commander to two psychiat-ric examinations following leaks to Fulbright. In a more explicit appli-cation President Johnson characterized Senate adversaries of the period as "Nervous Nellies," a disrespectful nickname first used in the Coolidge administration.(12) Orwell's novel abounds in negative epithets — to name a few, "swine," "thought-criminal," and "animals."

Another classic mind-conditioning principle is the Bandwagon effect, the tendency to conform, imitate, or follow the crowd when in doubt. In the Tonkin emergency, despite the warnings of Senator Morse, the Senate voted 88-2 to approve what amounted to a waiver of its war-making power. In a climate of uncertaintly and apparent urgency, few senators risked seeming to be unpatriotic. We are uncomfortably reminded of the almost competitive conformity of Orwell's characters during Two-Minute Hates and massive rallies.

A third principle is that of association, as when "virtue words" or glittering generalities are applied to suggest that virtue is associated with a person or cause being promoted. Thus fed only a smattering of the Tonkin dispatches but none that contained doubts about the second alleged attack, media people from Time, Life, and the New York Times jumped on the bandwagon, referring to the reprisal air raiders as "the nation's newest battle veterans," "heroes of the Tonkin Gulf," and "Policemen of the Pacific."(13) Equally adept were Orwell's thought-manipulators, who in Nineteen Eighty-Four used as slogan words and names of government agencies an array of glittering abstractions: "Peace," "Freedom," "Strength," "Plenty," and "Truth."

Newspaper and magazine reports of inroads on individual privacy in America in past decades also have an Orwellian ring. (Sources appear after end notes).

A federal judge fines an auto dealer for bugging his showroom to eavesdrop on customers; the defense attorney claims it is a common regional practice.

An electronics company markets a closed-circuit telescanner enabling supervisors to look in on branch offices or even to time workers' coffee breaks.

A chemical company markets the ultimate in deodorizers — Veilex. It anesthetizes nerve endings, making it impossible to smell bad odors while leaving intact nerve endings that sense "good" smells. One wonders: why clean up foul-smelling odors in a factory or city when the noses of people can be readjusted?

A state successfully uses a toll-free hotline on which citizens can anonymously accuse relatives, neighbors, and others of welfare cheating.

An Orwellian measure seems to cause a sharp decline in shoplifting losses. Subliminal commands not to steal are transmitted along with a department store's background music.

An increasing number of snooping devices of the do-it-yourself variey bring 1984 closer in 1978. Radio Shack offers a pocket lie detector kit for $11.95; for $1500 one can monitor the responses of friends or business competitors over the phone -- to determine the amount of stress in their voices -- using a mendacity indicator.

In 1979 a magazine disclosed that the CIA operated entrapment apartments in Greewwich Village and San Francisco using prostitutes, see-through mirrors, cameras, microphones disguised as electrical outlets, and tape recorders.

A midwestern state's department of transportation finally got around to removing "Big Brother" see-through mirrors installed in interstate highway rest stop buildings in 1969 to allow an observer hidden in a storeroom to watch parking lots and sidewalks to reduce vandalism.

Press reports described many of the foregoing developments as Orwellian, or used the term "Big Brother." Such ominous descriptors also were applied to misleading uses of language. So effectively did Orwell warn of "duckspeak," "Newspeak," and "doublethink" that "truth squads" such as the Doublespeak Committee of the National Council of Teachers of English focused public attention upon self-serving language smoggers. An Air Force spokesman attracted attention by calling the Cambodian bombings "air support" and tactical rocket and napalm attacks "surgical air strikes." In a short semantic leap bombing was renamed "protective reaction strikes."(14) Since 1967 many have pondered Senator Mike Mansfield's euphemism for all-out atomic war, which was "open-ended conflict."(15) President Reagan received NCTE Doublespeak recognition for naming a multiple-warhead missile "Peacekeeper." Finallly, for U.N. watchers there was Ambassador Kirkpatrick's distinction between friendly ("authoritarian") and unfriendly ("totalitarian") repressive governments.

And then there was Watergate. A Philadelphia columnist reflected on the basket of semantic snakes dumped into the public domain by that affair. It was bad enough that such terms as "loyalty," "law and order," "national security," and "in the national interest" were bent beyond recognition in a mockery of the communications process. However, the Watergate coverup language became so convoluted that apparently the Nixon group became unable to think about their situation in clear, honest

terms. Making an explicit connection with Orwell's "Politics and the English Language," journalist Bob Lancaster commented:

> Thus the one policy alternative that might have gotten Nixon
> off the hook -- telling the truth to the public -- was spoken
> of as policy of "letting it all hangout." That quickly
> transformed into a "limited hang out." "That in turn became
> a "modified limited hangout." And that, of course, was an
> absurdity. Because of this sheer degenerate incompetence of
> the language, the policy was never even seriously consid-
> ered.(16)

Nuclear power and nuclear arms advocates have coined many Orwellian
euphemisms. In place of the frightful term "explosion" we have "energet-
ic disassembly," and instead of "fire" we are apt to find "rapid oxida-
tion."(17) One concerned gentleman, Steven Hilgarten, coined a term for
such phraseology: "Nukespeak." Even the military is learning the lingo.
Typical examples are "clean bombs," "devices," and "nuclear exchanges."
For those who are reassured by phallic imagery we have "deep penetra-
tors," "full spikes," and "soft laydowns."(18)
   The field of education also is keeping pace. In the United States
bicentennial year United Press carried without comment a harrowing example of language abuse in one of our schools. A sixth grader was called
a "nonperson," confined to a topless and bottomless appliance carton for
ninety minutes, and jeered at. The offense? Talking to a girl in class.
School officials defended the punishment as "reality therapy." A spokes-
person for the school system referred to the penalty box as a "social ad-
justment center."(19) Elsewhere, in 1981 there was a literally shocking
example. A summer Bible school teacher got his youngsters to pay attention by seating them on his "electric stool," pressing a button and giving them a twelve-volt shock -- to aid them in "hearing the word." Few
parents objected. One even said she was not worried because her eight-
year-old son was "learning about God."(20)
   Where does all of this leave us on the thirty-fifth anniversary of
the publication of Nineteen Eighty-Four? Because of Orwell's concern we
are more aware of the awesome power and responsibility of the media, more
alert to the danger of blurring the information and entertainment functions, better able to recognize the ease with which government agencies
routinely preempt the propagandist's principles to try to manipulate the
media, and more likely to recognize the increasing incursions upon privacy in ostensibly "free" societies as well as the widening parameters of
obscurity and misdirection in the language of officialdom.
   We are uncomfortably close to Orwell's Nineteen Eighty-Four. Consider some recent developments. According to a Time cover story the National Opinion Research Center has found that from 1976 to the present
time now the percentage of the population having "a great deal of confi-
dence in the press" has slipped from 29 to 13.7. Proof of popular mis-
trust of the press came when the Reagan administration invaded Grenada
and excluded reporters without causing a national outcry. After sounding
the alarm on NBC's Nightly News, John Chancellor was probably astounded
when, in 500 letters and calls, the public supported the press restric-
tion 5 to 1. Time's 225 letters on the matter ran almost 8 to 1 against
the press.(21)
   Those of us who look to Japan as a model of efficiency, a precursor
of improved productivity, should consider what happed at the Fujitsu
Fanuc factory. The plant became so automated that management and the
labor union agreed to allow attrition to reduce the size of the work
force. However, the union was to regret its cooperation. As robots replaced dues-paying union members, the treasury suffered. But a solution
was found. Management agreed to pay union dues for each robot.(22)

There have been disquieting examples of doublethink. Roman Catholic theologians have offered a revisionist view of Martin Luther as a "father in the faith."(23) Soviet authorities are removing the "nonperson" status of Joseph Stalin and reglorifying him.(24) And there has been a curious marriage of business and education. An academic dean at Moravian College received a letter from a man whose company sells term papers. The writer wanted the dean to know that a graduating senior had not paid the bill for his term paper. The term paper vendor explained that he was not writing because of money — it was the principle of the thing!(25) Perhaps the crucial question is not are we in Nineteen Eighty-Four? but rather, to what extent is Nineteen Eighty-Four in us?

We are missing Orwell's purpose if we try to Nostradamusize Nineteen Eighty-Four and grade Orwell for percentage of accurate predictions. What he gave us in that novel was not intended as a self-fulfilling prophecy but its opposite. By extrapolating his fears into both a literary and popular success, Orwell created an instant myth — a construct that has made us aware of the deeper implications of otherwise random-seeming events, trends, and language barbarisms in the media. By doing so he helped us shape a Big Brotherless future — at least as of the real 1984.

NOTES

Brief portions of this essay appeared in the author's April 1983 English Journal article, "Slouching toward Relevance, or What to Do with Nineteen Eighty-Four until 1984," and are used here with the permission of the National Council of Teachers of English, publisher of the Journal.

1.   Paul Gray, Anne Hopkins, and John Saar, "That Year Is Almost Here," Time, November 28, 1983, p. 46.

2.   Todd Gitlin, Inside Prime Time (New York: Pantheon, 1983).

3.   David Chagall, "Only as Good as His Skin Tests," TV Guide, 26 March 1977, pp. 6, 8.

4.   Phillip Knightley, The First Casualty (New York: Harcourt Brace Jovanovich, 1975), p. 391.

5.   Ibid., p. 392.

6.   Seymour Hersh, "The Story Everyone Ignored," Readings in Mass Communication: Concepts and Issues in the Mass Media, ed. Michael C. Emery and Ted Curtis Smythe (Dubuque: Wm. C. Brown, 1974), p. 152.

7.   Knightley, The First Casuality, p. 395.

8.   Don Stillman, "Tonkin: What Should Have Been Asked,"   Our Troubled Press: Ten Years of the Columbia Journalism Review, ed. Alfred Balk and James Boylan (Boston: Little, Brown, 1971), pp. 112-114.

9.   Ibid., p. 118.

10.   Joseph C. Goulden, Truth Is the First Casualty: The Gulf of Tonkin Affair — Illusion and Reality (Chicago: James B. Adler/Rand McNally, 1969).

11.   Ibid., pp. 202-219.

12.   Ibid., p. 178.

13. Stillman, "Tonkin," pp. 113–114.

14. David Goodman, "Countdown to 1984: Big Brother May Be Right on Schedule," Futurist XII (December 1978): 351.

15. Goulden, Truth Is the First Casualty, p. 174.

16. Bob Lancaster, "Inexact Language Is an Invitation to Corrupt Politics," Philadelphia Inquirer, October 14, 1974.

17. Fred M. Hechinger, "Committee on Doublespeak: The Muck Stops Here," Philadelphia Bulletin, January 24, 1982.

18. Ellen Goodman, "'Nukespeak': The Language of Manipulation," Wilmington (Del.), Evening Journal, November 29, 1982.

19. "Teacher Puts Boy in Penalty Box," Philadelphia Daily News, October 21, 1976, p. 40.

20. "Religion a Shocking Experience," Philadelphia Inquirer, July 10, 1981, p. 6A.

21. William A. Henry III, "Journalism under Fire," Time, December 12, 1983, p. 76.

22. "Off Beat News Stories of 1983," The World Almanac and Book of Facts: 1984 (New York: Newspaper Enterprise Association, Inc., 1983), p. 696.

23. Richard M. Ostling. "Luther: Giant of His Time and Ours," Time, October 31, 1983, p. 100.

24. Dusko Doder, "Book Prize Seen as Rehabilitation Step for Stalin," Philadelphia Inquirer, November 24, 1983, p. 20-D.

25. (AP) "Cheating Is Common in Campus Life," Philadelphia Inquirer, November 24, 1983, p. 1-WB.

Sources of "Orwellian" newspaper and magazine items:

A federal judge. . . . "Auto Dealer Fined for Showroom Bug," Philadelphia Bulletin, June 9, 1974.
An electronics company. . . . "A TV Monitor to Time Coffee Breaks?" Item about Photo-Scan Company in a Delaware County (Pa.) newspaper, circa 1976.
A chemical company. . . . "Gag Orders in Secaucus," New Times, May 27, 1977, p. 17.
A state successfully. . . ."Little Pitchers," New Times, September 2, 1977.
An Orwellian measure. . . . "Sweet Nothings in Shoplifter Ears," Philadelphia Inquirer, October 8, 1978, pp. 1-A, 12-A.
An increasing number. . . . "Technology, Big Brother Are Invading Your Privacy," Philadelphia Bulletin, January 22, 1978, p. 10 XE.
In 1979 a. . . . John Marks, "Sex, Drugs, and the CIA," Saturday Review, February 3, 1979, pp. 12-16.
A midwestern state's. . . . Undated item in news roundup column, Philadelphia Inquirer.

15.
Nineteen Eighty-Four as Dystopia
LEAH HADOMI

George Orwell called <u>Nineteen Eighty-Four</u> a "Gestalt." By that he was probably referring to more than merely the compact organization of the novel's elements into a cohesive whole; he meant the close interplay between the novel and the real world, which is of a kind that whenever any of the novel's elements is found in reality, it instantly summons to mind, the work in its entirety.(1) Or, to state the case in terms of Jan Mukarovsky's theory of structure, "the entire construction of the work, and not just the part called 'content' enters into active relation with the system of life-values which govern human affairs."(2) This concentrated intensity of reciprocal relation between fiction and reality is a characteristic of satire in literary utopias and is a dominant feature of satire in dystopian compositions.

If we accept the premise that literary utopias are based on the idea of a satiric attack on imperfect reality by confronting it with a portrayal of an ideal world that is its opposite, then we may propose that dystopias represent a metamorphosis of utopian form wherein the butt of satire is both the world as it is and a parodic juxtaposition of the proposal for its redemption.(3) Dystopian criticism, however, involves more than the rejection of particular concrete manifestations of social existence; it is aimed at the entire ethical and social consciousness of the times.(4) So the criticism contained in <u>Nineteen Eighty-Four</u>, conceived as a Gestalt, is directed not so much at specific historical phenomena as, say, at fascism in its Nazi guise, or Marxism as it has been realized in communism, but at the totalitarian principle underlying all such systems. Monolithic ideologies aim at nothing short of a total regeneration of the world.(5) As a dystopian composition, Orwell's novel comprehends a contemporary reality that includes the consciousness that the historically programmatic ideologies of the nineteenth century ultimately failed to fulfill their promise, coming in our own times to constitute a threat to the very survival of humanity — a consciousness of what Ernst Bloch described as the "hope principle" (<u>Prinzip Hoffnung</u>) ending in the "murder of hope" (<u>Hoffnungsmord</u>).(6)

Summing up, therefore, we can say that both the utopian and dystopian forms rely on the dynamic interplay between an imaginary world and reality. They differ, however, in this: the utopia represents a rejection of the existing world by an act of fictive redemption; of both the way things are and the utopian proposal for setting them right.(7) The former is a satiric rejection of the current state of the world; the latter satirically repudiates both our judgment of the reality we inhabit and our vision of the world redeemed. The social utopia is recognized by its resolution of three ethical polarities in human attitudes towards oneself and one's society. The polarity of reason vs. passion is resolved in the ideal utopia by the dominance of reason. The needs of the individual coincide with those of the society, thus resolving the second polarity. The third one, the tension between social order and individual freedom, is resolved by the postulate that the ideal social organization is the one that coincides with the freedom of each of its citizens.

In the dystopia portrayed in Nineteen Eighty-Four the humanistic utopian resolution of these polarities undergoes satiric distortion. The process can be illustrated with reference to the first polarity, which is apparently resolved in Oceania on the utopian pattern, by asserting the primacy of reason. Yet in his campaign to reducate Winston Smith, O'Brien accounts for absolute state rule in Oceania by asserting a solipsist postulate -- namely that all knowledge of reality resides in the self, and that neither one's fellow man nor the external world exists independently of their representations in one's private consciousness. "Reality is in the skull," O'Brien tells Winston, "Nothing exists except human consciousness." [p. 213](8) It is on this point that satiric distortion is brought into play, wrenching the utopian principle of the dominance of reason out of all recognition. In the process the postulate of cogito ergo sum (Descartes) is displaced from its position in individual consciousness and shifted over into the domain of the collective, which imposes its will on every individual within its purview, thereby abrogating entirely the individual's right to autonomous thought. Satirical distortion therefore is made total, involving as it does a complete volte-face of the direction of normal solipsist epistemology. For no longer does the merging of the self with one's fellow man and the external world take place in the consciousness of the individual; it is accomplished by the annulment of private consciousness altogether.

The utopian resolution of the second polarity, which is achieved by striking a balance between private will and the general good, depends on an optimistic assessment of the potentialities of human nature. In this case dystopian transformation operates by way of satiric inversion. In both the utopia and dystopia human nature determines the character of society; and in both the maintenance of social cohesion depends on gratifying private desire. But in a dystopia of the kind represented by Oceania, love and mutual understanding and the equal distribution of material wealth are sources of pain rather than gratification, and pleasure is obtained not from doing good to one's neighbor but from the spectacle of his suffering and degradation.

The utopian method's resolution of the third polarity entails the establishment of social order as the precondition of personal freedom. In Orwell's novel the principle behind this resolution undergoes dystopian transmutation by satiric exaggeration. Society in Nineteen Eighty-Four is organized by a ruling hierarchy that maintains absolute supervision and control of every aspect of the conduct of all citizens. Oceanian societies defy rational explanation; nor are they of a kind that could possibly contribute to the happiness and freedom of the citizens of the state.

The most explicit statement in Nineteen Eighty-Four of the antipodal reversal of utopian values is made by O'Brien when he speaks to Winston Smith of the Party's master plan for Oceanian civilization:

It is the exact opposite of the stupid hedonistic Utopians that the old reformers imagined. A world of trampling and being trampled upon, a world which will grow not less but more merciless as it refines itself. Progress in our world will be progress towards more pain. (p. 214)

The three ethical polarities of the social utopia are implemented as ideal traits of the imaginary reality known as the Utopian World. The Utopian World is characterized by three attributes: isolation from the

empirical world, harmony between society and its members, and stasis as
the stability resulting from ideal ultimate perfection. In a Dystopian
World such as that of Nineteen Eighty-Four, these attributes are satirically inverted or intensified ad extremum. The isolation of the utopian
world evolves into confinement, the utopian harmony is exaggerated to dystopian coersion, and stasis turns into stagnation both of individual and
society.

In the dystopian world of Nineteen Eighty-Four, temporal and spatial
isolation are satirically distorted. Geographically Oceania is neither
remote nor secluded in any literal sense. It is a great power of vast
territorial extent, sharing the known world with two other great powers,
Eurasia and Eastasia, with which it alternately enters into alliances to
make war on the third. But these three superstates are all organized
along the same totalitarian lines, so that no qualitative difference exists among them. In effect, therefore, the world portrayed by Orwell offers no avenue of escape, either physically to the sanctuary of another
place or mentally into the future. [p. 125](9) Isolation in Oceania is
therefore complete, extending to the dimension of time as well as of
space. The very title of the novel is an ironic reference to the mean-
inglessness of the passage of time in the reality that the novel portrays. Time, indeed, can hardly be said to exist in a world that has
been projected into a future so immediate that our own present still
resonates it.

Hence the world created by Orwell contains no basis upon which a
comparison might be drawn between it and a qualitatively different locus,
since the author's satirically paradigmatic treatment of utopian isolation excludes the existence of an alternate reality that might function
as a foil for the imagined one. Nor does the work contain any basis of
comparison between the time into which Oceania has been projected and the
past, or the world known to the reader. Oceanians are therefore thrown
back entirely on themselves in judging their existence and are exposed
only to others who are no different from themselves. The consequence of
all this is the sense of confinement that is the universal experience of
all Oceanians. The inhabitants of Orwell's dystopia are imprisoned in a
unidimensional reality and are constrained to accept existence in an eternal here-and-now created by party ideology and obtained by the annihilation of the memory of all things past that were different and by the
extinction of any hope for change in the future. "And when memory failed
. . . there did not exist, and never again could exist, any standard
against which [the conditions of life] could be tested." (p. 78) Moreover to contemplate even the possibility of escape was to indulge in a
delusion.

The harmony of a utopian world is the direct consequence of applying
the utopian principle of complete identity between the aspirations of the
individual and the interests of the collective. Citizens of a utopia
identify wholly with the values and norms of their community, and their
involvement in the life of the collective is total and unreserved. Disagreement among individuals, or between individuals and the collective,
would be unthinkable in a utopia. Nor, for that matter, does there exist
the remotest chance of the individual's being harmed or his private needs
being overridden by utopian institutions. In the dystopian world of
Nineteen Eighty-Four, however, utopian harmony undergoes a satiric transformation not unlike the conversion of utopian isolation into dystopian
confinement. In Oceania the individual's submission into the values of
the collective is obtained by the forceful suppression of independent
thought and personal autonomy. "We shall squeeze you empty," O'Brien
tells Winston Smith, "and then we shall fill you with ourselves." (p.
206) Hence the concord between the individual and the collective is the
achievement of coercive indoctrination, and the individual's role in society is something to which he has been condemned by edict rather than

being a result of voluntary association deriving from his sense of communal identity. Oceanian citizens simply obey, either out of apathy or out of fear of retribution, to fulfill their appointed role in a society consisting entirely of "swarms of workers engaged in an unimaginable multitude of jobs." (p. 37)

The individual's integration into society in Oceania does not come about as a result of a person's free ethical choice derving from his natural disposition. Rather, the individual's nature is conditioned by his enforced submersion in the collective. According to the doctrine expounded by O'Brien, the State creates human nature; (pp. 216–217) this it does by channeling the deviant and intractable impulses inherent in people so that they should serve the goals of the Party and reinforce collective unity. The social bond is therefore maintained in Oceania by appealing to the very worst in human nature through an official policy of incitement to hatred of the enemy abroad and within, whether real or imagined. (pp. 14–15)

The satiric treatment of dystopian social concord is especially strong in Orwell's portrayal of a state machinery capable of creating and destroying identities at will. At the Ministry of Truth fictitious heroes like Comrade Ogilvy are created (by Winston Smith) and heretics like Withers "vaporized" and turned into "unpersons" overnight. (pp. 40–41) O'Brien's assertion that the "command of the totalitarians was 'Thou shalt'. Our command is 'Thou art,'" (p. 205) has a profoundly ironic significance in regard to the humanistic utopian ideal of perfect consonance between allowing the private self ample scope of expression and maintaining the public good.

The absurdity of dystopian pseudo-harmony is evident as well in Orwell's depiction of Oceanian social organization. Society in Nineteen Eighty-Four is a pyramidal hierarachy presided over by Big Brother and divided into three classes consisting of an Inner Party elite, Outer Party workers, and the submerged majority of proles. A similar model of pyramidal social organization headed by a guiding elite is adopted in many utopias, where its purpose is to maintain communal harmony. But in Oceania social concord is secured by coercion and the systematic suppression of private and social consciousness. "Big Brother," we are told, "is the embodiment of the Party." (p. 208) And although he may owe his existence entirely to the skewed logic of "doublethink," his absolute rule is faithfully maintained by his acolytes in the Inner Party, for whom the entire rationale of statecraft is "power over human beings. Over the body — but above all, over the mind." (p. 212) That power is exerted through terror directed at members of the Outer Party to ensure their obedience and unreserved conformity to the established organizational norms. Paradoxically this regimented social order, being based on terror, depends for its survival on the existence of a fictitious Brotherhood of anti-State conspirators in order to create the impression of "an endless pressing . . . upon the nerve of power" (p. 216) to legitimize its routine use of violence in its own defense.(10)

We learn from the book of the heresiarch, Emmanuel Goldstein, that the 85 percent of the population of Oceania consists of proletarian masses. (p. 168) These "proles" are socially and ideologically unconscious and condemned by their vegetal existence to ignorance of even their own misery. (p. 136) So that notwithstanding their overwhelming numbers, they remain politically inert, constituting the most oppressed section of the populace and the one with the least to gain from the coerced civic harmony of Oceanian society. (p. 59) Thus in the dystopian world of Nineteen Eighty-Four, the ideal of harmony between the individual and the collective is doubly distorted by the suppression of autonomous consciousness on the one hand and its complete absence on the other. In regard to both, the principle of harmony is exaggerated to the extreme limit of absurdity.

Winston Smith asserts the primacy of autonomous empirical thought against collective solipsism. His is a struggle in behalf of private experience, the of which significance derives from individuals' memory of the past and their hopes for the future. To this end he creates islands of privacy for himself within the pubic domain that is under the surveillance of the protectors of the State.(11) Thus at times he retreats into the sanctuary of "another place," such as the clearing in the wood where he and Julia first consummate their love, or their trysting place over Charrington's shop. At other times he withdraws mentally into another time -- either into the past through his memories of childhood or into the future through his dreams and visions of the Golden Country. These private islands of the self constitute, as it were, the novel's alternate ethical realm, parallel to the second realm in the utopian paradigm. However, in Orwell's work there ultimately exists no possibility of making a free choice between ethical realms, and the destruction of such sanctuaries of privacy as the individual is able to establish is only a matter of time.

The static ideal world of the Utopia in its ultimate perfection is inverted in the dystopian world to a suspense of progress and a halt of change. Enforced stagnation is the Party's way of perpetuating the present, which it does by harnessing the past to its will and rejecting the future. "Who controls the past," so runs the Party slogan, "controls the future: who controls the present controls the past." (p. 31)

And just as the passage of time is brought to a halt in the life of the collective, so too is it stopped in the life of the individual. All that exists is pure duration, originating in nothing and leading nowhere. With all recollection of the past expunged, and in the absence of any hope for the future, private identity is of no account and individual existence entirely contingent upon the existence of the collective. Personal memories fall into the category of "crimethink"; since they express desires they are proscribed by the Party; and any thought of change in the future can never be realized, merely condemning those who contemplate such change to extinction at the hands of the guardians of the social order. In the world of Nineteen Eighty-Four stasis, which in the utopia is the outcome of the attainment and perpetuation of an ideal mode of life, degenerates into a physical and spiritual stagnation that engulfs everyone, so that even such as Winston Smith and Julia are ultimately constrained to submit and say of themselves, "We are the dead." (p. 177)

The process in which the personality of the individual is broken down and his freedom of choice extinguished is connected with his acceptance of the precept "Freedom Is Slavery" as an article of faith and his willingness to suspend his critical faculties to the point of believing that "two and two make five." The State's control of the private perception of reality, and its annihilation of every vestige of knowledge deriving from empirical experience, results in the individual's coming to regard every event that he thinks happened but is at variance with what is officially said to have happened to be a hallucination: truth is only "whatever happens in all minds." (p. 224)

In conclusion we may refer back to the author's own comment on his novel, mentioned in the beginning of this discussion. What Orwell called the "Gestalt" of his novel depends not only upon the work's internal structural coherence but upon the integration, in a work of fantasy, of referents belonging to a world of the reader's own experience. In Orwell's novel satire establishes a link between a utopian imaginary world and menacing reality. Especially forceful in this regard is Orwell's portrayal of physical and moral frailty, which gives his tale its high degree of credibility. Moreover the anxiety the work inspires depends not so much on the author's frightening vision of the future as on the reader's realization that the seeds of the horror described in the novel are already sown in his own time. Hence the novel's warning has more to do with its relevance to immediate reality than with the fear it may arouse concerning what the future might hold in store. The establishment of mutually hostile blocks of nations in the twentieth century, the steady increase in the use of the technology of surveillance along with the growing influence of the mass communications media in our lives, the ongoing erosion of traditional ethical values and the attendant rise in personal and civic violence -- all these point to the very real inroads that the dystopian attributes of confinement, coercion, and stagnation have already made in the contemporary world.

A fitting close to this discussion is provided by the following quotation from Winston Smith's diary that seems to encapsulate the substance of our theme:

> To the future or to the past, to a time when thought is free, when men are different from one another and do not live alone -- to a time when truth exists and what is done cannot be undone:

> From the age of uniformity, from the age of solitude, from the age of Big Brother, from the age of doublethink — greetings! (p. 26)

NOTES

1.   Alex Zwedling, "Orwell and the Technique of Didactic Fantasy," in Twentieth Century Interpretations of Nineteen Eighty-Four, ed. S. Hynes (New Jersey, 1971), p. 92.

2.   Jan Mukarovsky, Aesthetic Function: Norm and Value as Social Facts (Ann Arbor, 1979), p. 89.

3.   On the utopia as an intellectual exercise with respect to possible modes of existence in the future, see R. Ruyer, L'utopie et les utopies (Paris, 1950), p. 9, or the German translation of the relevant passage in Utopie: Begriff und Phanomen des Utopischen, ed. A. Neususs (Neuwied, 1968), esp. p. 339; and for the image of the ideal world, see R. Gerber Utopian Fantasy: A Study of English Utopian Fiction since the End of the Nineteenth Century (London, 1959), p. 122, H. U. Seeber, Wandlungen der Form, in der literarischen Utopie (Goppingen, 1970) pp. 20 ff., and H. Schulte-Herbruggen, Utopie und Anti-Utopie: Von der Strukturanalyse zur Strukturtypologie (Bochum, 1960).

4.   Brief accounts of the shift from the utopian to the dystopian point of view may be found in C. Walsch, From Utopia to Nightmare (New York, 1962), pp. 166-171, and in J. L. Morillas, "From 'Dreams of Reason' to 'Dreams of Unreason,'" Journal of East and West Studies 82 (1972): 47-62. According to Schulte-Herbruggen, Utopie und Anti-Utopie, p. 119, the dystopian attitudes already in evidence in earlier centuries assumed importance in the nineteenth. Others argue, however, that this did not take place until the twentieth century. For the latter view, see L. Borniski, "Kritik der Utopie in der modernen englischen Literatur," Die Neueren Sprachen, Beihefte 2, p. 5; and J. C. Garrett, Utopias in Literature since the Romantic Period (Canterbury, 1968), pp. 46-63, and W. Vozkamp (Hrsg.) Utopie-Forschung (Stuttgart, 1982), esp. vol. 1.

5.   Hans Freyer, Theorie des gegenwartigen Zeitalters (Stuttgart, 1955), p. 75 conceives of the utopia as an intellectual protection into the future on the basis of the "apriorische Prinzip des Fortschritts" (a priori principle of progress").

6.   Ernst Bloch, Das Prinzip Hoffnung (Frankfurt-am-Main, 1959), p.
511. Schulte-Herbruggen, Utopie und Anti-Utopie, pp. 206-207, regards
Thomas More's Utopia to represent an "optimistische Bejahung der naturli-
lchen Weltordnung" (an "optimistic affirmation of the natural order of
the world") and the paradigm of such a work as Orwell's to be a "pessi-
mistische verneinung" (a "pessimistic negation") of the order of the
world.

7.   A. Zwerdling, "Orwell and the Technique of Didactic Fantasy,"
in Twentieth Century Interpretations, p. 91, observes, "Only an anti-
utopia could displace a utopian vision; only the fear of hell was as
powerful as the need for heaven."

8.   Page references to all citations in this paper from Nineteen
Eighty-Four are taken from the 1982 Penguin Books edition.

9.   "Orwell's profoundest insight is that in a totalitarian world
"man's life is shorn of dynamic possibilities"; see Irving Howe, "History
as Nightmare," in Twentieth Century Interpretations, p. 45.

10.   E. Kahler, The Tower and the Abyss (New York, 1967), p. 77,
distinguishes between individual sadism and collective political sadism
in the twentieth century. What he has to say has a bearing on George Orwell's novel: "The frightening feature in modern atrocities is exactly
the lack of such personal focus in which conflicting faculties can still
cohere."

11.   On the symbolic code reflecting this motif see Leah Hadomi, "A
Look an 'a Word an' the Dreams They Stirred!" Dutch Quarterly Review of
Anglo-American Letters 15 (1985): 73-91.

16.
More to Orwell: An Easy Leap from
Utopia to *Nineteen Eighty-Four*
JANICE L. HEWITT

When Thomas More wrote Utopia in 1515, he started a literary genre with
lasting appeal for writers who want not only to satirize existing evils
but to postulate the ideal state, a kind of Golden Age in the face of
reality.(1) The word "utopia" is itself More's coinage, a combination of
the Greek ou topos, meaning "no place," and eu topos, "good place." The
very term playfully enacts man's longing for an unattainable good life.
"Utopia", says Robert C. Elliott,

> is man's effort to work out imaginatively what happens — or
> what might happen — when the primal longings embodied in the
> myth [of the G olden Age] confront the principle of reality.
> In this effort man no longer merely dreams of a divine state
> in some remote time; he assumes the role of creator him-
> self.(2)

A utopia, then, by its very nature incorporates satire of the existing
situation and a plan for an "ideal commonwealth."(3) More does indeed
show both aspects in Utopia, putting into Hythloday's mouth enthusiastic
praise of the commonwealth "Utopia," which he has visited and by comparison criticizing many of the evils in Henry VIII's England. A dystopia
such as Orwell's Nineteen Eighty-Four, then, should be a kind of mirror
image, an anti-utopia, a utopia carried to its reasonable and extreme
conclusion.
   Thomas More, however, is a more multilayered trickster than he is
often credited with being, and he goes a step beyond the division between
satire and ideal state. Beatus Rhenanus, More's contemporary, characterized him as "every inch pure jest,"(4) a description that fits the man
who puns with the book's title and who sets up an elaborate hoax with
letters to and from Peter Giles and Jerome Busleiden to establish the
"actual" existence of Hythloday and the geographic location and alphabet
of Utopia.(5) What is not so easily noted, however, is that while Hythloday praises Utopia and thereby criticizes sixteenth-century England, he
unknowingly mouths criticism of the very Utopia he admires. Those evils,
unintentionally presented by Hythloday and not even commented upon by the
persona "More," represent powerful arguments against Utopia. They also
give evidence of More's imaginative ability to step outside his culture's
organic and hierarchical thinking in order to follow the Utopian ideals
to their logical conclusion. Similar conclusions are the basis of much
of the horror depicted in the realistic dystopia George Orwell will publish more than four hundred years later. Nineteen Eighty-Four is not so
much an anti-utopia as it is More's Utopia carried to the extreme.

Edward Surtz recognizes and comments on some of those dystopian elements but explains them away in what he perceives as the potential Christian paternalism of Utopia. He states that "Utopian absolutes are Christian values thinly veiled."(6) Elliott, however, disagrees with this Roman Catholic interpretation and points to divorce and euthanasia, both
acceptable to Utopians but not to Catholics. "The major problem," Elliott says, "is one of method," of seeing Utopia as a prose version of
formal verse satire. If so, a "Catholic" interpretation is no more valid
than a Marxist one, or any interpretation that rests solely on an ideological look at the work. Looking at the same work in which Surtz finds
a Catholic commonwealth, for example, Karl Kautsky concludes that More
"was a Socialist."(7)

In a very real way both Surtz and Kautsky, though diametrically opposed, are correct. Hythloday tells "More" that the Utopians were very
much impressed with Christianity when he and his friends introduced them
to the teachings of Christ. He adds,

But I think they were also much influenced by the fact that Christ
had encouraged his disciples to practice community of goods, and
that among the truest groups of Christians, that practice still pre-
vails.(8)

Surtz's Christian emphasis, therefore, has a good grounding in the text.
But there are also references to "community of goods" in this passage and
elsewhere, especially in Hythloday's stirring conclusion to book II, to
enable Kautsky to make his "roots of socialism" case. To achieve such
rigid positions, however, both critics must ignore important portions of
the text and both must assume that author Thomas More agrees with Hythloday's approval of Utopia.

If Thomas More's position is so clear, however, why is there so wide
a gap between critical responses? J. H. Hexter, disagreeing with Kautsky, writes, "More simply did not believe that all the evil men do can be
ascribed to the economic arrangements of society" and sees More as a
Christian man fighting the good medieval fight against the monster
Pride.(9) C. S. Lewis, on the other hand, concentrates on the text's
wit and jokes and concludes that it is "not a consistently serious philosophical treatise, and all attempts to treat it as such break down
sooner or later."(10) R. W. Chambers sees More as a reformer yearning to
return the entire country to the discipline of a medieval monastery.(11)
Although he seems to equate More's views with those of Hythloday, Chambers does recognize that Utopia is not entirely desirable, and chides
those of us who use More's catchy name incorrectly:

Utopia is depicted as a sternly righteous and puritanical
State, where few of us would feel quite happy; yet we go on
using the word 'Utopia' to signify an easy-going paradise,
whose only fault is that it is too happy and ideal to be
realized.(12)

But is author Thomas More the persona "More"? The autobiographical
beginning would indicate so, but it is not unusual for the author of a
satirical work to try to establish such veracity at the beginning. Just
as the word "utopia" is a playful witticism, "Hythloday" may come from
Greek words meaning "nonsense peddler." The word morus is Greek for
"fool," Chambers points out, so that More's use of his own name also may
be a joke. There is perhaps good correlation between author More and
persona More in book I in the debate between "More" and Hythloday over
the pros and cons of serving the king, a problem that More himself was
internally debating.(13) In book II, however, "More" has little to say

in reply to Hythloday's impassioned enthusiasm, even at the end of the
book when "More" states:

> My chief objection was to the basis of their whole system,
> that is, their communal living and their moneyless economy.
> This one thing alone takes away all the nobility, magnifi-
> cence, splendor, and majesty which (in the popular view) are
> considered the true ornaments of any nation. (p. 91)

More weakens the thrust of the argument by grammatical sloppiness --
"More's" "one thing alone" has two referents, "communal living and their
moneyless economy." He weakens the statement further by inserting the
modifying "in the popular view," and then he finally reduces the whole
issue to one of less importance than going in to supper.

Although the thrust and parry are evenly matched in book I and no
clear conclusion drawn, "More" is very much overmatched in book II. Elliott observes that in book II, "More" becomes a gull and that the conclusion leaves "Hythloday riding high, his arguments unanswered, his eloquence ringing in our ears. . . . More has given to Raphael Hythloday
all the good lines."(14) That would certainly seem to give credence to
the view that author More is sympathetic to Hythloday's position but cannot openly espouse Utopian reform because Henry VIII would not welcome
criticism. "More's" mild objections would be enough to defuse court objections to the satiric portions that call for reform of such abuses as
enclosures, depletion of the treasury for the glories of war, statutes of
laborers, poor housing, and a king who listened only to flatterers. What
is important to note, however, is that during Hythloday's glowing endorsement More undercuts him at crucial points with Hythloday's own
words. The flaws inherent in Utopia are so smoothly inserted that there
is no need for "More" to raise objections. The seeds of dystopia are already embedded in the discourse and need only sprout in the reader's
mind.

In his description of Utopia Hythloday says, "There is not a happier
people or a better commonwealth anywhere in the whole world" (p. 61).
And from the beginning of his description to the end he sees no flaws.
It is, however, but a short step from his description of Utopia to Orwell's broadly dystopic <u>Nineteen Eighty-Four</u>. In both, for example,
there is a total lack of privacy. In Utopia, "The doors . . . open easily and swing shut automatically, letting anyone enter who wants to --
and so there is no private property" (p. 38). An enigmatic definition of
private property! Although Utopia includes no technology such as the
telescreen through which Winston Smith is constantly watched, heard, and
preached to, forty men and women live in each of Utopia's rural houses,
and there are thirty families in each of the "spacious halls" in town.
Given the number of people in each dwelling, and with a phylarch watching
over each group, and given the communal dining and leisure activities,
little goes on in Utopia without a witness. The functions of Big Brother
and telescreen are effectively carried out by community and the public
officials called "fathers." It could be argued, of course, that this approach is patterned after monastic life and that individualism was not
highly regarded in a hierarchical society in which the members were still
organic parts of the body, the head of which was the king appointed by
God. But More daringly satirizes the flaws in such an interdependent
system.

The community and the "fathers" work together to assure the physical, mental, and moral well-being of every member of Utopia. Everyone
has enough to eat, and even if everyone eats in regimented fashion, the
food is clearly better than the starvation diet common in sixteenth-century England. Warm clothing is available to all Utopians, too, but as in
Oceania, men and women dress alike and in uniform colors, with rough mat-

erial deemed good enough. (This might, of course, not be a drawback to More, who secretly wore a hair shirt.) Any attempt at individuality in dress would be frowned upon in both cultures. But in both, too, the elite, a group that is supposed ideologically not to exist, get preferential treatment. When Winston and Julia visit O'Brien, for example, they are served wine and fragrant coffee, available only on the Black Market or not at all to those who are not members of the Inner Party. More also subtly indicates elitism when he talks of food distribution:

> When the hospital steward has received the food prescribed
> for the sick by their doctors, the rest is fairly divided
> among the halls according to the number in each, except that
> special regard is paid to the prince, the high priest, and
> the tranibors, as well as to ambassadors and foreigners. (p.
> 46)

Another form of elitism in this communal society centers on the Financial Factors, who live in those areas that the Utopians have conquered. Since those Factors live in "great style and conduct themselves like great personages" (p. 78), I suspect that those selfishly decadent positions were highly sought after.

Members of Utopia are also well housed, but no individual choice of dwelling can be made because "every ten years, they change houses by lot" (p. 38). Since the houses all look alike, just as all the cities are "built on the same plan, and have the same appearance" (p. 35), a move would have little effect except to assure that no one could get attached to a particular group of friends or neighborhood. Such a move would be disruptive even in small villages. Nineteen Eighty-Four takes it further, of course, because Winston, in quarters barely furnished with necessities, is neither warm nor well fed, though the government assures him that he is. And because both cultures forbid private discussion of political issues or dissenting opinions, watchful neighbors are more hazard than help.

Both Oceania and Utopia also control the leisure activities of their inhabitants. The reference in Utopia to "no chances for corruption; no hiding places; no spots for secret meetings" (p. 49) could apply equally well in Nineteen Eighty-Four. And although Hythloday says that no pleasure is forbidden, if a Utopian were not to like public lectures, working at his inherited trade, gardening, music, walking through the countryside, or playing the two approved games, one of which teaches mathematics and the other virtue, he would have few other choices. If he were to prefer to sleep during the mandatory five hours of leisure time that occur between the mandatory 4 A.M. rising time and the mandatory 9 A.M. beginning of the work day, that is not possible. As Robert Adams wryly points out, "There may be problems with this timetable, but boredom is only one of them."(15) Winston Smith's regimented work, compulsory exercise period, and the highly recommended attendance at evening lectures and political rallies are of the same ilk.

Even so seemingly innocent an activity as a walk in the country is hauntingly similar in both cultures. Winston is "free" to travel a certain distance from London but must avoid hidden microphones. A Utopian can get permission to travel, but only in groups and for a fixed length of time. And Hythloday adds:

> Anyone who takes upon himself to leave his district without
> permission, and is caught without the prince's letter, is
> treated with contempt, brought back as a runaway, and severe-
> ly punished. If he is bold enough to try it a second time,
> he is made a slave. (p. 49)

Big Brother would surely approve of that.

Another of the "freedoms" that Hythloday praises is that of religion, but this proves to be very like the freedom of travel. Although there are "different forms of religion throughout the island," the Utopians, being reasonable people, "are coming to forsake this mixture of superstitions, and to unite in that one religion which seems more reasonable than any of the others" (p. 78). This sounds tolerant, but there is a "strict law against any person who should sink so far below the dignity of human nature as to think that the soul perishes with the body, or that the universe is ruled by mere chance, rather than divine providence" (p. 80). He is not allowed to express his opinions to the "common people" but is encouraged to talk with priests and other important persons. "For they are confident that in the end his madness will yield to reason" (p. 81). If he tries to talk to anyone else, the punishment is death. Fear is a weapon in Utopia as in Oceania, and unacceptable thoughts are "madness."

The totalitarian society in *Nineteen Eighty-Four* no longer concerns itself with religion but *is* avidly concerned with conformity. In a clear parallel to the Utopian belief that wrong religious thinking is "madness" that will yield to reason, O'Brien tells Winston, "Shall I tell you why we have brought you here? To cure you! To make you sane!"(16) As William Steinhoff points out, however, O'Brien, for all his cold logic, is not reasonable but is, instead, mad.(17) Both Utopia and Oceania want total, willing compliance with ideology, whether religious or political. One of the great ironies, of course, is the fact that the thirty-nine-year-old More who could write "no man can choose to believe by a mere act of will" (p. 81) will later officially persecute Protestants.

Another area both societies try to control is the entire realm of love and sexuality. Hythloday reports that sex is one of the lesser pleasures, simply an adjunct to the higher pleasure of health, and as a pleasure it is listed between bowel movements and scratching to relieve an itch (p. 59). Orwell picks up on the same association with bowels: "Sexual intercourse was to be looked on as a slightly disgusting minor operation, like having an enema" (p. 57). Love between parents and children is also tainted by both states. Children in *Nineteen Eighty-Four* are taught by the state to spy on their parents and turn them in for deviant behavior. More hints the same thing in *Utopia.* If people are not allowed to talk about political matters in private, or to discuss dissenting religious views, on pain of death, how do the authorities learn about such behavior? Friends and children must inform.

The ultimate attempt to control any individual is the attempt to control his thoughts, a control achieved in *Nineteen Eighty-Four*. In the book's first chapter even Winston Smith knows the outcome: "Whether he wrote DOWN WITH BIG BROTHER, or whether he refrained from writing it, made no difference. . . . The Thought Police would get him just the same" (p. 19). The only aspect that Winston is unable to predict is that not only will Big Brother's Thought Police be able to detect his deviant thoughts, but they will also be able to control them. In the midst of torture and deprivation Winston consoles himself with the thought, "To die hating them, that was freedom" (p. 231). That, too, is denied. Total slavery of body and mind becomes the only route for him, so that one of the Party's slogans is realized: "Slavery is freedom."

In Utopia, too, Hythloday says, "They think that a crime attempted is as bad as one committed" (p. 68), and private discussion of forbidden ideas is punishable by death. Although there are few laws, "all laws are promulgated for the single purpose of teaching every man his duty" (p. 69). As in Oceania, there are no rights, only duties. The same was true in the court of Henry VIII. The court taught political conformity; the Church taught religious conformity. If a man went along with both, he was safe in the hierarchy. But deviation could be a capital offense there, too. "Slavery is freedom."

More may have given all the best lines to Hythloday, but Hythloday unwittingly mouths all the worst ones, so that the dangers of an authoritarian state are voiced equally with the advantages. Those dangers add up — whether in Utopia, Oceania, sixteenth-century England — or twentieth-century England, to a profound official distrust of the individual. The organic, hierarchical medieval view was beginning to show hairline cracks, and Thomas More wanted, despite the wit, the jokes, and the purported appeal of the Utopian way, to warn sixteenth-century England against unthinking acceptance of authority. He is neither "More" nor Hythloday but the author who can see beyond the weaknesses of both. While satirizing specific abuses in Henry VIII's England, More can also imagine the bleak consequences of carrying countermeasures to their logical extreme. For a Christian and a courtier that was radical thinking, but More had lived through the violent acquisition of kingship by Henry VII and the continuing power struggle of Henry VIII with church and nobles. Orwell had experienced the state's increasing control of the individual in the growth of such nineteenth-century institutions as the prison, the workhouse, the asylum, and their culmination in the socialist welfare state of the twentieth century, and he feared communist control. Orwell carried to an extreme what More could see was the logical extension of authoritarian methods. Writing four hundred years apart both men would agree, even though Thomas More speaks from the medieval ethos and George Orwell from a modernist one, that slavery is not freedom. Freedom is essential to human well-being.

NOTES

1.   Robert C. Elliott, The Shape of Utopia (Chicago: University of Chicago Press, 1970), p. 8.

2.   Ibid., p. 89.

3.   Ibid., p. 22.

4.   Ibid., p. 36.

5.   Dale B. Billingsley, "The Messenger and the Reader in Thomas More's Dialogue Concerning Heresies," Studies in English Literature 24 (Winter 1984): 5-22.

6.   Thomas More, Utopia, ed. Edward Surtz (New Haven: Yale University Press, 1964), p. xxix.

7.   Karl Kautsky, "The Roots of More's Socialism," in Utopia, ed. Robert M. Adams (New York: W. W. Norton and Co., 1975), pp. 140-148; 147.

8.   Thomas More, Utopia, ed. Robert M. Adams, p. 79. All citations will be taken from this text.

9.   J. H. Hexter, "The Roots of Utopia and All Evil," in Utopia, ed. Adams, pp. 170-77; 170.

10. C. S. Lewis, "A Jolly Invention," in Utopia, ed. Adams, pp. 217-220; 217.

11.   R. W. Chambers, Thomas More (London: The Bedford Historical Series, Jonathan Cape, 1938), p. 137.

12.   Ibid., p. 125.

13.   See Stephen J. Greenblatt, "More, Role-Playing, and _Utopia_," _The Yale Review_ LXVII, no. 4 (June 1978): 517-536.

14.   Elliott, _The Shape of Utopian_, pp. 47- 48.

15.   Thomas More, _Utopia_, ed. Adams; note, p. 41.

16.   George Orwell, _Nineteen Eighty-Four_ (New York: Signet Classics, 1983), p. 209. All citations will be taken from this edition.

17.   William Steinhoff, _The Road to Nineteen Eighty-Four_ (London: Weidenfeld and Nicolson, 1975), pp. 208-212.

17.
Nineteen Eighty-Four:
A Novel of the 1930s
JEFFREY MEYERS

> The Anschluss, Guernica -- all the names
> At which those poets thrilled or were afraid
> For me meant schools and schoolmasters and games;
> And in the process someone is betrayed.
>
> -- Donald Davie, "Remembering the Thirties"

Nineteen Eighty-Four is a projection of the future that is based on a concrete and naturalistic portrayal of the present and the past. Its originality is rooted in a realistic synthesis and arrangement of familiar materials rather than in prophetic and imaginary speculations.(1) The numerical title is thought to be a reversal of the last two digits of the year in which the book was completed (1948), but it was probably influenced by Yeats's poem "1919" and certainly inspired Alberto Moravia's 1934, Anthony Burgess' 1985, and Arthur C. Clarke's 2001. If the novel had been completed a year later and the title transposed to 1994, we would have had to wait another ten years for the momentous revaluation of Orwell's work. It is notoriously difficult to predict the future accurately in a world that is rapidly transformed by technology. Who could have imagined 1949 in 1914? How precisely can we imagine 2019 in 1984?

Most of Orwell's statements about the future were not prophecies but descriptions of events that had already taken place. He looked backward in time as much as he looked forward. The portrayal of Airstrip One reflects the defeated and hopeless air of postwar London. Britain had won the war but suffered a loss of colonies and an economic decline that made the country seem worse off than its defeated enemies. The ruined, squalid, and depressing postwar city was vividly portrayed by Wyndham Lewis in Rotting Hill (1951). When Lewis returned to London in 1945, after six years of exile in North America, he found himself in "the capital of a dying empire -- not crashing down in flames and smoke but expiring in a peculiar muffled way."(2) In 1948, the year Orwell completed his novel, Russia -- recently an admired ally -- had taken over all of Eastern Europe and was actively threatening the West. In that year Gandhi was assassinated, Jan Masaryk was killed (or killed himself), Yugoslavia was expelled from the Comintern, the Berlin airlift began, Count Bernadotte was murdered in Palestine, and civil war raged in China. "It was the coup in Czechoslovakia" in 1948, writes Irving Howe, "that persuaded many people that there could be no lasting truce with the Communist world."(3)

Orwell failed to predict urban guerrillas, industrial pollution, ecological problems, oil shortages, genetic engineering, organ transplants, computers, sophisticated spy equipment, spaceships, satellites, nuclear submarines, intercontinental missiles, and the hydrogen bomb as well as the dissolution of empire and the postcolonial era that followed

World War II. England and America today bear no significant resemblance to Oceania. Yet his very act of prophecy tended to induce its own fulfillment, for readers have adopted his terms and sought his portents. In the year 2000, as surely as we are now watching for Orwellian omens, masses of new believers will be standing on mountain tops waiting for the apocalypse at the end of the second millennium.

Orwell predicted in Nineteen Eighty-Four three hostile superstates (America, Russia, China; or Nato, Warsaw Pact, and Nonaligned countries) engaged in permanent but limited and indecisive warfare. He said that they would use conventional weapons, that the war would be confined to peripheral territories (Central America, Africa, the Middle East, and South Asia), and that there would be no invasion of the homeland of the principal powers.(4) The Vietnam war was a classic example of America and Russia supporting foreign armies in an alien battleground. The ruthless suppression of personal freedom, the rigid indoctrination and the widespread elimination of hostile elements during the Cultural Revolution in China, the Pol Pot regime in Cambodia, and the Khomeini autocracy in Iran have made Nineteen Eighty-Four a reality in our own time. But the horror of the Gulag Archipelago, which had existed for nearly two decades, is far worse than anything portrayed by Orwell. Russia was like Eurasia in 1948 and still is: a totalitarian power opposed to the West.

Nineteen Eighty-Four is composed of five poorly integrated elements. Orwell would have artistically refined and perfected them if he had not been desperate to finish the book before his death. He was terminally ill when he wrote the novel, had great difficulty completing it, and tried to make his task easier by repeating what he had written in his previous books. Orwell usually wrote clear drafts of his work, but more than half of the typescript of Nineteen Eighty-Four was crossed out and completely rewritten.(5)

The five elements are a conventional Orwellian novel of poverty, frustrated love, and flight to the countryside for solitude and sex; a satire on conditions in postwar England; an anti-utopian projection of an imaginary political future; an almost detachable didactic argument in Goldstein's testament and the appendix on Newspeak; and (the least successful and most horrible part) a portrayal of the torture and pain that are used to suppress political freedom -- clearly based on his knowledge of Nazi extermination camps and his personal experience in sanatoria during 1947-1948. The novel is artistically flawed because each element has a different novelistic and political purpose. How, then, do we account for the great strength of the novel, for the source of its overwhelming impact?

I have argued elsewhere that Nineteen Eighty-Four was influenced by Swift, Dostoyevsky, Zamyatin, and Trotsky; was a culmination of all the characteristic beliefs and ideas expressed in Orwell's works from the Depression to the cold war; was a paradigm of the history of Europe for the previous twenty years; and expressed the political experience of an entire generation. I would now like to show that if we read Nineteen Eighty-Four in its cultural context -- the literature of the 1930s -- we can see how Orwell's various elements are connected by a unified theme. His novel is a collective text that abstracts and synthesizes all the regular and recurring elements of Thirties literature. It explains the world of 1948 -- and by extension of 1984 -- by describing the conditions and ideologies that led to World War II.(6) In Nineteen Eighty- Four the 1930s were the prerevolutionary past, the final phase of capitalism that led to atomic warfare, revolution, purges, and the absolutism of Big Brother. Nineteen Eighty-Four is about the past as well as the future and the present.

The Past is one of the dominant themes of the novel. The Party confidently believes: "Who controls the past controls the future: who controls the present controls the past." The Party can not only change the past but also destroy it and authoritatively state: "it never hap-

pened."(7)   By creating a new as well as destroying the old past, the
Party can also arrange to predict events that have already taken place.
Winston spends a great deal of time conversing with proles, trying to recall and reestablish the personal and historical past that has been officially abolished. For he believes that the past may still exist in human
memory.   When Winston plots with O'Brien, they drink "to the past."
O'Brien gravely agrees that the past is more important than the future
because under a system of organized lying only a remembrance of the past
can prevent the disappearance of objective truth.

     Orwell's ideas about the capacity of language to express complex
thoughts and feelings, to describe the dimensions of experience with accuracy and honesty, are central to Nineteen Eighty-Four.   These ideas
originate in Winston's desire to rediscover his own past — in his dreams
and his diary -- and are contrasted to Ampleforth's enthusiastic creation
of Newspeak. In pursuing these thoughts about language Orwell joined the
literary debate about modern prose.

     The Newspeak tendency to reduce language, to limit the meaning, and
to reject abstract words was originally a positive aspect of modern prose
that developed just after the Great War. Hemingway, who began his career
as a journalist, was fascinated by the language of telegraphic cables
that resemble the messages sent to Winston's desk at the Ministry of
Truth: "speech malreported africa rectify."   Hemingway told his col-
league Lincoln Steffens: "Stef, look at this cable: no fat, no adjectives, no adverbs -- nothing but blood and bones and muscle. It's great.
It's a new language."(8)   Influenced by Ezra Pound, Hemingway came to believe that "prose is architecture, not interior decoration, and the Ba-
roque is over."(9)

     Like Robert Graves, John Dos Passos, Erich Maria Remarque, and other
writers who had served in the Great War, Hemingway also learned to distrust patriotic rhetoric. In A Farewell to Arms he wrote: "I was always embarrassed by the words sacred, glorious, and sacrifice and the expression in vain. . . .   Abstract words such as glory, honor, courage, or
hallow were obscene beside the concrete names of villages, the numbers of
roads, the names of rivers, the numbers of regiments and the dates."(10)
The abstractions were lies. Only the actual places where men had fought
and died had any dignity and meaning. The bitter disillusionment of the
Great War is connected to the betrayal of principles in Nineteen Eighty-
Four by Winston's prophecy of doom: "We are the dead," which is repeated
by both Julia and the telescreen when they are arrested. For Winston's
grim phrase is an ironic echo of an accusatory line, spoken by a corpse,
from John Macrae's popular poem of World War I, "In Flanders Fields":

We are the Dead. Short days ago
We lived, felt dawn, saw sunset glow,
      Loved and were loved, and now we lie
            In Flanders fields.(11)

     In the Thirties this need to reject meaningless abstractions was
combined with the desire to find a basic vocabulary and create a proletarian literature. Though Hemingway's short words, limited vocabulary,
and declarative sentences -- his bare, clear, and forceful style -- had a
salutary effect on modern prose, he was criticized by Wyndham Lewis in
"The Dumb Ox" for choking off the possibilities of thought: "Hemingway
invariably invokes a dull-witted, bovine, monosyllabic simpleton . . . a
super-innocent, queerly-sensitive, village-idiot of a few words and fewer
ideas."(12) Nineteen Eighty-Four demonstrates how the modern tendency to
reduce language to its essential meaning can, when carried to the extremes of Newspeak, make the expression of unorthodox opinions almost impossible.

     Orwell's essay "Politics and the English Language" demonstrates the
connection between inaccurate expression and dishonest thought.   It de-

bunks political pomposity, criticizes fuzzy thinking, and shows the corruption that comes from the use of cliches, hackneyed diction, and dead language. Nineteen Eighty-Four, however, criticizes the opposite tendency to oversimplify language so that it limits the range of human expression. While expounding the principles of Newspeak and creating the brilliant neologisms that have taken a permanent place in our speech (Big Brother, Thought Police, doublethink, facecrime, vaporized, unperson), Orwell also predicted the radical deterioration of language and the perversion of meaning. In our time the influence of technology, bureaucracy, television, and journalism has debased the language. Dangerous euphemisms have diminished the reality of all unpleasant concepts: prison, torture, war, disease, old age, and death. Vague but condemnatory words -- Communist, Fascist, racist, sexist -- have been indiscriminately attached to anything that anyone dislikes. Orwell would have deplored the primacy of visual over verbal media in our culture -- television and video over books and magazines -- and the corruption of language by computer jargon. All these tendencies have produced words that seem to be written on a typewriter by a typewriter.

Many of the characteristic literary themes of the Thirties appear in Nineteen Eighty-Four: schools, cinema, advertising and propaganda, public issues, self-deception, Marx and Freud, violence and war. And aspects of Orwell's reportage -- his anatomy of Burma, France, and England in the 1930s in "A Hanging," "How the Poor Die," and The Road to Wigan Pier -- are incorporated in Nineteen Eighty-Four to provide the documentary basis of the future world.

The writers of the thirties had intense feelings about the conventions and codes of schools and schoolboys, which were often based on personal experience as a teacher as well as a pupil. The headmaster became the embodiment of social and political power, and the austerity and sadism of the school were contrasted to the civility and kindness of the home. Auden expressed this theme when he wrote, "the best reason I have for opposing Fascism is that at school I lived in a Fascist state."(13) Anthony West, who described his own horrible schooldays in the autobiographical novel, Heritage, was the first to notice that "most of these [terrors], in Nineteen Eighty-Four, are of an infantile character, and they clearly derive from the experience described in Such, Such Were the Joys. . . . What he did in Nineteen Eighty-Four was to send everybody in England to an enormous Crossgates to be as miserable as he had been."(14)

Nineteen Eighty-Four explores the complex mixture of nostalgia, fear, and self-hatred that Orwell felt when writing about his schooldays. By drawing on these intense early experiences he convincingly portrays the psychological effects of totalitarian oppression: isolation, enforced group activities, physical discomfort, desire to suck up to those in power, lack of identity, feelings of guilt. The physical exercises, sexual propaganda, songs, processions, banners, and drills all derive from school. Parsons, who resembles a large boy, is an athletic Hearty. Winston dislikes Julia at first "because of the atmosphere of hockey-fields and cold baths and community hikes and general clean-mindedness which she managed to carry about with her." Even Winston's compulsive repetition of DOWN WITH BIG BROTHER in his diary recalls the lines written out as punishment at school.

Nineteen Eighty-Four reflects the Thirties ritual of cinema-going and the cult of film stars; the interest in advertising and the use of propaganda. In Keep the Aspidistra Flying, Gordon Comstock hates the movies and seldom goes there. But a recurring image in Nineteen Eighty-Four is the bombing of Jewish refugees in the Mediterranean which Winston sees at the cinema on April 3, 1984. Several hundred victims are killed when a rocket bomb falls on a crowded film theater in Stepney, East London. The obligatory Two Minutes Hate, with Goldstein as the star performer, is projected on a gigantic telescreen before a hysterical anti-Semitic audience.(15)

Winston dimly recalls an advertisement for wine in which "a vast bottle composed of electric lights seemed to move up and down and pour its contents into a glass." Virtually all the Outer Party members are swallowers of slogans: "War is Peace/Freedom is Slavery/Ignorance is Strength." (Should not it logically be "Ignorance is Wisdom"?) As in a modern political campaign, the head of Big Brother (whose image is an amalgam of Stalin and Kitchener) appears "on coins, on stamps, on the covers of books, on banners, on posters, and on the wrapping of a cigarette packet -- everywhere."

The writers of the Thirties dealt with public themes. It was a decade of economic depression throughout the world; massive unemployment and poverty; the misery of democracies and the rise of Fascism; wars in Manchuria, Ethiopia, and Spain; the Nazi seizure of territory in Austria, Czechoslovakia, and Poland. Russia experienced the forced collectivization of the Kulaks (1929-1933), the Ukraine famine (1933), the exile and murder of Trotsky (1940), and the Great Purge Trials (1936-1938). Writers fared badly under totalitarianism; Mayakovsky, Babel, and Mandelshtam were killed during Stalin's regime. The decade of hatred between the Nazis and the Communists culminated in profound disillusionment with the Hitler-Stalin nonaggression pact (August 1939), which was repudiated by Germany's invasion of Russia (June 1941). This abrupt alteration of political alliances was portrayed in Nineteen Eighty-Four when "it became known, with extreme suddenness and everywhere at once, that Eastasia and not Eurasia was the enemy. . . . The Hate continued exactly as before, except that the target had been changed."

As in 1930s literature, intellectuals in Nineteen Eighty-Four lie to support their cause and protect their own position, agree to accept and practice immoral acts. Orwell once condemned Auden for his phrase "the necessary murder." In Nineteen Eighty-Four O'Brien asked Winston: "If it would somehow serve our interests to throw sulphuric acid in a child's face -- are you prepared to do that?" and he unhesitatingly answers: "Yes." In both the 1930s and Nineteen Eighty-Four the ruling class betrays the principles of the revolution -- the deceivers are themselves deceived.

The committed writers of the 1930s developed a new moral awareness and literary strategy to deal with the dreadful conditions of the time. They became socially and politically conscious and abandoned private art for public communication. They adopted a new tone and rhetoric in which to express their new convictions and often embraced left-wing or Communist ideology. The two main intellectual influences of the Thirties, Marx and Freud, are faithfully reflected in Nineteen Eighty- Four. The Marxist dialectic, expressed in Trotsky's style, appears in the forbidden tract, The Theory and Practice of Oligarchical Collectivism. Winston embraces the Marxist belief: "If there was hope, it must lie in the proles." His hope is not based on their real or theoretical virtue but on the fact that they comprise 85 percent of the population and are the only force that seems strong enough to overthrow the Party. But the proles lack a Marxist political awareness and a desire to revolt against oppression.

Orwell suggests a Freudian interpretation of Winston's dreams to depict his inner life. They concern Winston's guilt about the sacrificial death of his mother, which foreshadows his betrayal of Julia. Winston realizes that the political hysteria stirred up by the Two Minutes Hate is an emotional outlet for "sex gone sour." And the last line of the children's poem, which he has been vainly trying to remember, is supplied by the voice on the telescreen when he and Julia are arrested in their secret bedroom. The line suggests the threat of castration after sexual pleasure: "Here comes a candle to light you to bed, here comes a chopper to chop off your head!"

In the Thirties violence was used to achieve political ends. The strong dictator replaced God as the omnipotent figure and ruled with ab-

solute and intimidating power.   There were constant threats of bombing
civilians and of global war.   Gordon Comstock eagerly awaits this destruction in Keep the Aspidistra Flying; George Bowling dreads it in Coming up for Air.   In Nineteen Eighty-Four the rocket bombs are fired on
the people by their own government in order to arouse continuous hatred
of the enemy.   The confrontation of Communism and Fascism in Spain was,
for most intellectuals, their first real experience of politics and warfare.   Auden and Spender attended propaganda conferences in Spain;
Hemingway and Koestler went as journalists; Francis Cornford and Julian
Bell were killed.   But of all the major writers involved in the war, only
Orwell fought as a common soldier, was seriously wounded, and survived to
record his experiences.   He came from the generation that had failed The
Test by being too young to participate in the Great War, but he brilliantly passed The Test in Spain.   Orwell (and his wife) knew from personal experience what it felt like to be hunted by the secret police.
His honesty and integrity shine through Nineteen Eighty-Four as they did
in the literary persona of the more openly autobiographical works of the
Thirties.   All his books project what Malcolm Muggeridge has called "his
proletarian fancy dress, punctilious rolling of his cigarettes, his rusty
laugh and woebegone expression and kindly disposition."(16)

Even more effective than evoking the past world of the Thirties to
explain the evolution of 1948 and 1984 is Orwell's ironic and cruel reversal of the dominant political themes of the period: homosexuality,
frontiers, spies, technology, Mass Observation, change of consciousness,
collective action, justification of Communism, and intellectual polarities.   Winston affirms Orwell's own commendable heresies of the 1930s his
refusal to adopt the orthodoxy of the left about the Socialist intelligentsia in England (criticized in The Road to Wigan Pier) and about the
Communist party in Spain (condemned in Homage to Catalonia).   Nineteen
Eighty-Four contains two opposing strains: Orwell's truthful revelations
about the horrors of both Fascism and Communism, and his despair about
the destruction of the hopes and ideals of the Thirties.

The homosexual theme, founded on adolescent love affairs in school,
portrayed as a protest against the oppressive educational system and
idealized in poems such as Auden's "Lay your sleeping head," becomes perversely twisted in Nineteen Eighty-Four.   Winston's intense attachment to
O'Brien takes on homosexual overtones and verges on sexcrime. (When tortured, Winston freely but falsely admits he is a sexual pervert.)   When
he first comes to his hero's flat, "a wave of admiration, almost of worship, flowed out from Winston towards O'Brien."   When O'Brien tortures
him to the point of lunacy and death, "it made no difference.   In some
sense that went deeper than friendship, they were intimates."   And just
before he faces his final degradation in Room 101, "the peculiar reverence for O'Brien, which nothing seemed able to destroy, flooded Winston's
heart again."   Like the young favorite of the Head Boy at school, Winston
vacillates between craven submission and a lust for vicarious power.

O'Brien's Irish name may have been inspired by the surname of Orwell's first wife, Eileen O'Shaughnessy, by her brother, Dr. Eric Lawrence O'Shaughnessy (who had the same Christian name as Orwell) and by
Eric's wife, Dr. Gwen O'Shaughnessy.   The name may have expressed Orwell's fears about the power, domination, and sexual demands of women,
which the passive Winston is scarcely able to deal with.   Eileen, as
closely attached to her brother as to her husband, was deeply grieved by
Eric's death at Dunkirk in 1941.   Both Eric and Gwen O'Shaughnessy
treated Orwell for tuberculosis in the 1930s.   Orwell may have trans-
ferred his antagonism for the doctors -- who seemed to be torturing him
while trying to cure him during the unsuccessful treatment with strepto-
mycin in 1948 -- to the authoritarian figure of O'Brien.   While curing
Winston of thoughtcrime, O'Brien destroys his body exactly as the doctors
had done.

The map, the frontier, and the geographical context of the literary work were recurrent metaphors in the poetry of Auden and his followers. The marked increase of this imagery coincided with the obsolescence of the frontier, which was easily overrun by tanks, planes, and modern armies. (Goldstein declares: "the main frontiers must never be crossed by anything except bombs.") Orwell sets his novel in a global context by describing two vast land masses that are alternately opposed to and aligned with Oceania. A Flying Fortress lies between Iceland and the Faroes in the north; victories are announced on the Malabar front in the south; and the permanent land wars take place in the rough quadrilateral covered by Tangier, Brazzaville, Darwin and Hong Kong. Julia gives Winston precise directions to their secret meeting place "as though she had a map inside her head." And Orwell is concerned, more profoundly than the Thirties writers, with the inner psychic frontier at which man can be broken and made to betray.

In the literature of the 1930s spies secretly cross the frontier and operate independently against the alien population. In Nineteen Eighty-Four Goldstein is said to control spies and saboteurs; but the real Spies (the name of a youth group) work in the home against their own parents. Parsons, the most enthusiastic Party hack, is proud of the fact that his daughter has betrayed him for uttering "Down with Big Brother" in his sleep (another example of the Freudian unconscious at work). All the principal characters in the novel are either arrested (Winston, Julia, Parsons, Syme, Ampleforth) or work for the Thought Police (O'Brien, Charrington, Parsons's daughter).

The Thirties writers, following the Italian Futurists, were fascinated by modernism, airplanes, and technological advance. Auden liked industrial landscapes and advocated "New Styles of architecture, a change of heart." Orwell, who "loved the past, hated the present and dreaded the future,"(17) opposed modern change and longed for the familiar cosiness of the decent past. In Nineteen Eighty-Four a dehumanized London is called Airstrip One and hovering helicopters snoop into people's windows. Technology either breaks down and causes chaos or operates efficiently and leads to repression.

The characteristic mode of social inquiry in the 1930s was Tom Harrisson's Mass Observation, which "tried to understand social behaviour by accumulating disparate [factual] observations about what given groups of people were doing."(18) This is also ironically reversed in Nineteen Eighty-Four, where Mass Observation is a mode of surveillance carried on by the Thought Police to identify and vaporize potential opponents of the regime.

The writers of the 1930s advocated a change of heart and new awareness that would lead to revolutionary commitment. In Nineteen Eighty-Four there is also an alteration of consciousness and a commitment to the revolution -- but of an entirely different kind. In the last part of the novel O'Brien tortures Winston -- using a process that resembles Electro-Convulsive Therapy -- in order to humiliate him and destroy his powers of reasoning. He makes Winston believe that two plus two equals five, forces him to betray Julia, crushes him until he loves Big Brother.

The idea of collective action was a major preoccupation of the Thirties. Writers were concerned with relating the public and private dimensions of their lives, with creating a Popular Front, with establishing a secure defense against Fascism by immersing themselves in the collective security of the Soviet Union. In the 1930s there "was an attempt to deny utterly the validity of individual knowledge and observation."(19) Unlike most writers of the 1930s, Orwell (who had served as part of a unit in the Burma Police) rejected the idea of collective action and almost always stood alone. The only group he ever joined -- the Anarchists in Spain -- were an underdog minority, destined for destruction. Like all left writers of the Thirties, Orwell hoped for a new social order; but he did not believe that Communism would help mankind progress toward that goal. In Nineteen Eighty-Four the Party embodies the collective mind and all members are forced to participate in communal activities. Winston, locked in loneliness, becomes a lunatic, a minority of one, the only man still capable of independent thought. He is "The Last Man in Europe" (the original title of the book) precisely because he adheres to the importance of the individual mind. Orwell shows that totalitarianism paradoxically intensifies solitude by forcing all the isolated beings into one overpowering system.

Thirties' writers idealized and justified the Soviet Union -- even after the transcripts of the Purge Trials had been published and the pact with Hitler signed. They argued that any criticism of Russia was objectively pro-Fascist. This belief was carried to a typically ludicrous extreme in a line of Day Lewis's "The Road These Times Must Take": "Yes, why do we all, seeing a communist, feel small?" Winston feels small when he sees O'Brien, not only because he admires and loves him but because he craves O'Brien's power ("The object of power is power") and is reduced by his torture to a rotten, suppurating cadaver who resembles "a man of sixty suffering from some malignant disease." In Nineteen Eighty-Four Winston's physical disease symbolizes his intellectual "illness": his heretical hatred of the prevailing ideology.

Finally, the political conditions of the 1930s led to an intellectual polarity between catastrophe and rebirth, a contrast between economic and industrial collapse and revolutionary hope for the future, a belief in the destruction of the old social order for the sake of a new Communist world. Nineteen Eighty-Four combines and transforms these polarities. The revolution is followed by betrayal and repression; catastrophe leads only to catastrophe; the new order is far worse than the old. In Orwell's novel the "endless catalogue of atrocities, massacres, deportations, lootings, rapings, torture of prisoners, bombing of civilians, lying propaganda, unjust aggressions, broken treaties" are attributed to Eurasia (or Eastasia), but they actually take place in Oceania.

After World War II, the destruction of much of England, the reaffirmation of the class system, and his own illness, Orwell realized that the totalitarian states he had written about in his essay on James Burnham had come into permanent existence. The ideas of the 1930s had led to the chaos of postwar Europe, and his hopes had been destroyed. Orwell's disillusionment and disease help to account for the political ideas and the artistic flaws of the novel. Nineteen Eighty-Four is at once a warning about the future, a satire on the present, and an ironic parody of the literary and political themes of the Thirties. The Past, as a theoretical concept and a historical reality, is crucial to the meaning of the novel. "The best books, [Winston] perceived, are those that tell you what you know already."

NOTES

1.   See Jeffrey Meyers, "The Genesis of Nineteen Eighty-Four," A Reader's Guide to George Orwell (London, 1975), pp. 144-154. See also Jeffrey Meyers, George Orwell: The Critical Heritage (London, 1975), and Jeffrey and Valerie Meyers, George Orwell: An Annotated Bibliography of Criticism (New York, 1977).

2.   Letter from Wyndham Lewis to Geoffrey Stone, January 15, 1948, quoted in Jeffrey Meyers, The Enemy: A Biography of Wyndham Lewis (London, 1980), p. 286.

3.   Irving Howe, Celebrations and Attacks (London, 1979), pp. 208-209.

4.   Since 1948 wars have been fought in Korea, Vietnam, Cambodia, Laos, Malaya, Indonesia, Israel, Egypt, Jordan, Syria, Lebanon, Cyprus,

Yemen, Iran, Iraq, the Congo, Kenya, Sudan, Nigeria, Ethiopia, Somalia, Angola, Mozambique, Rhodesia, Chad, Chile, Nicaragua, El Salvador, and the Falkland Islands.

5.   I have examined a microfilm copy of the typescript of Nineteen Eighty-Four in the Orwell Archive at University College, London University. The original is in a private collection in America and was published in a facsimile edition by Harcourt, Brace in 1984.

6.   The standard works on this period are Samuel Hynes, The Auden Generation (London, 1976) and Bernard Bergonzi, Reading the Thirties (London, 1978).

7.   George Orwell, Nineteen Eighty-Four (London, 1972), p. 31.

8.   Letter from George Seldes to Jeffrey Meyers, April 2, 1983.

9.   Ernest Hemingway, Death in the Afternoon (New York, 1932), p. 191.

10.   Ernest Hemingway, A Farewell to Arms (New York, 1969), pp. 184-185.

11.   John McCrae, "In Flanders Fields," Best Loved Poems of the American People (N.Y., Garden City: Doubleday Inc., 1936), p. 429.

12.   Wyndham Lewis, "The Dumb Ox," in Life and Letters (April 1934), reprinted in Jeffrey Meyers, Hemingway: The Critical Heritage (London, 1982), pp. 196-197.

13.   W. H. Auden in The Old School, ed. Graham Greene (London, 1934), p. 14.

14.   Anthony West, "George Orwell," in Principles and Persuasions (London, 1958), pp. 156, 158.

15.   See Jeffrey Meyers, "Orwell as Film Critic," Sight and Sound 48 (Autumn 1979): 255-256.

16.   Malcolm Muggeridge, "Langham Diary," Listener, October 6, 1983, p. 18.

17.   Malcolm Muggeridge, quoted in Meyers, Reader's Guide to George Orwell, p. 144.

18.   Bergonzi, Reading the Thirties, p. 52.

19.   Julian Symons, The Thirties (London, 1960), p. 142.

18.
Orwell, Proudhon, and the Moral Order

AARON NOLAND

Karl Marx, in The Poverty of Philosophy, published in 1847, after decrying what he found to be the "ignorance" of economics and politics in the writings of Pierre-Joseph Proudhon (1809-1865), the leading nineteenth-century theorist of anarchosyndicalism and his rival for the allegiance of the French working class, summarily dismissed Proudhon as nothing more than petty bourgeois in spirit and outlook.(1) A little over a century later James Walsh, in The Marxist Quarterly, after decrying George Orwell's "ignorance of economics and politics," similarly dispatched the latter to the dustbin of history, declaring that "Orwell is little more than a mouthpiece for some of the most deep-seated petit-bourgeois illusions and prejudices."(2)

This juxtaposing of the names Proudhon and Orwell and the disparaging of both by Marx and one of his epigone is not arbitrary, a sheer happenstance. Proudhon and Orwell had a good deal more in common than the hostility of Marxists: they shared a common vision of the nature of the social orders they wrote about and sought to transform. Indeed, an examination of Orwell's social thought, his socialism, against the background of Proudhon's anarchism, even within the limitations of this paper, can prove heuristic, for it may not only serve to bring into focus some of Orwell's principal beliefs and the essential character of his socialism but aid in identifying certain traditions of nineteenth-century social reformism reflected in his thought that have not hitherto received even passing attention by students of Orwell's writings.

In strikingly similar ways Proudhon and Orwell were concerned above all with what each identified as a "crisis of civilization" that threatened in his own lifetime the very existence of the social order and the future of Western man. To Proudhon this crisis had its origins in the French Revolution and the incipient Industrial Revolution, both viewed by him as watersheds, turning points in human history.(3) Writing in 1858, Proudhon characterized contemporary French society as "menaced by dissolution," with instability, doubt, and social malaise all but universal and their corrosive effects on public morality and conduct everywhere apparent.(4) To Orwell World War I was the watershed that marked the beginning of our "decline and fall." Writing in 1940, Orwell noted the "disintegration of our society and the increasing helplessness of all decent people," and indicated that what was "quite obviously happening" was "the break-up of laissez-faire capitalism and of the liberal-christian culture."(5)

What was to be done? How was the dissolution of the social order and the descent into chaos to be brought to a halt, reversed, and hope and action for a better world engendered? In Proudhon's day, as in Orwell's, utopian schemes and grand, rationally stuctured programs for

social reconstruction were readily at hand — Marxism (in its many varia-
tions), Saint-Simonism, Fourierism, the programs advanced by Auguste
Comte, Louis de Bonald, Etienne Cabet, and other schools of social recon-
structionists.   As Proudhon put it; "systems abound; schemes fall like
rain."(6) In Orwell's time a similar plethora of programs and ideologies
were advanced, with perhaps Marxism receiving, at least among British intellectuals and progressive thinkers, the greatest attention and recruit-
ing the largest following. To both Proudhon and Orwell, however, these
proposed solutions were all more or less arbitrary constructions, projections of mere wishes and visions of possible new worlds, either unrealistic plans to resurrect a dead past or utopian leaps into a problem-free
future. The essential thing, to both men, was not to endeavor in some
arbitrary manner to legislate into existence any kind of "true order" of
society but, rather, to discover what are and, indeed, have always been
the fundamental principles, the "organizing principles" of a stable and
progressive social order — principles, in Proudhon's words, that were at
one and the same time organique, regulateur, and souverain.(7)
    Where were these "organizing principles" that govern and direct so-
cial reconstruction to be found? The answer that both Proudhon and Orwell gave was that they were to be sought in the history of man's past,
in what mankind had created for itself in the course of millennia of existence. Proudhon wrote of the necessity of "interrogating history" for
"all truth is in history" and "the laws of society are revealed by history."(8) Orwell again and again stressed the continuity of history. No
past was ever a closed book, something finished and done with, just as no
future was a tabula rasa, a completely new beginning for mankind. "The
past," he affirmed in Coming up for Air (1939), "is a curious thing.
It's with you all the time."(9) Elsewhere he reminded his readers that
"human beings are influenced by their past," and that for better or
worse, every viable social institution "will always bear upon it some
lingering memory of the past."(10)
    The principal elements of this usable past, elements that can be
dealt with in only the most summary fashion given the limitations of this
paper, were to Proudhon and Orwell alike essentially moral, ethical,
spiritual in the broadest sense — justice, family, liberty, work, patriotism, and "military virtues," as Orwell labeled certain moral imperatives.
    To Proudhon justice was one of the "essential attributes of human-
ity," the core organizing principle of any viable social order. He defined it as being "the respect, spontaneously experienced and reciprocally attested to, of dignity due an individual in whatever circumstances
he may find himself involved in, at whatever risks we may run in defending."(11) Proudhon wrote a four-volume study exploring all the ramifica-
tions of justice in society. Orwell was not as scholarly in this matter,
employing the notion of justice in a pragmatic manner. Justice was "decency," "fairness," "giving each individual his due," and "playing by the
rules of the game." No two words appear with greater frequency in Orwell's writings than the words "decent" and "decency," and Orwell spoke
of his principal objective as "a decent reconstruction of society."(12)
    To both Proudhon and Orwell the family was a moral entity, the core
element, the basic cell of the social order embodying, in their view, not
only the private interests of the connubial partners and their progeny
but those of society as well. In Proudhon's view the family was the em-
bryonic "organ of justice" and served as a moral agency, "the effective
core and foundation," as a Proudhonian scholar has put it, "of moral
life."(13) In Orwell's view the family defended and nourished individualism, exemplified loyalty, and guaranteed the continuity of generational
links. At its best family life nurtured a real concern for the feelings
of others, tolerance, self-sacrifice, and affection. In a society growing increasingly more fragmented, impersonal, and threatening, the family

retained its value as a place of refuge, of stability and hope. "Almost any situation is bearable," Orwell contended in his <u>A Clergyman's Daughter</u> (1935), "if you have a home to go back to and a family who will stand by you."(14)

It was this attitude toward the family as a moral unit which in large measure accounts for Proudhon's and Orwell's strong and often expressed hostility toward feminists and feminist movements, to divorce, abortion, and birth control -- and, specifically in Orwell's case -- to homosexuals and lesbians. At a time when almost all socialists and radical social theorists were supporters of feminist movements in France and elsewhere, Proudhon took an opposing stance, coining and propagandizing the slogan "Better confinement than emancipation." "How stupid this century is," Proudhon declared in print, "with its sophisms and its rantings about the emancipation of women."(15) According to Orwell, England after World War I "was full of half-baked antinomian opinions . . . feminism, free love, divorce-reform . . . birth control." He often ridiculed birth control "fanatics," and in his <u>Keep the Aspidistra Flying</u> (1936), when Gordon Comstock, Orwell's mouthpiece in the novel, is asked "what <u>would</u> Socialism mean, according to your idea of it?" Comstock's answer is "'Oh! Some kind of Aldous Huxley <u>Brave New World</u>; only not so amusing. . . . Community-hikes from Marx Hostel to Lenin Hostel and back. Free abortion clinics on all the corners.'"(16) Homosexuals are referred to frequently in Orwell's writings as "Nancy Boys," the "pansey crowed," "the pansey left." Lesbians come in for their share of mockery, as in the essay "Inside the Whale" (1940), where "gruff-voiced lesbians in corduroy breeches parade the boulevards of Paris."(17)

If Proudhon's and Orwell's views concerning the family and feminism set them apart from their contemporaries on the political left, their espousal -- and it was an enthusiastic one -- of patriotism could only serve to underscore their distinctiveness as social thinkers. Proudhon drew a distinction between nationalism, which could embody blind chauvinism or jingoism, and patriotism, a love for one's birthplace, one's native soil. In times of crisis, Proudhon affirmed, it was not doctrine or philosophy but patriotism that was of the utmost importance.(18) Likewise, Orwell insisted that patriotism was not to be confused with nationalism: "Patriotism is of its nature defensive, both militarily and culturally. Nationalism, on the one hand, is inseparable from the desire for power." To Orwell patriotism was a moral force, the expression of the deeply anchored, historically conditioned sense of unity of a people, "the bridge between the future and the past": it "runs like a connecting thread through almost all classes." Patriotism was "deeper than the economic motive" being "stronger than class-hatred."(19)

Both Proudhon and Orwell emphasized the central importance of work in the creation of a just and stable social order: for both it constituted one of the organizing principles of any viable society. To Proudhon and Orwell alike work was conceived as not only an indispensable means of obtaining the wherewithal to live but as literally an expression of the human spirit, the bedrock of community life. Proudhon considered work to be the most spiritual, creative, and exalting of all human activities. Moreover work, in Proudhon's words, was "nature's way of relating men to one another."(20) As Orwell saw it -- and, again, his views paralleled those of Proudhon -- the problem was to organize work in such a manner as to retain and even enhance its moral dimension, to achieve a balance between liberty and organization, between "technical efficiency" and individual, humane values. Both men envisioned some sort of mutualism, a reciprocity in work relationships, which would be based on a true "social contract" entered into by individuals of their own free will.(21)

How was the future "moral" social order to come into existence? Both Proudhon and Orwell rejected the Marxist notion of revolutionary action. Although an occasional reference to political violence can be

found in the writings of both men, and although neither ruled out completely the possibility of revolutionary action [Orwell, for example,
wrote in 1940 that "I dare say the London gutters will have to run with
blood"](22), the characteristic stand that both Proudhon and Orwell took
on this question was that the transformation of society would be carried
out through a protracted political struggle by an alliance of social
classes, in particular sectors of the middle classes -- farmers, shop-
keepers, entrepreneurs, managers, technicians, and other professional
people — and working-class strata. Writing in 1938, Orwell affirmed
that "there now exists a huge middle class whose interests are identical
with those of the proletariat." "In tastes, habits, manners and outlook," Orwell maintained, "the working class and the middle class are
drawing together."(23)
     It was at this point, on the question of the transition to the fu-
ture social order, that the last of the moral organizing principles designated by Proudhon and Orwell came into play. Neither man believed in
historical inevitability, in some dynamism of perpetual, assured progress
inherent in the very nature of human activity, in history. To Proudhon,
as to Orwell, the dynamic element in progress was human will and human
effort, and each individual had to take upon himself the burden of "making history," of disciplining himself or herself as a warrior did for the
struggle and for the victory.(24) The building of a new society would be
the result of conscious, concerted efforts: it would be, as Orwell saw
it, governed by a moral imperative ["'If men would behave decently the
world would be decent' is not such a platitude as it sounds"](25), and it
would call into play what Orwell identified as "military virtues" --
physical courage, dedication, discipline, tenacity, self-sacrifice: it
would be the political and moral equivalent of war itself. And as in
war, Orwell reminded his contemporaries, "toughness is the price of survival."(26)
     From this brief examination of George Orwell's social thought in
tandem with Pierre-Joseph Proudhon's, two aspects of Orwell's socialism
stand out: (1) its conservative cast and (2) its all-pervasive moral
inspiration and character. Orwell was a traditionalist; his outlook was
imbued with a reverence for the past. What is past to Orwell is indeed
prologue. He cherished old-fashioned individualism and independence, and
he distrusted modern, bureaucratic, and centralized political and economic structures. Finally, Orwell's vision of a viable, humane social reconstruction was deeply infused with traditional moral and ethical values. As he read history these values had been the inspiration and had
provided the driving force, the impetus for progress; they would be the
bedrock and the sustaining force of the more "decent" society to come.
To George Orwell, the social order was, above all else, a moral order.

NOTES

     1. Karl Marx, The Poverty of Philosophy (New York, 1963), pp. 126,
144; see also pp. 179-180, 190, 192-202, and passim.

     2. Vol. III, no. 1 (January 1956): 25, 33, 35, 36.

     3. On Proudhon's life and writings, see Robert Hoffman, Revolu-
tionary Justice: The Social and Political Theory of P. J. Proudhon (Ur-
bana, Ill., 1972); George Woodcock, Pierre-Joseph Proudhon (New York,
1956).

     4. Proudhon, De la justice dans la Revolution et dans l'Eglise
(Paris, 1930; first ed. 1858), I: 250-251. See also Proudhon, Les Con-
fessions d'un Revolutionnaire (Paris, 1929), pp. 87-88.

5.   George Orwell, A Collection of Essays (New York, 1954), pp. 253, 224, 254, The Collected Essays, Journalism and Letters of George Orwell, ed. Sonia Orwell and Ian Angus 4 vols. (New York, 1968), II: 203 — cited hereafter as CEJL; Orwell, The Road to Wigan Pier (New York, 1958), pp. 214, 219.

6.   Proudhon, Idée Générale de la Révolution au XIX Siècle (Paris, 1934), p. 157.

7.   Proudhon, De la justice, III: 280, 316-317; Orwell, The Road to Wigan Pier, pp. 172, 177, 186-187, 216, 224-230, and passim; Orwell, Dickens, Dali & Others (New York, 1973), pp. 75, 183; Orwell, Shooting an Elephant (London, 1950), pp. 90, 117, 140. See also CEJL, I: 336, 532; IV: 452; George Woodcock, The Crystal Spirit: A Study of George Orwell (n.p., 1968), pp. 29, 138; John Atkins, George Orwell (London, 1954), p. 394.

8.   Proudhon, Philosophie du Progrès (Paris, 1946), p. 123.   See also A. Noland, "History and Humanity: The Proudhonian Vision," in The Uses of History, ed. H. V. White (Detroit, 1968), pp. 59-105, and passim.

9.   George Orwell, Coming up for Air (London: Victor Gollancz, 1939) p. 31.

10.   Orwell, Shooting an Elephant, p. 30; idem, The Lion and the Unicorn (London, 1962), p. 85. See also William Steinhoff, George Orwell and the Origins of Nineteen Eighty-Four (Ann Arbor, 1976), p. 178; Woodcock, The Crystal Spirit, p. 234; David Kubal, Outside the Whale: George Orwell's Art & Politics (Notre Dame, Ind., 1972), p. 33. Writing in 1948, Orwell noted: "There is now a widespread idea that nostalgic feelings about the past are inherently vicious. One ought, apparently, to live in a continuous present, a minute-to-minute cancellation of memory, and if one thinks of the past at all it should merely be in order to thank God that we are so much better than we used to be." CEJL, IV: 445; see also p. 443.

11.   Proudhon quoted in Noland, "History and Humanity," pp. 83-84. See also Selected Writings of P. J. Proudhon, ed. S. Edwards (New York, 1969), pp. 249-251.

12.   Orwell, A Collection of Essays, p. 207; see also pp. 208, 212, 213; Atkins, George Orwell, 1, 186, 191, 388, 389; Peter Stansky and William Abrahams, Orwell: The Transformation (New York, 1980), p. 274; Christopher Small, The Road to Miniluv: George Orwell, the State and God (Pittsburgh, 1976), pp. 117, 118-135.

13.   Hoffman, Revolutionary Justice, pp. 251-252. See also Henri de Lubac, The Un-Marxian Socialist: A Study of Proudhon, trans. by R. E. Scantlebury (New York, 1948), p. 229.

14.   Orwell quoted in R. A. Lief, Homage to Oceania (Columbus, 1969), p. 90; Orwell, Nineteen Eighty-Four (New York, 1982), p. 22; Orwell, A Clergyman's Daughter (New York, 1960), p. 148.

15.   Quoted in Lubac, The Un-Marxian Socialist, pp. 49-50; see also pp. 51-52, 208; Hoffman, Revolutionary Justice, pp. 215, 250-252.

16.   Orwell, The Road to Wigan Pier, p. 138. See also pp. 174, 216; CEJL, I: 121; II: 201; Orwell, Keep the Aspidistra Flying (New York, 1957), p. 81.

17.   Orwell, Down and Out in Paris and London (New York, 1965), pp.
158, 160; Orwell, Burmese Days (New York, n.d.), pp. 191; Orwell, The
Road to Wigan Pier, p. 33; Orwell, Keep the Aspidistra Flying, p. 16; Orwell, Dickens, Dali & Others, pp. 141, 136; Orwell, A Collection of Essays, p. 216. Daphne Patai, in her book The Orwell Mystique: A Study in
Male Ideology (Amherst, 1984), examines at length Orwell's "profound mis-
ogyny" and "homophobia."

18.   Proudhon quoted in Lubac, The Un-Marxian Socialist, p. 59; see
also pp. 56, 57.

19.   CEJL, III: 6, 7, 362, 340, 363-380, and passim; IV: 12, 43,
311; Orwell, The Lion and the Unicorn, pp. 9, 23, 28, 85, 88, 55, 75, 27;
Orwell, The Road to Wigan Pier, pp. 187; Orwell, Dickens, Dali & Others,
pp. 95, 117. See also Peter Lewis, George Orwell: The Road to Nineteen
Eighty-Four (London, 1981), pp. 71, 85; Bernard Crick, George Orwell: A
Life (Boston, 1980), pp. 257, 380; Atkins, George Orwell, pp. 346, 29.
"It is in Orwell's patriotism," George Woodcock affirmed, "that the conservative elements in his life are most strongly evident." Orwell's Mes-
sage (Mediera Park, British Columbia, 1984), p. 128.

20.   Proudhon, De la Creation de l'ordre dans l'humanite (Paris,
1927), pp. 297, 329, 445; see also Noland, "History and Humanity," pp.
84-85.

21.   Orwell, The Road to Wigan Pier, pp. 208, 215; CEJL, I: 530; II:
25; III: 31, 33, 34, 118, 149; IV: 18, 372, 503; Orwell, Shooting an Elephant, p. 138; idem, The Lion and the Unicorn, pp. 76-86, and passim;
Woodcock, The Crystal Spirit, pp. 30, 285, 287; Proudhon, Systeme des
Contradictions economiques (Paris, 1923), I: 65-165, and passim, 213; II:
327; Proudhon, De la Justice, III: 15-16, 265-266; Noland, "History and
Humanity," pp. 85-86.

22.   CEJL, I: 539, 350. See also Orwell, The Lion and the Unicorn,
p. 58.

23.   CEJL, III: 4-23 and passim, 294; I: 305; II: 33, 39, 42; Orwell, The Lion and the Unicorn, pp. 40-43. See also Atkins, George Orwell, pp. 173-178; Selected Writings of P. J. Proudhon, pp. 72, 151, 162-
164, 176; "The Social Revolution Demonstrated by the Coup d'Etat of the
Second of December," in December 2, 1851, ed. J. B. Halsted (New York,
1972), pp. 279, 281, 290, 297; Hoffman, Revolutionary Justice, pp. 315,
324.

24.   Proudhon quoted in Hoffman, Revolutionary Justice, p. 281; Lubac, The Un-Marxian Socialist, p. 290; see also Orwell, The Road to Wigan
Pier, p. 172; CEJL, IV: 17.

25.   CEJL, I: 428.

26.   Orwell, The Lion and the Unicorn, pp. 88, 29, 94; CEJL, I: 540;
II: 14, 170, 239; IV: 19, 249; Orwell, Dickens, Dali & Others, p. 137.
See also Lionel Trilling, The Opposing Self (New York, 1979), pp. 139-
140; Atkins, George Orwell, p. 252. "Human society must be based on common decency, whatever the political and economic forms may be" (CEJL, I:
531).

19.

The Political Basis of Orwell's
Criticism of Popular Culture

WILLIAM T. ROSS

George Orwell, as John Coleman points out, not only wrote about popular culture in "Boys' Weeklies," "The Art of Donald McGill," and "Raffles and Miss Blandish" but seemed "positively to have enjoyed the forms" he studied.(1) For Mary McCarthy, Orwell "virtually invented" the study of popular culture, and for George Woodcock, the three essays just mentioned "have formed the foundation for a whole branch of contemporary British criticism -- represented particularly by Raymond Williams and Richard Hoggart -- devoted to the study of popular culture."(2) But Orwell was not one to write serious journalism about mere idiosyncratic enjoyments, nor, we can be fairly sure, was a professional journalist interested in starting a new academic discipline.   Instead his passions and energies were directed elsewhere, as he himself admitted in 1946 in a short sketch entitled "Why I Write":

> The Spanish war and other events of 1936-37 turned the scale
> and thereafter I knew where I stood. Every line of serious
> work that I have written since 1936 has been written, direct-
> ly or indirectly, against totalitarianism and for democratic
> Socialism, as I understand it.(3)

Despite this statement, Orwell makes no special political claim for his three essays, and the "significance" he overtly assigns to each study is hardly controversial or sectarian.

In "Boys' Weeklies" (1939) he is primarily interested in an analysis of the attitudes being inculcated in English schoolboys. In "The Art of Donald McGill" (1941) Orwell claims that a study of humorous postcard art has "only 'ideological' interest," by which he seems to mean that the cards reveal the "ideas" that form the thoughts and feelings of the English working class. In "Raffles and Miss Blandish" (1944) Orwell substitutes "sociological" for "ideological" as his criterion of value, and then proceeds to adumbrate what he perceives to be a shift in values -- as reflected in two popular crime novels -- between the early part of the century and the early 1940s.

The essays may well be classics among students of popular culture, but later adulation does not explain motive or preoccupation. I suggest that if we take Orwell's 1946 statement seriously, and if we try to place Orwell's three essays in a slightly wider context of some of his related writings, we will see that, far from being obsessed with popular culture for its formal values or possessed of the disinterested gaze of the academic student of culture, Orwell was committed to the eradication of totalitarianism, and his use of popular culture springs from a search for some viable alternative to the future of the totalitarians.

In the passage from "Why I Write," the key terms are clearly "socialism" and "totalitarianism." The Spanish Civil War taught Orwell about the nature of leftist (especially Russian) totalitarianism, but he had concluded even earlier that fascist totalitarianism could be opposed only by socialism. Unfortunately as he indicated in The Road to Wigan Pier (1937), socialism, specifically the English variety, was not completely to his liking either. Socialism, he insists in the confusing final chapter of that work, must be "humanised," by which he meant in large part that it must be taken away from the ideologues, the party-liners (who were more impressed with Russia's industrialization than with any "human" problem), and from the "earnest ladies in sandals, shock-headed Marxists chewing polysyllables, escaped Quakers, birth-control fanatics and Labour Party backstairs-crawlers."(4) The interesting thing about this catalogue is that it does not embrace the lower classes, the workers whom socialism was supposed to help. For Orwell the odious kinds of socialists, the ones scaring off honest working men and petit-bourgeoisie, were all associated with the higher classes and the intellectuals. Thus it is hardly surprising that it is not the achievements of intellectuals or of socialist societies but rather his memories of Edwardian working-class hearths that convince Orwell that "our age has not been altogether a bad one to live in" (pp. 113-118).

Given his biases, then, Orwell must search for humanizing tendencies among the populace at large. Hence while we remember Orwell's three major essays exploring forms of popular art, his true interest in popular culture is much more widespread. For example, he wrote a number of reviews, essays, and introductions to writers who were historically "popular" such as Charles Reade, Charles Dickens, Jack London, and Rudyard Kipling. In 1940 he published "My Country Right or Left," a declaration of his allegiance to a regrettably capitalist England in the fight against fascism and an essay that contains many comments on the character of the English people. In 1941 he published "The Lion and the Unicorn," a lengthy defense of the English character. Volume III of The Collected Essays, Journalism and Letters of George Orwell conveniently reprints (together and hence out of proper chronological sequence) six essays on things English: "The English People," "In Defense of English Cooking," "A Nice Cup of Tea," "Review of the Pub and People by Mass Observation," "The Moon under Water" (a description of an ideal — and imaginary — pub), and "Review of Cricket Country by Edmund Blunden." As the titles suggest, these efforts range from serious, thoughtful, and lengthy essays to fussy instructions on how to make a proper cup of tea, but they are all permeated with emotional attachment to English culture. When one examines the major themes of the more thoughtful and extended essays and the offhand comments of the minor journalism, one is not long in realizing how insular Orwell's socialism has become and how programmatic is his celebration of the cultural values of the English.

In summary, though he never forgot that England is a land of "snobbery and privilege," he still finds in it the liberal virtue of freedom (freedom that is preserved even in time of war, for example). All in all England, in its cultural unity, is like a family, a family with many virtues. Those virtues include the inability to be good haters and the tendency to admire folk-heroes such as Jack the Giant-killer. Orwell never got over his hatred of English privilege and upper-middle-class pretension, but he still found it possible to love many of the qualities of the "loose maritime democracy" even when those qualities made, as he had to admit, the working class less likely to insist that England turn socialist.

Orwell's interest in British culture culminates in Nineteen Eighty-Four. Winston Smith is aware that there is a past and that there are simple human pleasures and exchanges mainly through the proles, members of the lumpenproletariat who are bovine and incapable of revolution and

yet capable of an emotional life that Winston envies. Nine years before
he published <u>Nineteen Eighty-Four</u> Orwell, in a review of Malcolm Muggeridge's <u>The Thirties</u>, insists that "we have got to be children of God" —
that is, brothers — "even though the God of the Prayer Book no longer
exists" (II: 18). Orwell seems to make clear in <u>Nineteen Eighty-Four</u>
that what brotherhood the proles have will never really matter in a future world "founded on 'realism' and machine guns," but he at least still
thinks enough of traditional English culture to make it a sad counterpoint to the world of Big Brother. Observed from the wider perspective
of these comments on English culture, the motivation behind Orwell's
three essays devoted to specific popular forms becomes much clearer. In
"Boys' Weeklies," for example, Orwell has to face up to some real contradictions. In the first place, this form of "popular" culture is read
by the future leaders, all of whom, he is convinced, are being indoctrinated in reactionary values by the ruling class. But at least, he is
forced to concede, the "pre-1914" politics of the magazines he singles
out are without "Fascist tinge" (I: 471). Furthermore the more up-to-
date magazines feature "bully-worship and the cult of violence," although
"not to anything like the extent one would expect," and not to the extent
of the American "adventure" magazines (I: 476). In other words, the
world of the English boys' magazines, no matter how reactionary in values
and assumptions about class distinctions, is still closer to a world of
decency than much going on around him. If one must have future leaders
as well as the ordinary male public indoctrinated with right-wing values,
things could certainly be a lot worse.

But a greater ambivalence enters when Orwell considers a leftist alternative. "Why," he asks, "is there no such thing as a left-wing boys'
paper?" Coming from a leftist, his initial response is something of a
shock:

> At first glance such an idea merely makes one slightly sick.
> It is so horribly easy to imagine what a left-wing boys' pa-
> per would be like, if it existed.

He then goes on to recall a ponderous tract distributed to public schoolboys in the early twenties by "some optimistic person":

> Q. "Can a Boy Communist be a Boy Scout, Comrade?"
> A. "No, Comrade."
> Q. "Why, Comrade?"
> A. "Because, Comrade, a Boy Scout must salute the Union
> Jack, which is the symbol of tyranny and oppression etc.,
> etc." (I: 483)

In all its dreariness, he insists, this exchange would be the tonal model
for any left-wing boys' magazine. Furthermore while his objections on
the surface, are, aesthetic, he has genuine political reservations as
well. At the present time, he notes, any such publication would consist
of similarly tedious "uplift or it would be under Communist influence and
given over to adulation of Soviet Russia" (I: 483). No boy, he assures
us, would read it. And this hypothetical journal's content, one should
note, would involve a far greater worship of totalitarianism than English
schoolboys are currently getting. Orwell closes by observing that there
simply is no such thing as left-wing popular literature in England and
protests that the reasons for this would be far too complicated to consider in the current piece (I: 484). Clearly despite its shortcomings,
he would prefer the older English tradition to any juvenile left-wing
cult of bully worship.

"The Art of Donald McGill" reveals a vague, turn-of-the-century
"radicalism" in McGill's comic postcards (II: 158). But Orwell is mainly

interested in noting the absence of any of the "improving" strains of the Boys' Weeklies. Apparently the postcards do not "attempt to induce an outlook acceptable to the ruling class" (II: 159). And in the only one of the three major essays to be devoted to a genre intended exclusively for the working class, Orwell indulges in a great deal of class analysis. Working-class humor is properly contrasted with the sophisticated sexual jokes of Esquire, for example, and the postcard jokes about honeymoons are connected to the still extant village custom of sewing bells to the bridal bed.

Orwell seems to be drawing a valid distinction, but as usual he has one eye cocked on the world around him. For ultimately what working-class humor provides is a mild check to totalitarianism. "A dirty joke," he admits, "is not . . . a serious attack upon morality" (II: 163). But it is a way of rebelling against authority, against more than human expectations with which society burdens us. Society demands "faultless discipline and self-sacrifice . . . expects its subjects to work hard, pay their taxes and be faithful to their wives."

> The whole of what one may call official literature is founded on such assumptions. I never read the proclamations of generals before battle, the speeches of Fuehers and prime ministers, the solidarity songs of public schools and left-wing political parties, national anthems, Temperance tracts, Papal encyclicals and sermons against gambling and contraception, without seeming to hear in the background a chorus of raspberries from all the millions of common men to whom these high sentiments make no appeal. (II: 163-164)

A dirty joke, Orwell knows, is a private rebellion and not capable of standing up to fascism, but it at least represents a side of man that will not be comfortable under any official dispensation. Otherwise such postcards "are a sort of saturnalia, a harmless rebellion against virtue."

But despite his interest in class distinctions, Orwell's real interest seems to lie in integration, for he closes the essay by observing that jokes much like Donald McGill's could at one time be uttered "between the murders in Shakespeare's tragedies" (II: 165). Now they are banned from sophisticated literature, and literature has ceased to speak for one "corner of the human heart." Other art forms seem, however, to be more genuinely capable of transcending class differences. In a newspaper review that the editors of The Collected Essays, Journalism and Letters append as a note to "Donald McGill," Orwell describes "vulgar" music hall comedians, including Max Miller. The national appeal of such comedians reminds us of "how closely knit the civilization of England is, how much it resembles a family, in spite of its out-of-date class distinctions" (II: 161-162n). Once again Orwell had found in the popular culture an English habit of mind inconsistent with narrow ideology and, paradoxically in its delight with obscenity, an island of humanity in a dour, officious, and expedient world.

"Raffles and Miss Blandish" is a study of the values in an Edwardian and a modern crime novel, with the intent of pointing out the change in "popular attitude" that has taken place between the two periods. As John Coleman points out, the comparison of "the crickety gamesmanship" of Hornung's Raffles and the "sadistic sex ploys" of Chase's No Orchids for Miss Blandish is highly inappropriate: "They were always playing in different ball-parks."(5) The difference in the two is not simply a function of the passage of time.

But the faulty logic underlying the comparison does not obscure Orwell's basic aim. Indeed, that he would think such comparison justifiable and necessary simply shows how important he thought English popular opinion was and how dismayed he was at its implied deterioration.

And dismayed he was. For Raffles has a gentleman-criminal as its hero -- a man who is outside the law and yet manages to have a code of conduct by which he lives. He is even a cricketer, and cricket is a game in which "good form" is paramount, which, according to Orwell, is why the Nazis hated it.

As one might well imagine, the Nazis have far more to do with Miss Blandish than they do with Raffles. And the "struggle of power," as all the beatings, rapings, and stabbings in Miss Blandish make clear, is what the novel is all about (III: 218). The police are as immoral as the gangsters, and any sense of "expiation" for deeds committed or of fighting   heroically against the odds is lost. The book, in short, is "pure Fascism" (III: 223); but by 1945 Orwell cannot mention fascism without perceiving another totalitarian menace on the horizon:

> Fascism is often loosely equated with sadism, but nearly al-
> ways by people who see nothing wrong in the most slavish wor-
> ship of Stalin. The truth is, of course, that the countless
> English intellectuals who kiss the arse of Stalin are not
> different from the minority who give their allegiance to
> Hitler or Mussolini. (III: 222)

The common people, at least until recently, have never kissed any part of Stalin's anatomy or believed in hitting a man when he was down. But alas -- and this is what really frightens Orwell -- "the popularity of No Orchids" and like items indicates that the "world of absolute good and evil" of the common people is being eroded (III: 223).

Orwell was more than a little skeptical about the absoluteness of good and evil, but his preference for that simplistic worldview to the amorality of the intellectuals' indicates how frightened he had become. In order to keep Stalin at bay he will accept a world of simpleminded morality and unexamined slogans, or Raffles, an upper-class bandit whom, Orwell admits, "has no real moral code, no religion, certainly no social consciousness" (III: 224). Instead, in their place "he has set of reflexes -- the nervous system, as it were, of a gentleman." As the passage makes clear, Orwell is now ready to admit that the social code of a gentleman -- a far more suspect and less communal thing, for example, than a common music hall tradition -- is a useful inhibition on behavior. Take it away, he implies, and the world of unchecked sadism -- in literature and politics -- bursts upon us.

It is a commonplace criticism of Orwell that, in Richard Hoggart's words, he saw the working classes "through the fug of an Edwardian music hall."(6) But Orwell tended to evaluate everything in light of the Edwardian period in which, it must be remembered, he grew up. The Boys' Weeklies that interested him most had not changed since 1913, working-class postcards were stuck in a 1900-style radicalism, and Raffles the Edwardian burglar was preferable to the sadistic criminals of forty years later. Orwell would prefer left-wing boys' magazines: he would like a truly integrated literature that could include "low" sexual humor; he would prefer popular heroes with something more than a knee-jerk reaction to certain taboos. But the only alternatives that seemed to loom at him offered worse fates -- offered, in fact, whether one turned to right or left, a totalitarian state.

Although that totalitarian state has not arrived -- at least for the Western democracies -- we would be foolish to question the depth or belittle the validity of Orwell's obsessions. But we should also recognize that even obsessions can have unanticipated results. And one of the ironies of the recent history of critical taste is that George Orwell

managed to start a new critical tradition -- or at least enlarge the subject matter available to criticism -- while searching for an alternative
to Big Brother.

NOTES

1.   John Coleman, "The Critic of Popular Culture," The World of
George Orwell, ed. Miriam Gross (London: Weidenfeld and Nicolson, 1971),
pp. 102-103.

2.   Mary McCarthy, The Writing on the Wall and Other Literary Essays (New York: Harcourt Brace, and World, 1970), p. 162; George Woodcock, The Crystal Spirit: A Study of George Orwell (Boston: Little,
Brown, 1966), p. 162.

3.   Sonia Orwell and Ian Angus, eds., The Collected Essays, Journalism and Letters of George Orwell, 4 vols. (London: Secker and Warburg, 1968), I: 5. Volume and page numbers to all subsequent references
to items contained in The Collected Essays are included in the text.

4.   The Road to Wigan Pier (London: Secker and Warburg [orig.
pub., 1937], 1959), pp. 218, 215. Subsequent page references to Wigan
Pier are included in the text.

5.   Coleman, "The Critic of Popular Culture," p. 105.

6.   Richard Hoggart, The Uses of Literacy (London: Chatto and Windus, 1959), p. 17.

20.
George Orwell: The Politics of
Nineteen Eighty-Four
and Asian Ambivalences

KIRPAL SINGH

Unlike several of his contemporaries, George Orwell has not been subjected to critical scrutiny by Asian literary scholars. This is a matter
of both curiosity and regret; the more so when we realize that at least
Animal Farm and Nineteen Eighty-Four have become household terms among
most educated Asians. Two of his most widely anthologized prose pieces
-- "Shooting an Elephant" and "A Hanging" -- are set in Burma, and his
novel Burmese Days is often mentioned in discussions of Edward Morgan
Forster's A Passage to India. It is, of course, well known that Orwell's
experience as a police officer in the Indian subcontinent shaped, to a
considerable degree, his political outlook.(1) He does not frequently
refer to these early years, but scattered throughout his writings are
references -- whether implicit or explicit -- to the valuable lessons he
learned as a servant of the Imperial British Empire.
　　The road to Mandalay disillusioned Orwell, and far from taking up
the White Man's burden, his conscience was struck at the wrong that the
white man's rule was perpetrating. If in Kipling's work we notice a
deep-rooted ambiguity about the repercussions of the Raj, in Orwell there
is a forthrightness that disturbs. When one of the Raj's many apologists
took Orwell to task for a review in which Orwell pointed out the blatant
injustice and exploitation that the apologist's book had failed to mention, Orwell calmly replied:

> I think you have missed my point. It isn't what you did say
> about the British in Burma, but what you didn't say. No one
> would infer from your book that the British had done anything
> worse than be a little stupid and sometimes follow mistaken
> policies. Nothing about the economic milking of the country
> via such concerns as the Burma Oil Company, nor about the
> disgusting social behaviour of the British till very recent-
> ly. I do know something about this.(2)

Given all this, therefore, the question that readily comes to mind is,
why have Asian critics not bothered very much about Orwell's work? I do
not think the neglect to be merely accidental. After all, we in Asia do,
use liberally several terms that Orwell has given currency: Big Brother,
Newspeak, All animals are equal but. . . !
　　I will say at the very outset that one reason for the neglect of Orwell in Asia could be that in spite of his very incisive depiction of
some crucial aspects of contemporary reality, he remains a somewhat simplistic writer. I have in mind, for instance, the contrast we find between Orwell and Aldous Huxley -- the latter an author whom Asians have
not neglected. Huxley's own interests in Oriental culture notwithstand-

ing, in his work, there is, a complexity that is lacking in Orwell's. Take Nineteen Eighty-Four as an example. It is a nightmare world which we are presented. Two distinct images remain firmly embedded after one has read this horrific work: the image of the boot stamping on the human face -- forever, and the rats in Room 101. It so happens that according to Chinese zodiac, the year 1984 is the year of the rat. Indeed, it is the year of the Golden Rat — a rat that is going to bring prosperity to the world, a rat that promises hope and plenty, a rat which according to the almanac is going to begin a fresh sixty-year cycle. For more than a quarter of the world's population, therefore -- the Chinese — the rat does not belong to the category of fear-instilling animals. In fact, the rat is seen to be an intelligent, witty, and charming creature. To be born in the year of the rat is considered lucky; to be born in 1984, the year of the golden rat, is a bonus. If Huxley had written Nineteen Eighty-Four, I think he would have borne in mind these different — indeed, conflicting — associations, especially if one of the three major regions of his nightmare world was East Asia. Since Nineteen Eighty-Four is a political novel it is imperative that the author should have recognized the multifarious dimensions of the symbols he employed.

An author cannot be expected to take into account the varied cultural orientations of all his readers. But here is where we come up against a dilemma: Orwell was aware that in these days, with the English language colonizing practically the entire globe, his works would be read outside the Western world, and yet he seems to have taken very little trouble to make his books acceptable to readers who were not Occidental. Although he passionately spoke out against the immoral treatment of the coolie, he did not bother about the coolie's makeup. In wanting to be overtly political he forgot that man, while being a political animal, is also much more. And here, I think, lies the crux of the answer we are looking for: Orwell is too much a propagandist for the Asian mind.

The Asian does not reject the propagandist per se. By the same token, he finds it extremely embarrassing to pay homage to a propagandist. The Asian concept of the writer is, I think, closer to ancient Greece than modern Britain. All three important cultures of Asia -- the Chinese, the Indian, and the Nusantaran (the culture of the Malay Archipelago) -- have a long and respectable literary tradition. The most significant feature of this literary tradition is that the emphasis has almost always been on the spiritual well-being of man. Now as we know, Orwell was not, except in a very minimal way, concerned primarily with man's spiritual existence. Material well-being seems to be at the core of everything Orwell wrote. Hence his obsession with class, with economic man. His politics seem to have been markedly affected by his outrage at the manner in which man exploited fellowmen, at the manner in which some men remained in power while others groveled in poverty. In terms of his art, telling a story — always at the forefront of an Asian's expectation -- was secondary to exposing a lie. To an Asian the following confession may be admirable, but it will also be highly damaging: "My starting point is always a feeling of partisanship, a sense of injustice. When I sit down to write a book, I do not say to myself, 'I am going to produce a work of art'. I write it because there is some lie that I want to expose, some fact to which I want to draw attention, and my initial concern is to get a hearing."(3) For the Asian a writer must rise above partisanship, his initial concern being to produce a work of art, not to get a hearing. Orwell's confession is, by Asian standards, damnable. Not only does a confession of this sort seek endorsement of championship, it also presupposes that the speaker knows a lie from a truth. In other words, Orwell's confession is an arrogant assertion of his own self-righteousness. His writing therefore will be seen as an imposition rather than a persuasion. We see here a startling divergence of interpretation: to an

Occidental reader, Orwell's statement shows moral courage; to an Oriental
it shows hubris.

It would be wrong to think that the kind of writing Orwell aspired
to write is alien to the Asian character. It is not. What is alien,
perhaps, is the unabashed utterance that one is somehow privy to the nature of things — that one is, in some sense, God. The point, however,
remains that from an Asian perspective Orwell's work lacks subtlety, or
if one wants to see this in more negative terms, his work lacks cunning,
particularly the type of cunning by which an author disguises his own belief for the sake of involving his readers. Maybe this is the reason
most Asians find Animal Farm truly lovable. Here, in the guise of a
fable, an animal story, is a disturbing vision of human existence, of the
shattering of human dreams, of the realization that a revolution is precisely that: coming full circle. The Orient is fond of a cylical view
of things, as the Occident subscribes to a linear time frame. For once
Orwell produced a work of art and did it so beautifully that even children are fascinated. This is the kind of political writing to which the
Asian responds almost instinctively; it is a genre with which his own
literary tradition has made him most familiar.

When we think of specific political beliefs in Orwell's work and relate these to the Asian mind, we find, again, areas of disjuncture. Although commentators on Orwell are still debating the exact nature of Orwellian politics, it is clear that he was a socialist. But his brand of
socialism does not seem to be consistent with socialism as this political
ideology is commonly known. For Orwell, socialism grew out of deep personal encounters with life. One such encounter took place on his first
visit to Burma. As he was to tell readers of The Tribune in 1947, watching the behavior of the white quartermasters on board ship taught him
more than he could have learned from "half a dozen Socialist pamphlets."(4) Shall we say the Orwellian socialism champions the underdog?
And while there is to be centralized control, true socialism is achieved
only when there is "justice and common decency."(5)

Now no Asian would want to disagree with the realization of justice
and common decency, but centralized control is quite another issue. In
fact, as with so many other political labels, I do not think Asians feel
comfortable with socialism as an operational political tool. I do not
think that Asians even fully understand the concept of socialism as Orwell thought of it. There is always a danger of applying meanings to a
concept one is not familiar with, and when it concerns such a vexed topic
as Orwellian socialism, the Asian shies away. What, I believe, the Asian
will recognize in Orwell's socialistic writings is the anger of a man
frustrated to the core. Like Orwell, Asians would want to see the triumph of justice and common decency, but not necessarily at the expense of
class. The Asian would rightly view the mere abolition of class as a
very simplistic, if not naive, solution to political problems. Asia is
beseiged by complex issues of race, language, and religion. Then there
are differences in custom and manners even when race, language, and religion are common denominators. It will strike the Asian reader that much
of Orwellian political thinking is irrelevant to his situation, not because he would object to socialism as a doctrine but because he would
feel that in his passionate eagerness to stamp out fascism (or communism,
or capitalism), Orwell, like most political missionaries, ignored the
fundamental complexity which for the Asian defines human existence.

Closely connected to this would be Orwell's staunch stand on the
question of individuality. Here Orwell is in tune with the rest of the
great Western tradition, which has always asserted the inalienable right
of the individual. Edward Morgan Forster's famous remark that if he had
to betray his country or his friend, he would betray his country would
meet perhaps with unqualified approval in the West, particularly from
liberal quarters. But Forster's remark would need a lot of qualification

before it meets with approval in Asia. The Indian Bhagavad Gita -- a
literary text akin to the Gospels in Christianity -- is an anguished debate between Arjuna, the warrior, and Krishna, the god-incarnate. There
is a battle in progress and Arjuna has to lead his army for the fight.
He is in great pain and sorrow, as fighting would mean killing relations
and friends, people he loves. Krishna admonishes Arjuna and explains to
him that in life we often have to go through such suffering of the soul,
of doing things against our own desires. The conflict between duty and
desire is almost always resolved in Asia on the side of duty. To be dut-
iful means, to a large extent, to live up to the expectations of the society in which one finds oneself. A certain measure of compromise is
thereby inevitable. The individual and his personal beliefs are important, but they usually cannot override familial or societal expectations.
This is why, in India at least, true individuality is only to be sought
after one has been through the first three stages of being: child,
breadwinner, and husband and father. The fourth stage, when one searches
for one's true identity, really begins in the sixtieth year, when one can
usefully combine the lessons of knowledge with experience in order to at-
tain true wisdom. It would be rash and extremely disrespectful for an
Asian to assert his individuality in the face of family or social opposition. Hence conformity. Naturally the Western world has experienced
such crises too, but in the West, I feel, the individual has always had
more freedom from constraints such as we in Asia live under. Asians can
easily soar to epic heights with a Milton but would find it excruciating
to have to endorse a Blake.

     Individual worth is very precious in Asia, as it is in the West, but
it is seldom allowed to take precedence over collective worth. This is
why a person such as a writer is seen to be someone "special," a person
worthy of the Muse, a person inspired beyond ordinary human capabilities.
Because of this he enjoys the privileges denied the ordinary man or woman. But he has to prove worthy of this right in order to enjoy it without threat of withdrawal. For Western readers, part of the terror of
Nineteen Eighty-Four must reside in the fact that ultimately Winston
Smith is so thoroughly destroyed by O'Brien as to convert from being a
hater of Big Brother to one who understood and loved this dubious entity.
The reader would recoil at the way in which the individual is crushed.
For the Asian reader the real horror of the book would be the fact that
Smith betrays Julia, with whom he has an unwritten pact, a bond. I wonder how Western readers respond to this act of betrayal. Explanations
such as that he did it under extreme duress, under terrible tortures,
would not satisfy the Asian reader. This is a variation on the theme of
individuality. To preserve his own skin, Smith cries out bitterly "Do it
to Julia! Do it to Julia!" because Orwell writes, "there was one and
only one way to save himself. He must interpose another human being, the
body of another human being, between himself and the rats."(6) We are
talking about a fictive work, and it is potentially risky to infer from
such a work an author's personal convictions. Would Orwell have done the
same in similar circumstances? If not, why does he make his hero, the
man he has made the reader identify with throughout the book, do it?
These are questions an Asian reader asks. Even in a work of fiction it
would be considered wrong to allow total defeat of a hero. The Party's
victory over Smith would be laughed off as being juvenile because Smith
would be seen as a weakling, a man unworthy of another's trust. And it
would be the writer's moral duty to create a character who would stand up
and fight the Party even if this resulted in his death. There is true
heroism. The Asian would agree with Hemingway's Santiago that a man can
be destroyed but not defeated.

     We are told that in the world of Nineteen Eighty-Four sex had become
a political act, an act against the Party. O'Brien explains to Smith
that in the future the sex instinct will be eradicated, orgasm aboli-

shed.(7) Without going into any detailed discussion of the scientific
possibility of such an event, the Asian reader will put this aside as yet
another Western absurdity. Sex is sex for the Asian, it is not politics;
if anything it is religion. It is hard to imagine an Asian couple reg-
istering their protest against a power machine by making love. You make
love to engender -- either a child or your bond -- you do not make love
to demonstrate your hatred of an external condition. The very thought
itself is repulsive to Asian upbringing, let alone that actual act! Sex
is a private matter in Asia, something in which one indulges and enjoys
with one's loved one but without brandishment. Westerners would have
noticed that Asians rarely speak about sex openly -- it is not a fit subject for public discussion. This does not mean the Asian is squeamish or
embarrassed by sex and sexual activity; it only means that for the Asian
bed and politics do not mix. What will happen, one might well ask, if
Asia was ruled by a power that disallowed sex? The point being how would
an Asian couple react to the Party's strictures in Nineteen Eighty-Four.
I think the answer is that the Asian couple would not make love; they
would not give the Party the satisfaction of catching them at it; they
would prefer to forgo as a sacrifice their own pleasure to the humilia-
tion that Smith and Julia go through as a result.

From a Western viewpoint the abolition of orgasm may be seen to be
the ultimate violation of human individuality; from an Asian viewpoint
such an act would only be a futile exercise in ridiculousness; an act
that would reveal the extreme stupidity of the Party rather than one that
would deny the individual the right of sexual pleasure. Neurosurgery or
no neurosurgery, the Asian mind simply will not accept such a situation.
For the Asian orgasm does not reside in a nerve; it is an attitude, a
spiritual and mental state. No amount of tampering with the human brain
will nullify this.

And what about Orwell's politics of power? How does the Asian react
to the Party's program in Nineteen Eighty-Four? Power-crazy people will,
without question, arouse anxiety and suspicion, but power in itself is
not necessarily a bad thing. The opinion that power corrupts and absolute power corrupts absolutely is mainly a Western one; in Asia power
could be (and indeed has often been) used to better the welfare of the
people. It depends on the use that is made of power. The real horror
for the Asian reader in Nineteen Eighty-Four is not that there is a Big
Brother (a Big Brother can sometimes be very useful and welcome), not
that there is a Party that has absolute power, but that the proles live
in such squalid conditions. Both Big Brother and the all-powerful Party
have proved disappointing if they cannot and do not do something about
the proles. Without the backing and support of the majority -- the
proles, say -- Big Brother and the Party are vacuous: of what real use,
then, is the power they profess to possess? Here again the Western and
the Eastern understanding of power may differ. In the West power implies
the ability to do things the way one wants; usually through sheer force;
power becomes an instrument for bullying. In the East power implies the
ability to do things the way one wants but through winning people over --
not through force but through example. When we say someone is a powerful
man in Asia we mean he commands the respect of others, not that he can
use force to bully others into obedience. The way an Asian reader sees
it, Orwell has it all wrong from the very word go. If Big Brother and
the Party are to prove credible, they have to do more than break weak-
lings like Winston Smith. In a very real sense the whole thing would be
seen as a joke; one do not harness one's entire machinery to win a symbolic battle. Gandhi's life and philosophy bear ample testimony to the
way in which Asia can react to brute force: calm indifference and non-
cooperation. One simply can't kill off everyone -- as the Imperial British in India realized. And Asia is huge, it is teeming with millions of
human beings, each quite prepared to live and die without attaining ideal

conditions of existence. We are firm believers in time and we can be
very patient. If O'Brien thinks the Party can be patient, he has yet to
understand Asian patience.

Finally, what about lies, the distortion of truth, doublethink?
Like the Asian attitude toward power, lying may not be an evil in itself
-- it again depends on the context. Westerners may find it very difficult to lie because honesty is so highly prized. In Asia honesty is often equated with folly and naivete. The Asian can bear and suffer a lot;
he is not keen on winning every battle he confronts, whether it is a battle for truth or for power. He has learned, over thousands of years,
that ultimately it is better to lose the battles and win the war. If
telling a lie can prevent undue hurt, if it could bring about greater
tolerence and goodwill among men, if the lie can be put to good use, then
frequently it may be condoned. Since Asians are firm believers in the
dictum that no one possesses absolute truth and that lying is merely the
other side of truth, we do not always insist on the truth.

I know this is a rash and unkind thing to say and that it may, if
misunderstood, reduce Asians to liars and hypocrites. In reality the
situation is more complicated: there are different kinds of lies — a
political lie may not be seen as incriminating as a moral lie. Leaders,
Asians will recognize, sometimes have to lie in order that a greater evil
be prevented or a greater good be attained. Parents sometimes have to
lie to their children because the time has not come for the children to
understand the full meaning of the truth. Likewise with a leader and his
people. In Asia the respect for authority is deeply ingrained — people
look up to leaders as children look up to parents. Leaders are guardians, and guardians, by definition, know what is best. This does not,
however, mean that a leader can get away with lie after lie. In a
strange, frequently inexplicable way, Asians believe that each must carry
his own cross, and a leader who deliberately deceives will have to confront his own truth in good time.

Western readers of a novel like A Passage to India have often expressed their bewilderment at the apparent "lies" or "inconsistencies"
practiced by the Indian characters, but Forster himself seemed to have
realized that there was more to the characters' behavior. Some of the
lies in Animal Farm may be overlooked by the Asian reader -- he is ever
ready to give the leaders the benefit of the doubt. Such behavior may
imply a certain subservience to the Occidental reader, but for the Asian
it is only marking time: give a person enough rope and he'll hang himself. Since most Asians believe in the relative nature of truth -- absolute truth being known only to God himself — anyone has the right to put
forward his version of it. One is not obliged to accept any particular
version. So-called official versions only serve narrow, political ends,
and since man is more than merely a political animal, these "official"
versions do not affect his overall attitude or behavior.

Modern history has shown how large masses of Chinese, Indian, and
Nusantaran people have carried on stubbornly with their time-cherished
patterns of living in spite of official decree. This is why the distor-
tions of truth that offended Orwell so much as he experienced the Spanish
Civil War and, later, World War II do not offend the Asian to any marked
degree. Asians are quite at home with "doublethink" -- love does imply
hate; war, peace; truth, falsity. For us in Asia these are two facets of
the same reality -- ultimate reality being a mystery. So the four
fingers that O'Brien holds up could be seen as five — it is a matter of
perception. The rope in the dark could well be taken to be a serpent. I
am aware that Orwell was trying to get at something larger than such
quibbling, that Newspeak was intended "not only to provide a medium o
expression for the world — view and mental habits proper to the devotees
of Ingsoc, but to make all other modes of thought impossible."(8)
Throughout the ages different experiments have been tried to enslave hu

man freedom -- whether it is freedom of thought or of action. Newspeak
is but one such experiment. Like others before, it will frighten and
disrupt; it may even succeed in destroying other modes of thinking. But
the human mind and the human will are mysteries, and we in Asia, while
holding our breaths at the latest scientific and technological incursions
into these areas, do not really believe that we can discover their se-
crets. For us, in time to come, Newspeak will be replaced by something
else and the cycle of history will continue.

Does all this mean that Orwellian politics and, in particular, Nineteen Eighty-Four have little or no relevance to Asia? On the surface the
answer must be yes. For the greater part, Orwell would be seen as too
English in terms of political belief and too egoistic in terms of his
literary art to merit much attention from Asians. Burmese Days showed
tremendous promise in its treatment of intercultural conflict -- Asians
can involve themselves readily with Flory's plight. But after that Orwell began to move away from Asia and more and more into Europe and eventually into Britian. Though it was his anger at Russian communism that
spurred Animal Farm, for once literary art triumphed over the goal that
produced it. Nineteen Eighty-Four has the makings of a great book, but
it fails. It fails because, for us at least, it makes mountains out of
mole-hills, becomes farcical in its treatment of human love and shallow
in its vision of human existence. As a story it is unable to excite the
reader's imagination; as a political tract it is too imposing; and as a
prophecy it is too exclusive. Perhaps Orwell's earlier title for the
book -- The Last Man in Europe -- would be more apt: Winston Smith is,
indeed, the last man in Europe, but he cannot be said to be also the last
man in Asia.

NOTES

1.   See, in this respect, George Orwell, a Life, ed. Bernard Crick,
(Harmondsworth: Penguin, 1980), particularly chap. 5, "An Englishman in
Burma."

2.   The Collected Essays, Journalism and Letters of George Orwell,
4 vols. (Harmondsworth: Penguin, 1970), IV: 142.

3.   Ibid., I: 28.

4.   Ibid., IV: 308.

5.   The Road to Wigan Pier, (Harmondsworth: Penguin, 1962), p.
154.

6.   Nineteen Eighty-Four, (Harmondsworth: Penguin, 1954), p. 230

7.   Ibid., pp. 214-215.

8.   Ibid., p. 241.

21.
The Lure of Power in
Post-Orwellian Political Fiction

RICHARD I. SMYER

Caught in a "dense mass of people" filling Victory Square, an area domi-
nated by a towering statue of Big Brother, George Orwell's Winston Smith
feels as though he is being "ground to pulp."(1)   Here, as in other
scenes in Nineteen Eighty-Four, we hear a somberly dystopian note struck
that will reverberate through the works of many political writers over
the last three decades. We find, for example, an echo of Winston's dis-
tress in Milan Kundera's description of his characters' dilemma in The
Joke (1967): "Lured on by the voice of utopia, they have squeezed . . .
through the gates of paradise only to find, when the doors slam shut behind them, that they are in hell."(2)
      However, what we find in Kundera and other writers of political fic-
tion is not simply a case of malevolent ruler and abjectly victimized
subjects but, rather, an authoritarian, sometimes totalitarian, system
holding out to the individual a strength to compensate for his own mortal
limitations. At first appearance Orwell's Winston is Lear's "poor . . .
forked animal" -- middle-aged, afflicted with an ulcerated ankle, his
physical "meagerness" emphasized by his bulky Party overalls. With "chin
nuzzled into his breast," as though bent under the barely supportable
weight of existence itself, Winston hurries into his apartment building,
Victory Mansions, to escape from the insistent reminders of mankind's
subjection to time and mortality (the chill April wind whipping clouds of
dust through the streets of Airstrip One), only to encounter another reminder of weakness in the literal powerlessness of the lift to carry him
up to his flat (p. 3).
      The state is what the lone individual is not. Confronting a Winston
too small for his uniform is a picture of Big Brother, an "enormous face"
on a poster "too large for indoor display"; in contrast to the broken
elevator is O'Brien's promise that the submergence of Winston's individuality into the Party's collective body will enable him to be "lifted
clean out" of the "stream of history," to be made "all-powerful and immortal"; and finally Winston discovers that behind the down-curving mus-
tache of a menacing Big Brother is the upward curve of the leader's bene-
volent smile (pp. 3, 165, 257, 267, 300).
      In C. J. Koch's The Year of Living Dangerously (1978), set in Indo-
nesia during the months prior to the outbreak of civil war in September
of 1965, it is in the strength of a Far Eastern Big Brother, Bung ("elder
brother") Sukarno, that Billy Kwan -- patronized when not pitied because
of his dwarfishness and ambiguous ethnic identity -- discovers a new,
heroic self. "Sometimes," Billy reveals, "I almost feel we share the
same identity. . . . I could have been him."(3)
      The totalitarian political system fascinates by embodying the fan-
tasy of permanence in a world of change. Like monumental representations

of the Party boot that O'Brien excitedly envisions forever "stamping on a
human face" (p. 271), the four massive concrete pyramids (the ministries
housing the Party's knowledge and power) press down upon the passive surface of Oceanian society (pp. 5-6). Just as determined to assert through
architectural grandiosity a power as seemingly absolute as that of bet-
ter-known dictators, the Somali strongman of Nuruddin Farah's Sweet and
Sour Milk (1979) has his own "showy pieces of tumorous architecture"
fashioned after building projects from the time of Mussolini and Stalin.(4) The Moscow of Topol and Neznansky's Red Square, a Gorky Park
with more serious political significance, is a stone and steel proclamation of the state's durability. Only rarely during the police investigation into the death of Premier Brezhnev's brother-in-law do we glimpse
the unofficial human reality of the all-too-mortal human flesh -- such as
in the forest-enclosed special cardiac clinic where aging and ailing "men
of the Kremlin" secretly reveal their failing powers and in the morgue
where a dead general, a hero of the revolution, is reduced to a cadaver
with sawn-open skull, to a brain spilled onto a surgical dish.(5) Official reality is the imposing statue of Felix Dzerzhinsky (the organizer
of the Soviet secret police) that, unlike Winston Smith fleeing the chill
wind of an Oceanian April, stares with a "look of stone" down Marx Prospect, unmoved by the Russian "blizzard-laden wind" (p. 203).
      Orwell's dystopian vision is that of a society systematically trying
to turn itself into a completely closed system, a "world of total integration . . . deprived of accident [and] contingency."(6) "Who controls
the past," runs a Party slogan that points to such a goal, "controls the
future: who controls the present controls the past" (p. 35). A flaw in
the developing "pattern" of total control, Winston cannot be considered
fully integrated into the Party's grand design until he has submitted to
the state not only physically but also internally, with "heart and soul"
(p. 258).
      The Party's refusal to tolerate the independent existence of any
type of mental or emotional experience finds its geopolitical counterpart
in the empire's aggressiveness in J. M. Coetzee's fable Waiting for the
Barbarians (1980). Opposed to the frontier ideal — with its acceptance
of differences and the coexistence of self and other — is the totalitarian compulsion to violate boundaries, to subjugate. The vast unexplored
wilderness inhabited by the free-spirited nomad is reduced to the soldier's bloody cartography slashed into the back of a captive.(7) The aim
of the interrogator-torturer is to possess the victim as fully as a musi-
cian possesses his instrument: "A certain tone enters the voice of a man
who is telling the truth," claims an interrogating officer; "training and
experience teach us to recognize that tone" (p. 5).
      There is no basic difference between the Empire's ruthless determi-
nation to thrust its power outward and the almost routine display of
power through acts of anal penetration practiced by white prison authorities on imprisoned blacks in the novels of other South African writers --
bodily violations symbolically reenacting the Europeans' massive violation of the black Africans' ancestral lands. For the white man, physical
abuse is a claim of property right: urinating on the face of a captive
black man is the Afrikaners' primitive, even animalistic, gesture of
ownership.(8)
      As an important and complex aspect of political fiction, the themat-
ic relationship between sexuality and social regimentation has been explored by a number of writers, with the general tendency being to stress
the incompatibility of eros and ideology. However, the fact that in some
cases sexual attitudes and behavior are presented as the expressions of
an authoritarian environment suggest that it may be an oversimplification
to view Winston Smith's carnal interest in Julia only as healthy lust un-
ambiguously opposing the patriarchal state's life-denying anti-eroticism.
Just as the Anti-Sex League sashes wrapped around the bodies of young

party women tend to call attention to their shapeliness (p. 11), within
the males "whose sex instincts" are judged to be "less controllable than
those of women" (p. 132), the Party's official hostility toward sensual
pleasure must result, one feels sure, in the compression of the males'
sexual energy, its intensification, and its consequent transformation into a compensatory fantasy of limitless power to be manifested through the
unrestrained use — and violation — of the female.

The "scores" of sexual encounters Julia mentions in a rather matter-
of-fact manner are instantly exaggerated in Winston's imagination into
the wild fantasy of a Julia of almost unlimited penetrability ("hundreds-
thousands" he wishes), of a woman who, "corrupt to the bones," is primed
for total violation. The fact that by the end of the novel Julia's once
sensually vibrant body, now violated to its depths by O'Brien's psycho-
surgical technology, is corpselike in its deroticized condition, indicates the possibility that behind Winston the self-proclaimed rebel
against the apparent puritanism of Big Brother is another Winston, sub-
missive and loyal, engaged in offering to the ruling patriarchy for a
final violation his lover's one sacrosanct area of personal integrity and
selfhood, which Julia has defined by her adamant refusal to yield her
body to "those swine," the Inner Party members [pp. 126, 294].(9)

The raped mother of the Ugandan Robert Serumaga's Return to the
Shadows (1969) is old Africa assaulted by the destructive force of modern
revolutionary politics.(10) The rural Indonesia of The Year of Living
Dangerously is an ancient Mother, the Goddess of Rice, violated from one
age to the next by foreign political and cultural intrusions and, by the
1960s, to the figure of the Jakarta slum woman whorishly posturing to
trick white men into grudging acts of charity for her starving child (pp.
97, 128). In Koch's novel sexuality symbolizes a land exploited by for-
eigner and native alike — the depraved whores in a Jakarta cemetary trying to attract business by wearing Western clothing (p. 182)); the be-
gowned Indonesian "boy-girls" whom the Australian pederast Wally O'Sul-
livan obessively pursues (pp. 54, 61); and Sukarno himself, cultivating
the myth of his inexhaustible sexuality (p. 54) to enhance his political
prestige. Although Salim, narrator and central character of V. S. Naipaul's A Bend in the River, presents himself as potential victim of anti-
Indian feeling, the content of his sexual imagination — "brothel fantasies of conquest and degradation, with the woman as the willing victim"(11) — is an emblem of the newly independent black Arican nation in
which he seeks refuge. Old humiliations return as the appearance of
government-hired white mercenaries reawakens in the supposedly liberated
Africans a look of "abject" servility; and as though crushed beneath the
physical weight of the nation's "Big Man," a young follower standing beneath a "larger-than-life" picture of the President, like Winston before
the Big Brother poster, looks "ill," "shrunken, and characterless" (pp.
76, 271).

In George Konrad's The Loser (1980) repeated references to political
activity (specifically that of the men pushing post-World War II Hungary
into the embrace of Soviet Russia) as a form of sexual experience(12)
imply that, like Machiavelli's Fortune, the nation's history is, as one
Communist puts it, a woman on whom "we have to force ourselves" (p. 214).
However, the females' uninhibited, sometime adulterous sexuality (pp. 4,
11, 18, 128, 232, 273, 276, 314) suggests that the Hungarian Fortuna is
not so easily controlled, as is borne out by the 1956 uprising and later
surprising twists and turns of the nation's history. The instances of
male violence against women (pp. 116-117, 278, 284), as well as the beat-
ing inflicted on the central character (a male) while strapped to a gyne-
cological chair (p. 193), mark the degeneration of revolutionary man into
a whoremaster attempting to force the gift-giving Fortuna into the brothel of ideological orthodoxy.

For the provincial Peruvian half-bread, Cayo Bermudez, who, in Varga Llosa's Conversation in the Cathedral (1969), suddenly finds himself appointed Director of Security in a militantly anti-leftist government, the most gratifying reward is the opportunity to use the women in his power -- Hortensia, the light-skinned kept lesbian, and Queta, the dark-complexioned prostitute from a brothel he controls - to act out the profoundly subversive and utopian fantasies that his move from country to capital city has brought into consciousness. Fulfilling the half-breed's desire to see reversed the centuries-long superiority of white South American over nonwhite is the supine passivity of Hortensia as the dark-skinned woman, assuming the posture of the sexually dominant male, descends on her. Responding to an even more primitive dream, of the South American continent as an egalitarian Eden, the intimately entwined bodies of the two lovers are indistinguishable in the shared intensity of erotic excitement.(13)

There is another variety of political fiction that probes into the authoritarian preconceptions and tendencies of a society as a whole through the private, personal behavior of individuals far removed from centers of power. The misadventures of the title character of Heinrich Böll's The Lost Honor of Katharina Blum (1974), an obscure West German whose very ordinary, even humdrum, private life is roughly forced onto the stage of public attention, reveal a destructive leader-worship near the surface of the national consciousness. The sudden breaching of Katharina's emotional reserve by her chance encounter with Götten, an army deserter, and the shattering of her door by police storming into her apartment in pursuit of the fugitive, set in motion a series of assaults on the woman's moral identity and her public transformation into slut and leftist radical in the outrageous journalistic campaign of innuendo and smear led by the idolized reported Tötges.(14)   Like Thomas Mann in "Mario and the Magician," Böll is dramatizing the linked obsessions of a people — victimization and unbridled power.   Implicit in both Katharina's penchant for domestic service and the exaggerated importance attributed to her housekeeping by a grateful employer ("she has released us from . . . chaos" [p. 39]) is an ominous servility and hankering after a savior-leader, a figure of destiny — for Katharina, "the One who was to come" (pp. 60, 82). This "One" is both Götten, who, in calling forth Katharina's latent capacity for passionate commitment, prepares her for the role of victim, and Tötges, the hypnotic effect of whose articles (p. 62) makes possible the transformation of helpless victim into avenging deity -- into the sheet-shrouded Atropos, deadliest of the Fates, whose "ritual murder" of the handsome Tötges is the ceremonial transmutation of spellbinding "hero" into sacrifical lamb offered up to the German public [pp. 13, 137].(15)

It has been pointed out that in Kundera's fiction the characters' experience of an oppressive political system tends to make them "master practitioners of the art" in their private relationships.(16)   Victimized by the Communist party's humorless rigidity, Ludvik Jahn, the central figure in The Joke, rewards the devoted but sexually timid Lucie, the only outsider who takes an interest in him during his confinement in a labor camp, with an attempted seduction that quickly turns into violence and a near rape; and a coolly calculating Ludvik deceives and humiliates Helena, a neglected wife who has passionately yielded to his adulterous advances simply to avenge himself on her husband, supposedly the agent of Ludvik's disgrace fifteen years earlier (pp. 98-99, 151).

To some extent post-Orwellian political fiction can be regarded as a corrective to Nineteen Eighty-Four. For example, Kundera's exposure of the authoritarian imperatives within even intimately personal interactions of individuals in a regimented society partially closes a gap for which Erika Munk has criticized Orwell's novel -- its lack of "detailed models of totalitarian family and sexual life" (p. 52). In Burger's

Daughter (1979), July's People (1981), and a number of short stories
Nadine Gordimer reveals, through a careful probing into the ironies of
romantic and familial relationships, the internal contradictions of a
political and social system built on an ideology of racial supremacy. In
Gabriel Garcia Marquez's The Autumn of the Patriarch (1975) the two-di-
mensionality of Big Brother's poster image becomes an in-depth exploration of the psychological, sociological, and even mythic roots of the
leader's charismatic power. Thus in post-Orwellian fiction we find in-
dications that even if Nineteen Eighty-Four is not a model to be slavish-
ly imitated, it is still able to suggest areas of political experience to
be mapped.

NOTES

1.   George Orwell, Nineteen Eighty-Four (New York: Harcourt Brace
& World, 1949), p. 116.

2.   Milan Kundera, author's preface to The Joke, trans. Michael
Henry Heim (Harmondsworth: Penguin, 1982), p. xii.

3.   Christopher J. Koch, The Year of Living Dangerously (Harmondsworth: Penguin, 1983), p. 99.

4.   Nuruddin Farah, Sweet and Sour Milk (London: Heinemann, 1980),
pp. 73, 130

5.   Edward Topol and Fridrikh Neznansky, Red Square, n. trans. (New
York: Quartet Books, 1983), pp. 76, 108.

6.   Irving Howe, "The Fiction of Antiutopia," in his Decline of the
New (New York: Harcourt Brace, 1970), p. 68.

7.   J. M. Coetzee, Waiting for the Barbarians (Harmondsworth: Penguin, 1983), pp. 10-12 and passim.

8.   Lauretta G. Ngcobo, Cross of Gold (London: Longman, 1981), pp.
48, 113,; D. M. Zwelonke, Robben Island (London: Heinemann, 1973), pp.
14, 33, 71, 87, 145; Alex La Guma, In the Fog of the Season's End (London: Heinemann, 1972), p. 7.

9.   Winston's power-oriented relationship with Julia is discussed
in Erica Munk's "Love Is Hate: Women and Sex in '1984,'" The Village
Voice, February 1, 1983, pp. 50-52, and Daphne Patai's "Gamesmanship and
Androcentrism in Orwell's Nineteen Eighty-Four," PMLA 97 (1982): 856-870.

10.   Robert Serumaga, Return to the Shadows (New York: Atheneum,
1970), p. 54

11.   V. S. Naipaul, A Bend in the River (New York: Knopf, 1979),
pp. 55, 174.

12.   George Konrad, The Loser, trans. Ivan Sanders (New York: Harcourt Brace Jovanovich, 1982), pp. 175, 177, 179, 180, 192, 193, 212,
228, 235, 255.

13.   Mario Vargas Llosa, Conversation in the Cathedral, trans. Greg-
ory Rabassa (New York: Harper & Row, 1975), pp. 295, 322.

14.   Heinrich Böll, The Lost Honor of Katharina Blum, trans. Leila
Vennewitz (New York: McGraw-Hill, 1976), pp. 18, 37, 42-43.

15.   Katharina's insistence on precise wording becomes a dangerous confusion of word and meaning: repeated linkages of Katharina's name with Götten mesmerizes the word-struck woman into an identification with the nearly homonymous Götten "goddess"; and her response to Tötges' request for a sexual "bang" is the real "bang" of her pistol (pp. 29-30, 137).

16.   Helen Pochoda, "Introduction," The Farewell Party by Milan Kundera, trans. Peter Kussi (Harmondsworth: Penguin, 1977), p. x.

22.
Jack London and George Orwell:
A Literary Kinship

VICTOR R. S. TAMBLING

Since George Orwell's untimely death in 1950, many critics and scholars have compared some of his writings to those of the American author Jack London, who died when Orwell was a teenager. The principal comparison between the authors are London's The People of the Abyss and Orwell's Down and Out in Paris and London; and London's The Iron Heel, and Orwell's Nineteen Eighty-Four. It is these works I shall be principally concerned with in this paper.

There is no doubt whatsoever that London's The People of the Abyss had a profound effect on the young Orwell, who read this book while still at Eton.(1) In the summer of 1902 Jack London lived in the East End of London doing on-the-spot research for what was to become a classic sociological study of conditions in the slum areas of the capital of the British Empire. To enter the "Abyss" (as London called it), he first had to obtain the appropriate attire, and so he went into one of the many second-hand clothes shops. London wrote:

> I selected a pair of stout though well-worn trousers, a frayed jacket with one remaining button, a pair of brogans which had plainly seen service where coal was shovelled, a thin leather belt, and a very dirty cloth cap.(2)

In such a way did London enter into the world of the poor and deprived of the East End. He now looked like an East-Ender, but what of his American accent? This was bound to reveal his nativity, so London concocted a story that he was an American sailor down on his luck. He now had this disguise and his alibi, but would it fool the population and, most of all, those with whom he came into contact? London soon found that his clothes were the badge of the class he wanted to be part of, and that people no longer addressed him as "sir" or "governor," but as "mate." The expression "governor," London wrote, "smacked of mastery, and power, and high authority, the tribute of the man who is under to the man on top," whereas "mate" was, "a fine and hearty word, with a tingle to it, and a warmth and gladness."(3) So London was accepted, and for six or seven weeks he was able to visit the low spots of East London, the casual ward, the spike, the workhouse, and many doss houses of the metropolis. London finished his sojourn with a visit to the hop fields of Kent.(4)

Orwell returned to England from Burma in September 1927, on leave from the Indian Imperial Police, and shortly afterward he resigned his position. In the fall of that year he made the first of many ventures into the East End of London. Orwell obtained tramp's clothes and walked into the East End to Limehouse. These trips by Orwell were to become the

"London" part of <u>Down and Out in Paris and London</u>, published in 1933. Orwell followed the trail recorded by Jack London in 1902, and many of Orwell's experiences appear to be borrowings from London. Orwell too, obtained a change of clothes for his descent into the "Abyss," and like London, he went to a second-hand clothes shop and sold the clothes he was wearing in exchange for "a shilling a coat, once dark brown, a pair of black dungaree trousers, a scarf and a cloth cap."(6)

Orwell wandered the streets until late at night, afraid to speak in case someone noticed a disparity between his clothes and his accent. Orwell was an Old Etonian, and his accent would be difficult to disguise, and in his own words Orwell was "a thoroughly bad actor."(7) However, no one ever remarked on his accent, and he had no searching inquiries from those he encountered. Orwell tells us that he helped a hawker pick up a barrow that he had upset:

> 'Thanks, mate', he said with a grin. No one had called me
> mate before in my life — it was the clothes that had done
> it.(8)

Orwell now followed literally and physically Jack London's trail: doss houses, the spike, the casual ward, and the workhouse, talking to and living with the inhabitants of the "Abyss." Orwell too, went hop picking in Kent, but this was after he had completed his manuscript of <u>Down and Out in Paris and London</u>.(9) His essay on hop picking was not published until after his death, but some of the experiences of his trip to Kent were used in <u>A Clergyman's Daughter</u>, published in 1935.

Replying to an inquiry as to which was the favorite of his own books, London replied: "that is a hard question to answer. I think I put more of my heart into <u>The People of the Abyss</u> than into any other book.(10) Orwell never wrote in any length about <u>The People of the Abyss</u>, but he had obviously read it thoroughly both at Eton and before his own ventures into the "Abyss." <u>Down and Out in Paris and London</u> was Orwell's first published book; six months before his death, Orwell's last book was published, the dystopian novel <u>Nineteen Eighty-Four</u>.

George Orwell's first published reference to Jack London's <u>The Iron Heel</u> was in the essay entitled "Prophecies of Fascism," published in <u>Tribune</u> on July 12, 1940.(11) In this essay, Orwell compares <u>The Iron Heel</u>, H. G. Wells's <u>The Sleeper Wakes</u>, and Aldous Huxley's <u>Brave New World</u>. Orwell agreed to a large extent with London's opinion of the "capitalist class," but he maintained that London had "a Fascist strain in him" that enabled him to foresee the rise of fascism. London's interpretation of history was better than that of the Marxist socialists. In <u>Horizon</u> (August 1941), Orwell wrote:

> The people who have shown the best understanding of Fascism
> are either those who have suffered under it or those who have
> a Fascist streak in themselves. A crude book like <u>The Iron
> Heel</u>, written nearly thirty years ago, is a truer prophecy of
> the future than either <u>Brave New World</u> or <u>The Shape of Things
> to Come</u>.(12)

In 1945 Geroge Orwell wrote an introduction to <u>Love of Life and Other Stories</u> by Jack London, which was published by Paul Elek in 1946. This collection contains fifteen of London's short stories, including three of Orwell's favorites, "Just Meat," "The Chinago," and "The Apostate," the last being a story about child labor in America. In October 1945 Orwell made a broadcast entitled "Jack London," which included a brief biography, a short dramatization of the opening paragraphs of "The Apostate," and a critical view of London's works. <u>The Iron Heel</u> is referred to, and listeners are urged to read this particular novel, or at least

Chapter xxi of the book -- analysing the mentality of the new
rulers of the world. It's one of the best statements of the
outlook of a ruling class -- of the outlook that a ruling
class must have if it's to survive -- that has ever been
written.(13)

The same statement was used in an almost identical broadcast with the
same title in November 1946. Around the time that Orwell made his first
"Jack London"(14) broadcast, he had started work on what was to be his
last work, Nineteen Eighty-Four.(15)   The most interesting thing about
Orwell's introduction to Love of Life and Other Stories is not his critical appraisal of the stories and Jack London but a lengthy (over two hundred words) quote from The Iron Heel. The quote is also from Orwell's
favorite chapter in that novel. Which London had titled "The Roaring
Abysmal Beast."
        The Iron Heel is filled with footnotes, and this gives the novel the
appearance of an authentic historical document. London wrote the novel
at white heat -- he began it on August 29, 1906, and finished it on December 17 of the same year -- as he was pressed for funds for his "Snark"
voyage.(16)   Chapter 21 contains just four footnotes, and it is the third
footnote that is most significant:

Ardis was completed in 1942 A. D., while Asgard was not completed until 1984 A. D. It was fifty-two years in the building, during which time a permanent army of half million serfs
was employed. At times these numbers swelled to over a million -- without any account being taken of the hundreds of
thousands of the labour castes and the artists.(17)

The tyrants in The Iron Heel are known as "the Oligarchs," and their
secret police were "the Mercenaries." In Nineteen Eighty-Four the tyrant
is Big Brother and his secret police are the Thought Police. Winston
Smith, Orwell's hero in Nineteen Eighty-Four manages to obtain a copy of
a banned book written by Emmanuel Goldstein entitled The Therory and
Practice of Oligarchical Collectivism.(18) Orwell had two working titles
for his last novel: The Last Man in Europe and Nineteen Eighty-Four.(19)
He chose the latter title, I believe, because London's work had left a
lasting impression upon him. A chapter in The Iron Heel is entitled
"Lost Oligarch"-- the term "oligarch" is nowadays more likely to be used
by a sociologist than a socialist.
        Orwell had read London's work, had studied the low life of the East
End of London, and wrote about it. He also wrote the introduction to a
collection of London's short stories and did at least two broadcasts
about London's life and work. All writers are influenced in some way by
the books they have read -- London, for example, was influenced by Kipling, and this influence can be seen in many of London's early stories.
The debt has been remarked upon by many scholars and critics of London.
The publication of London's The Son of the Wolf in 1900 saw him hailed in
the literary press as "The Kipling of the Klondike."(20) Orwell wrote a
lengthy essay about Kipling which was published in Horizon in 1942; London too wrote a lengthy essay on Kipling which was published in 1903.
Both Orwell and London defended Kipling's ideas about race and patriotism
despite their "socialist" leanings.(21)
        Orwell's Nineteen Eighty-Four and Down and Out in Paris and London
and London's The Iron Heel and The People of the Abyss are written in the
same mold and style and are worthy of closer scrutiny by scholars and
critics.
        Both writers died quite young -- Orwell was forty-six and London
only forty -- yet their works are still read today by millions of people.

They inspire the up-and-coming writer, just as Jack London inspired the young Eric Arthur Blair all those years ago at Eton.

NOTES

The Collected Essays, Journalism, and Letters of George Orwell were edited by Sonia Orwell and Ian angus. The four volumes have been reprinted many times, and are an invaluable source on Orwell.

1.   George Orwell, The Road to Wigan Pier (Harmondsworth: Penguin, 1971), p 12.

2.   Jack London, The People of the Abyss, (Arco Publications, 1962).

3.   Ibid., p. 23.

4.   Ibid., pp. 103-109, chapteer XIV: Hops and Hoppers.

5.   George Orwell The Road to Wigan Pier (Harmondsworth: Penguin, 1971), p. 132.

6.   George Orwell, Down and Out in Paris and London (Harmondsworth: Penguin, 1977), p. 114.

7.   George Orwell, The Road to Wigan Pier (Harmondsworth: Penguin, 1971), p. 132.

8.   George Orwell, Down and Out in Paris and London (Harmondsworth: Penguin, 1977), p. 115.

9.   Bernard Crick: George Orwell: A Life (London: Secker and Warburg, 1980); p. 133. What is interesting at this stage, however, is that his most sustained period of tramping, to and from the hopfields of Kent in August and September 1931, came after the submission of the Down and Out or The Scullin's Diary manuscript to Cape. He did not tramp Kent for the book. See also The Collected Essays, Journalism and Letters of George Orwell, vol. 1 (Harmondsworth: Penguin, 1971), pp. 75-95.

10.   Letter from Jack London to Loen Weilskov October 16, 1916, reprinted in Letters from Jack London ed. King Hendricks and Irving Shepard (London: MacGibbon & Kee, 1966), p. 475. Jack London died on November 22, 1916, and this was one of his last letters to a "fan."

11.   Reprinted in The Collected Essays, Journalism and Letters of George Orwell vol 2. (Harmondsworth: Penguin, 1970), pp. 45-49.

12.   Ibid., pp. 166-172, Wells Hitler and the World State.

13.   Ibid., Volume Four, pp. 41-48.

14.   See The Jack London Newsletter, vol. 11, Nos 2-3 (May-December 1978) (Carbondale IL: Southern Illinois University), pp. 33-40. Forces Educational Broadcast "Jack London" by George Orwell.

15.   Letter to Celia Kirwan, August 17, 1946 reprinted in CELJ, IV: 235. (Harmondsworth: Penguin, 1970).

16.   In April 1907, Jack London left San Francisco to make a "seven year voyage" around the world aboard his yacht The Snark, using advanced

royalties on as yet unwritten stories and novels, this dream turned into a nightmare. Late in 1908, after many tribulations the Snark voyage was abandoned, ill with a tropical skin disease, London and his wife Charmian returned to their ranch in Glen Ellen, California in eary August, 1908.

17.   Jack London, The Iron Heel (Arco Publications, 1973), p. 150.

18.   George Orwell, Nineteen Eighty-Four (Harmondsworth: Penguin, 1973), p. 150.

19.   Letter to F. J. Warburg. October, 22, 1948, reprinted in CEJL, VI: 507. (Harmondsworth: Penguin).

20.   See for example Books of the Week (The Son of the Wolf), Anon., San Francisco Bulletin, April 29, 1900.

21.   Jack London, These Bones Shall Rise Again, reprinted in Revolution and Other Essays, (New York: Macmillan, 1910), and George Orwell: Rudyard Kipling, in Horizon (February 1942) reprinted in CEJL, II: 215-229. (Harmondsworth: Penguin, 1970).

George Orwell International Conference

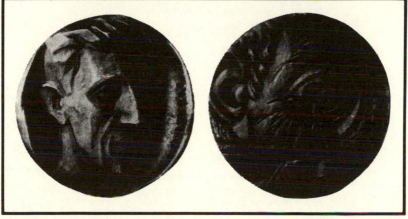

GEORGE ORWELL by Alex Shagin   3" Bronze Medal

Thursday, Friday, Saturday
October 11, 12, 13, 1984

HOFSTRA
UNIVERSITY
HEMPSTEAD, NEW YORK 11550

HOFSTRA UNIVERSITY CULTURAL CENTER

Director

JOSEPH G. ASTMAN

Assistant Directors

NATALIE DATLOF
ALEXEJ UGRINSKY

Assistant to the Director

CAROLYN SCHNECK

Special Assistant to the Director

BARBARA LEKATSAS

Development Coordinator

DONNA TESTA

Conference Coordinators

JO-ANN GRAZIANO
KARIN BARNABY

Secretaries

MARILYN SEIDMAN
ATHELENE A. COLLINS

Assistants

SAMUEL AMAYA	TARA STAHMAN
DORIS KEANE	JOHN SYSAK
PATRICK H. MAHONEY	SINAIDA U. WEBER
SUSAN REGINE	

Galleries

David Filderman Gallery

MARGUERITE M. REGAN
Assistant to the Dean of the Library Services

NANCY E. HERB
ANNE RUBINO

Emily Lowe Gallery

GAIL GELBURD
Director

MARY WAKEFORD
Directorial Assistant

Musical Organizations

American Chamber Ensemble

BLANCHE ABRAM
NAOMI DRUCKER
Directors

Hofstra String Quartet

SEYMOUR BENSTOCK
Artistic Coordinator

Conference Director

COURTNEY T. WEMYSS

Conference Coordinators

NATALIE DATLOF
ALEXEJ UGRINSKY
JO-ANN GRAZIANO

George Orwell Conference Committee

MEYER BARASH
JEANNE FUCHS
JOHN T. MARCUS
HERBERT D. ROSENBAUM
HENRY SIKORSKI

ROSALIE H. STILLWELL
ALEXEJ UGRINSKY
JOHN E. ULLMANN
COURTNEY T. WEMYSS

DIRECTOR'S MESSAGE

I think it important that the life and works of George Orwell come to hold a
secure, proper niche in the noble body of literature which has been generated in the
English tongue over many centuries. Mention of his name in the far future should evoke
in educated men that same breed of respect which the names Fielding, Goldsmith and
Sterne evoke in us. These names suggest the rank to which I trust Orwell will be assigned by scholars of other ages.

To my mind, Orwell's niche is at risk because of the current overemphasis of
some facets of the man at the expense of certain others, these latter being of a more
enduring quality. My fear is that Orwell the Patron Saint of Poverty and Bard of
Apocalypse will, in the long run, tire people of the future and consequently subvert
them into neglecting Orwell the ligand -- the connection between the higher and lower
grades of literature -- and of Orwell the preserver of the twentieth-century milieu.

I have long been struck by the fact that Orwell is a much more significant figure
than his mere literary accomplishments -- which are modest -- suggest. Furthermore, he
is honored here and elsewhere this year because of a novel which is not his best. The
greatest virtue of Nineteen Eighty-Four -- this taut, well brewed and commanding horror
story -- is that it directs us or should direct us to his other offerings. Then the
other novels (Burmese Days, Coming Up for Air, etc.), the superb literary criticism
(Kipling, Dickens, etc.) the book reviews, the documentaries (Down and Out in London
and Paris, The Road to Wigan Pier, Homage to Catalonia) will bring forth to us the
English milieu of the first half of this century with at least the accuracy with which
Pepys presented the milieu of the Restoration -- without, I judge, the particular intent
of the diarist himself.

Burmese Days -- fine novel that it is -- cannot touch Coming Up for Air, Orwell's best ever, of which one seldom hears mention today or for that matter heard mention of forty years back. Yet in it we meet England about to face Hitler -- the Vlad Dracula of modern Europe. We also meet George Bowling, the incarnate spirit of the decent Englishmen who shortly afterward made "a pact of death"* with Winston Churchill.

These works also contrive to send us up to Swift, over to Defoe and Chesterton and down to Jack London and George Gissing. George Orwell's works are, in short, marvelous points of departure. His BBC broadcast of 1941 or thereabouts in which he analyzed Gerard Manly Hopkins' poem "Felix Randal" is of a quality such as to inspire the interested young to take up the study of prosody.

His 1941 essay on the mind of H.G. Wells -- written because Wells, a month or so earlier, had been so foolish as to tell the press that the Wehrmacht was finished and that Herr Hitler had shot his wad -- not only accounts for the mentality which could reach such a fatuous conclusion but also, at least by implication, explains the intellectual lesions of the Webbs, George Bernard Shaw and others of that kidney.

In putting down someone whose notions were not rooted in reality Orwell frequently resorted to the flat, unadorned statement: "He does not know how things work." He then set out to prove as much, almost always successfully. Among the notable instances are those of Wells, Dickens and in lesser degree of Kipling. His regard for Jack London -- such as it was -- stemmed from the fact that London clearly realized that bravery was not a monopoly virtue of fighters in righteous causes.

As far as I know Orwell never addressed himself to the works of Anthony Trollope who did indeed know how things work and who never mentioned matters the workings of which he did not understand. I wish to God that Orwell had turned his attention to Trollope.

To conclude, preoccupation with his immediate importance should not ultimately cause scholars of the future to underrate George Orwell.

Courtney T. Wemyss
Professor of Biology
Conference Director

* These apt words are -- alas -- those of A.J.P. Taylor and not my own.

Thursday, October 11, 1984

Conference Opening: 9:00 - 10:30 a.m.	Registration: David Filderman Gallery Department of Special Collections Hofstra University Library - 9th floor

10:30 a.m.   Greetings from the Hofstra University Community

Sanford Hammer
Provost & Dean of Faculties

Joseph G. Astman
Director
Hofstra University Cultural Center
Professor of Comparative Literature & Languages

Courtney T. Wemyss
Professor of Biology
Conference Director

11:00 a.m.   Keynote Address: Jeffrey Meyers
Professor of English
University of Colorado
Boulder, CO

"Nineteen Eighty-Four: A Novel of the 1930's"

11:30 a.m.   Invitational Address: Alex Shagin, Sculptor
Los Angeles, CA, formerly leading
staff artist of the Leningrad Mint,
Leningrad, USSR

Creator of the official George Orwell
Conference Medal

Opening of Conference Exhibit

"George Orwell: His Works, His World"

Reception

12:00 noon - 1:30 p.m.   Lunch: Student Center Cafeteria

1:30 - 3:30 p.m.   PANEL I - LITTLE BROTHER

                        Moderator/Commentator: John E. Ullmann
                                                Dept. of Management & Marketing
                                                Hofstra University

                        "Orwell and Little Brother"
                        Walter Poznar
                        Saint Leo College, Saint Leo, FL

                        "The Political Basis of Orwell's Criticism of
                            Popular Culture"
                        William T. Ross
                        University of South Florida, Tampa, FL

                        "George Orwell's Political Themes: Asian Ambivalences"
                        Kirpal Singh
                        National University of Singapore, Kent Ridge, Singapore

3:30 - 4:30 p.m.   PANEL II - DOCUMENTARY FICTIONS

                        Moderator/Commentator: Jeanne Fuchs
                                                English Language Program
                                                Hofstra University

                        "The Lure of Power in Post-Orwellian Political Fiction"
                        Richard I. Smyer
                        The University of Arizona, Tucson, AZ

                        "George Orwell and the Problematics of Non-Fiction"
                        Howard Wolf
                        SUNY/Buffalo, Buffalo, NY

4:30 - 5:30 p.m.   William J. West
                        Exeter, England
                        Editor of the forthcoming Orwell, The War Broadcasts and
                            Orwell, The War Commentaries

                        "A Dialogue with William J. West: The New BBC Orwell
                            Manuscripts"

                        Moderator/Commentator: Howard Fink
                                                Department of English
                                                Concordia University
                                                Montreal, Quebec, Canada

                        Question and Answer Period

5:30 - 6:30 p.m.   Dinner: Student Center Cafeteria

Thursday, October 11 (Cont'd.)   School of Law, Moot Courtroom, Room 308, South Campus

6:30 - 8:00 p.m.   PANEL III - POLITICAL COMPARISONS

                                Moderator/Commentator: John T. Marcus
                                                        Department of History
                                                        Hofstra University

                                "Commitment and Identity: Orwell's Reflections of
                                   Arthur Koestler in Nineteen Eighty-Four"
                                Howard Fink
                                Concordia University, Montreal, Quebec, Canada

                                "Raymond Williams versus Orwell"
                                Martin Green
                                Tufts University, Medford, MA

                                "Orwell, Proudhon, and the Moral Order"
                                Aaron Noland
                                Professor Emeritus
                                The City College/CUNY, New York, NY

8:00 p.m.   ROUNDTABLE WITH FACULTY FROM THE HOFSTRA UNIVERSITY
                                SCHOOL OF LAW

                                "Privacy and Government: 1984 and After"

                                Introductions:

                                Eric J. Schmertz
                                Dean, Hofstra University School of Law and
                                Edward F. Carlough Distinguished Professor of Labor Law

                                Moderator/Commentator:

                                Burton C. Agata
                                Max Schmertz Distinguished Professor of Law

                                Participants: John DeWitt Gregory
                                                Professor of Law

                                                Leon Friedman
                                                Professor of Law

                                                Ronald H. Silverman
                                                Professor of Law

                                Reception: Faculty Lounge

Friday, October 12, 1984   Dining Rooms ABC, Student Center, North Campus

9:00 a.m. - 5:00 p.m.   Exhibits: David Filderman Gallery:

                                    "George Orwell: His Works, His World"

10:00 a.m. - 5:00 p.m.   Emily Lowe Gallery:

                                    "George Grosz: An Artist for 1984"

9:00 - 10:30 a.m.   PANEL IV - LITERARY COMPARISONS I

                         Moderator/Commentator: Meyer Barash
                                                 Department of Sociology
                                                 Hofstra University

                         "Nineteen Eighty-Four and Gravity's Rainbow:
                            Two Anti-Utopias Compared"
                         J. Bakker
                         University of Groningen, Groningen, The Netherlands

                         "Past and Present in Coming Up For Air and Nineteen Eighty-Four:
                            A Comparison with R. Warner's The Aerodrome"
                         Maria Teresa Chialent
                         Istituto Universitario Orientale, Naples, Italy

                         "George Orwell and Iris Murdoch: Patterns of Power"
                         Amin Malak
                         The University of Alberta, Edmonton, Canada

10:30 a.m. - 12:00 noon PANEL V - LITERARY COMPARISONS II

                         Moderator/Commentator: Henry Sikorski
                                                 Department of English
                                                 Hofstra University

                         "G.K. Chesterton and Nineteen Eighty-Four"
                         Louis Burkhardt
                         Metropolitan State College, Denver, CO

                         "Jack London and George Orwell: A Literary Kinship"
                         Victor R.S. Tambling
                         Birmingham, England

                         "Orwell as Poet"
                         Rosaly DeMaios Roffman
                         Indiana University of Pennsylvania, Indiana, PA

12:00 noon - 1:30 p.m.   Lunch: Student Center Cafeteria

1:30 - 3:00 p.m.   PANEL VI - LINGUISTICS

Moderator/Commentator: Alexej Ugrinsky
                        Department of Comparative Literature
                           and Languages
                        Hofstra University

"Beyond Orwell: Clarity and the English Language"
Madelyn Flammia
Monmouth College, West Long Branch, NJ

"The Rhetoric of Down and Out in Paris and London"
John P. Frazee
The University of Texas of the Permian Basin, Odessa, TX

"Some Aesthetic-Based Similes in Orwell"
James McNally
Old Dominion University, Norfolk, VA

3:00 - 5:00 p.m.   PANEL VII - LEVIATHAN

Moderator/Commentator: Joseph Cassar
                        Academy for The Development of a
                           Democratic Environment
                        Sliema, Malta

"'Sugarcandy Mountain': Thoughts on George Orwell's Critique
   of the Christian Doctrine of Personal Immortality"
James Connors
University of Hawaii at Manoa, Honolulu, HI

"Nineteen Eighty-Four and George Orwell's Other
   View of Capitalism"
Arthur Eckstein
University of Maryland, College Park, MD

"Orwell: From 'Clerisy' to 'Intelligentsia'"
Jasbir Jain
University of Rajasthan, Jaipur, India

"Orwell the Self-Educated Student of English History"
R.L. Patterson
Castleton State College, Castleton, VT

Friday, October 12

5:00 - 6:00 p.m.   Emily Lowe Gallery, South Campus

                          SPECIAL VIEWING AND RECEPTION

                          "George Grosz: An Artist for 1984"

6:15 p.m.   Dining Rooms ABC, North Campus

                          GEORGE ORWELL CONFERENCE BANQUET

                          Cash Bar

                          Greetings: Linton S. Thorn
                                      Associate Dean, Hofstra College of Liberal Arts
                                      and Sciences
                                      Chair, Department of History

                                      Courtney T. Wemyss
                                      Department of Biology
                                      Conference Director

8:30 p.m.   John Cranford Adams Playhouse, South Campus

                          CONCERT: HOFSTRA STRING QUARTET

                                        PROGRAM

                          Quartet No. 1 in D minor..................... Arriaga
                          Quartet No. 1............................... Shostakovich
                          Quartet in F minor, Op. 95 (Serioso)........ Beethoven

                                    Harry Glickman, violin

                                    Ray Kunicki, violin

                                    Harry Zaratzian, viola

                                    Seymour Benstock, 'cello

Saturday, October 13, 1984   Dining Rooms ABC, Student Center, North Campus

9:00 a.m. - 1:30 p.m.   Exhibits: David Filderman Gallery

                         "George Orwell: His Works, His World"

1:00 - 5:00 p.m.   Emily Lowe Gallery:

                         "George Grosz: An Artist for 1984"

8:00 - 9:00 a.m.   Continental Breakfast

9:00 - 10:00 a.m.   PANEL VIII - UTOPIA AND DYSTOPIA

                         Moderator/Commentator: Herbert D. Rosenbaum
                                                 Department of Political Science
                                                 Hofstra University

                         "More to Orwell: An Easy Leap from Utopia to
                             Nineteen Eighty-Four"
                         Janice L. Hewitt
                         Rice University, Houston, TX

                         "George Orwell 'Down and Out' to Catalonia:
                             A Socialist's Progress"
                         Lora Lerman
                         New York University, New York, NY

                         "Ideology, Revisionism and the British Left:
                             Orwell's Marx and the Marxists' Orwell"
                         John Rodden
                         University of Virginia, Charlottesville, VA

10:30 a.m. - 12:30 p.m. PANEL IX - NINETEEN EIGHTY-FOUR

                         Moderator/Commentator: Jonathan Rose
                                                 Department of English
                                                 Drew University
                                                 Madison, NJ

                         "Primal Guilt: The Genesis of Nineteen Eighty-Four"
                         Catherine B. Burke
                         Western Washington University, Bellingham, WA

                         "Nineteen Eighty-Four and the Massaging of the Media"
                         W. Russel Gray
                         Delaware County Community College, Media, PA

                         "George Orwell's Nineteen Eighty-Four:
                         The Dystopian Paradigm as Satire"
                         Leah Hadomi
                         University of Haifa, Oranim, Tivon, Israel

Saturday, October 13 (Cont'd.)   Dining Rooms ABC, Student Center, North Campus

10:30 a.m. - 12:30 p.m.   PANEL IX - NINETEEN EIGHTY-FOUR
(Continued)
                            "'Rats!' to Nineteen Eighty-Four"
                            Michael Orange
                            University of Sydney, New South Wales, Australia

                            "Nineteen Eighty-Four: How Near? How Far?"
                            Leon Martel
                            Author, Lecturer
                            New York, NY

1:00 p.m.   Brunch

GEORGE GROSZ

AN ARTIST FOR 1984

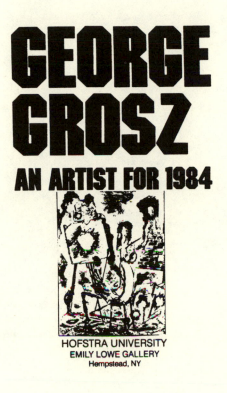

HOFSTRA UNIVERSITY
EMILY LOWE GALLERY
Hempstead, NY

SEPTEMBER 9 - OCTOBER 21, 1984

COOPERATING INSTITUTIONS

Abraham & Straus
Hempstead, NY

CBS News
New York, NY

Coliseum Motor Inn
East Meadow, NY

Marriott Hotel
Uniondale, NY

Maryland Center for Public Broadcasting
Owing Mills, MD

Nassau Library System
Uniondale, NY

New York Public Library
New York, NY

Numismarketing Associates
Woodland Hills, CA

Suffolk Cooperative Library System
Bellport, NY

University College London Library
London, England

HOFSTRA UNIVERSITY CULTURAL CENTER

Conference Schedule and Publications Listing

*George Sand Centennial—November 1976
*Heinrich von Kleist Bicentennial—November 1977
+ The Chinese Woman—December 1977
*George Sand: Her Life, Her Works, Her Influence—April 1978
*William Cullen Bryant and His America—October 1978
 The Trotsky-Stalin Conflict in the 1920's—March 1979
 Albert Einstein Centennial—November 1979
 Renaissance Venice Symposium—March 1980
+ Sean O'Casey—March 1980
 Walt Whitman—April 1980
 Nineteenth-Century Women Writers—November 1980
 Fedor Dostoevski—April 1981
 Gotthold Ephraim Lessing—November 1981
 Franklin Delano Roosevelt: The Man, The Myth, The Era—March 1982
 Johann Wolfgang von Goethe—April 1982
 James Joyce—October 1982
 Twentieth-Century Women Writers—November 1982
 Harry S. Truman: The Man from Independence—April 1983
**John Maynard Keynes—September 1983
 Romanticism in the Old and the New World-Washington Irving, Stendhal, and Zhukovskii—October 1983
 Espectador Universal: Jose Ortega y Gasset—November 1983
 Dwight D. Eisenhower: Soldier, President, Statesman—March 1984
+ Victorian Studies—April 1984
 Symposium on Eighteenth-Century Venice—April 1984
 George Orwell—October 11-13, 1984
 Friedrich von Schiller—November 8-10, 1984
 John F. Kennedy: The New Frontier—March 28-30, 1985
 Fourth Annual Edward F. Carlough Labor Law Conference—April 16, 1985
 Evaluating Higher Education—April 18-19, 1985
 Harlem Renaissance—May 2-4, 1985
 New York State History Conference—June 7-9, 1985
 Manzoni Symposium (Como, Italy)—June 1985
 Evolution of Business Education—September 19-21, 1985
 Eighteenth-Century Women Writers—October 10-12, 1985
 Johann Sebastian Bach—October 24-26, 1985
 Law School Conference: The United States Supreme Court (The Burger Court), 1969-1985—November 6, 1985
 Avant Garde Art and Literature—November 14-16, 1985
 Television 1985: Past, Present, and Future—November 19-21, 1985
 Lyndon B. Johnson—March 1986
 Conference on Human Rights—April 1986
 Fifth Annual Edward F. Carlough Labor Law Conference—April 1986
 Conference on the Disabled—June 1986
 George Sand: Her Life, Her Works, Her Influence—October 1986
 Miguel Unamuno/Frederico García-Lorca—November 1986
 Carl Gustav Jung and the Humanities—November 24-26, 1986
 Richard M. Nixon—Spring 1987
 Bicentennial of the United States Constitution—October 1987
 Aleksandr Sergeevich Pushkin—November 1987
 Gerald R. Ford—Spring 1988
 Byron and His Contemporaries—Spring 1988
 Madame de Staël—October 1988
 Jimmy Carter—Spring 1989
 Bicentennial of the French Revolution—Fall 1989
 Ronald Reagan—Spring 1990

*Volumes available from AMS Press
**Volume available from Sharp & Armonk
+ No publication
All other volumes forthcoming from Greenwood Press

For further information and "Calls for Papers":
Hofstra University Cultural Center
Hofstra University
Hempstead, NY 11550
(516) 560-5669/5670

CREDIT for the success of the Conference goes to more people than can be named herein, but those below deserve special commendation:

HOFSTRA UNIVERSITY OFFICERS: James M. Shuart, President
                                Sanford Hammer, Provost & Dean of Faculties
                                Robert C. Vogt, Dean, Hofstra College of
                                    Liberal Arts & Sciences

CUSTODIAL & GROUNDS SERVICES: Ken Tietze, Resident Manager
                                Harry Meisenholder, Director of Grounds

DAVID FILDERMAN GALLERY: Marguerite M. Regan, Assistant to the Dean of Library Service
                           Nancy E. Herb
                           Anne Rubino

DEPARTMENT OF COMMUNICATION ARTS: William R. Renn, Chairman
                                    Kit Hunt, Faculty Program Coordinator WRHU

DINING SERVICES: Tony Internicola, Director
                   Dawn Smith, Assistant Director & Catering Manager

EMILY LOWE GALLERY: Gail Gelburd, Director
                      Mary Wakeford, Directorial Assistant

FACILITIES MANAGEMENT: Charles L. Churchill, Facilities Manager
                         Dorothy Fetherston, Director of Scheduling

HOFSTRA UNIVERSITY LIBRARY: Charles R. Andrews, Dean
                              Wayne Bell, Associate Dean

MAIL SERVICES: Dolores Pallingayan, Administrator
                 George McCue, Supervisor
                 Mail Room Staff

OPERATIONAL SERVICES: James Fellman, Vice President of Operational Services & Staff

PLANT ENGINEERING & MAINTENANCE: Richard J. Drury, Director of Physical Plant
                                   Charles Rubel, Associate Director
                                   Physical Plant Staff

PUBLIC SAFETY & TELECOMMUNICATIONS: Robert L. Crowley, Director
                                      Ed Bracht, Deputy Director
                                      Margaret A. Shields, Operations Manager

PUBLICATIONS OFFICE: Jack Ruegamer, Director, Printing and Publications
                       Vicki Anderson
                       Margaret Mirabella
                       Veronica Fitzwilliam

                       Doris Brown, Supervisor, Printing Department
                       Printing Department Staff

SCHOOL OF LAW: Eric J. Schmertz, Dean
                 Staff of the Xeroxing Office

SPECIAL SECRETARIAL SERVICES: Stella Sinicki, Supervisor
                                 Staff

TECHNICAL & MEDIA SERVICES: Elizabeth Weston, Media Services Librarian
                               William Gray
                               Ray Tynn

UNIVERSITY RELATIONS: Harold A. Klein, Director
                         James Merritt, Assistant Director
                         M.F. Klerk, Editor/Writer
                         Frances B. Jacobsen, Administrative Assistant

                         GERMAN CLUB

                    John Sysak, President
            Patrick H. Mahoney, Vice President
                  Beth Nagel, Treasurer
                  Ron Jundor, Secretary

Forthcoming:

INTERNATIONAL CONFERENCE

Friedrich von Schiller Conference

**THURSDAY, FRIDAY, SATURDAY
NOVEMBER 8, 9, 10, 1984**

Co-Sponsored by:
**GOETHE HOUSE NEW YORK
LUFTHANSA GERMAN AIRLINES
PRO HELVETIA ZURICH**

FOR INFORMATION:

Alexej Ugrinsky, Conference Director
Natalie Datlof, Conference Coordinator

HUCC
(516) 560-5669, 5670

HOFSTRA UNIVERSITY

HEMPSTEAD, NEW YORK 11550

TRUSTEES OF HOFSTRA UNIVERSITY
as of December 1983

THE OFFICERS

Emil V. Cianciulli '52, *Chairperson*
Frank G. Zarb '57, *Vice Chairperson*
Lawrence Herbert '51, *Vice Chairperson*
Norman R. Tengstrom '48, *Secretary*
James M. Shuart '53, *President*

THE MEMBERS

Jack G. Clarke '49
Maurice A. Deane '81
John S. DeJose '41
George G. Dempster '61 *(Chairman Emeritus)*
Joseph L. Dionne '55
Milton M. Gardner, M.D.
Allan Gittleson
Eugene Goldman
Leo A. Guthart
Benjamin J. Jenkins
Florence Kaufman
Gerald Light
David S. Mack '67
Ann M. Mallouk '72
Walter H. Miller
Thomas H. O'Brien
Greta M. Rainsford, M.D.
Suzanne K. Schwerin

John Cranford Adams, *President Emeritus*
James Harper Marshall '58, *President Emeritus*
Donald E. Axinn '75, *Trustee Emeritus*
Eben Breed, M.D., *Trustee Emeritus*
Bernard Fixler '41, *Trustee Emeritus*
Raymond French, *Trustee Emeritus*
Jeanette Hosler, *Trustee Emerita*
Dana Storrs Lamb, *Trustee Emeritus*
Mary T. Martin, *Trustee Emerita*
Donald A. Petrie '42, *Trustee Emeritus*

HOFSTRA UNIVERSITY has been named the recipient of a $450,000 Challenge Grant from the National Endowment for the Humanities (NEH). Under the terms of the challenge, the funds raised through the Conference will generate an additional contribution by the federal government of one-third of the total raised. A portion of your admission fee will be used toward matching the challenge grant.

NOTES

Index

DARLA KOWALSKI

About the Editors and Contributors

J. BAKKER teaches American literature at the University of Groningen, the Netherlands. His most recent books are *Fiction as Survival Strategy* (1983, a study about Hemingway and Bellow) and *Ernest Hemingway in Holland, 1925-1981* (1986). He is also one of the cofounders and coeditors of *DQR* (*Dutch Quarterly Review of Anglo-American Letters*), in which many of his articles have appeared.

LOUIS C. BURKHARDT is currently a graduate student at the English Department of the University of Colorado, Boulder and was formerly (at the reading of this paper) an instructor at Metropolitan State College, Denver. He is studying Edmund Spenser and the English tradition of allegory.

MARIA TERESA CHIALANT is Associate Professor of English at the Istituto Universitario Orientale of Naples, Italy. She specializes in the nineteenth-century novel and women's fiction, studying the interconnections between cultural formations and narrative modes. She has written on Charles Dickens, George Gissing, and E. M. Forster, among others. Her current research interests include H. G. Wells's "scientific romances."

JAMES CONNORS is Associate Professor of History at the University of Hawaii at Manoa. He teaches world civilizations and European intellectual history. In 1986 he received the university's Excellence in Teaching Award. He has contributed articles on Orwell to *Modern Fiction Studies* and has delivered papers on Orwell at various scholarly meetings. His long-term Orwell project is a book-length study of the authors who played important roles in shaping the novelist's attitudes toward religion and politics.

A. M. ECKSTEIN is Associate Professor of History at the University of Maryland, College Park. He is especially interested in the history of individualism within Western civilization. He has written extensively both on the ancient world and George Orwell. His latest work is *Senate and General: Individual Decision-Making and Roman Foreign Relations* (1987).

HOWARD FINK is Professor of English at Concordia University in Montreal. He is also Director of the Concordia Centre for Broadcasting Studies. He has published frequently on modern literature and radio drama. His book *1984: George Orwell and Satire* is being readied for publication.

MADELYN FLAMMIA is a graduate student in the English Department at Rutgers University. She is currently working on a dissertation in the field of composition theory.

JOHN P. FRAZEE is Associate Professor and Chairman of Literature and Director of the Division of Humanities and Fine Arts at the University of Texas of the Permian Basin. He has published articles on Thackeray and Dickens. His principal research interest is in defining the ways that authorial intention shapes the materials of fiction.

W. RUSSEL GRAY is Professor of Liberal Arts at Delaware County Community College in Media, Pennsylvania, where he has served for eighteen years. He teaches courses in developmental English, writing about the mass media, novels of the future, and mystery literature, and has published or presented papers on *Nineteen Eighty-Four*, futuristic films, detective fiction, and Victorian prize-fighting.

LEAH HADOMI is Senior Lecturer of Comparative Literature at Haifa University. Her principal research interests and publications in books and articles have been directed toward the modern literary utopia as well as comparative studies in drama and the postwar German novel.

JANICE L. HEWITT, a graduate student at Rice University, has presented papers at the Utopian Studies Conference, Rice Symposium, and SCMLA, in addition to participating in the George Orwell Conference.

JASBIR JAIN chairs the Department of English, University of Rajasthan, Jaipur (India). Her principal research interests are contemporary drama and the sociocultural dimensions of liberal thought. She is the author of *Nayantara Sahgal, Colonial Encounter: Henry Derozio, George Orwell: Witness of an Age*, and *Stairs to the Attic: The Novels of Anita Desai*. Currently she is working on a book about contemporary American drama.

JEFFREY MEYERS, Professor of English at the University of Colorado, is the author of *A Reader's Guide to George Orwell* (1975), *George Orwell:*

The Critical Heritage (1975), and *George Orwell: An Annotated Bibliography of Criticism* (1977); biographies of Katherine Mansfield (1978), Wyndham Lewis (1980), and Ernest Hemingway (1985); *Fiction and the Colonial Experience* (1973), *The Wounded Spirit* (1973), *Painting and the Novel* (1975), *A Fever at the Core* (1976), *Married to Genius* (1977), *Homosexuality and Literature* (1977), *Hemingway: The Critical Heritage* (1982), *D. H. Lawrence and the Experience of Italy* (1982), *Disease and the Novel* (1985), and *Manic Power: Robert Lowell and His Circle* (1987). He has also edited *Wyndham Lewis: A Revaluation* (1980), *The Craft of Literary Biography* (1985), *D. H. Lawrence and Tradition* (1985), *The Legacy of D. H. Lawrence* (1987), and *The Biographer's Art* (1987).

AARON NOLAND is Professor Emeritus of History at the City College of New York. He has published books and articles on European socialism and anarchism. For many years he was managing editor of *The Journal of the History of Ideas*.

MICHAEL ORANGE is Senior Lecturer in the Department of English at the University of Sydney, New South Wales, Australia. He has published works on Shakespeare and E. M. Forster, and is currently writing about Jane Austen.

R. L. PATTERSON is Professor of History at Castleton State College, Vermont. During the 1970s he regularly taught the history of social reform movements and poverty and welfare. Currently, Professor Patterson is writing a book on an intellectual "outsider," Sir Lewis Namier, who, like Orwell, independently proclaimed the Whig outline of English history.

ROSALY DEMAIOS ROFFMAN is Associate Professor of English at Indiana University of Pennsylvania. In addition to composition and world literature courses, she has taught creative writing, mythology workshops for teachers, and Japanese and Chinese literature in translation courses. Her poetry and reviews have appeared in a number of magazines and journals. Currently she is working on a scholarly book on Robert Bly; and a book of her poems and creative writing exercises will be published in 1987.

WILLIAM T. ROSS is Chairman of the Department of English at the University of South Florida, Tampa. He is the author of *Weldon Kees* as well as a number of articles on Orwell and on rhetoric and style.

KIRPAL SINGH is Senior Lecturer of English at the National University of Singapore. He is an established poet and short story writer. Singh has published extensively on Commonwealth literature and on Huxley and Orwell. He has recently completed a booklength study of Huxley's work and is currently researching for a comparative study on Wells and Tagore. His publications include: *The Stellar Gauge: Essays on Science Fiction*; *Through Different Eyes—Studies in Indian Literature*; *Critical Engagements*; *The Writer's Sense of the Past*, and numerous articles in various books and journals.

RICHARD I. SMYER is Associate Professor of English at the University of Arizona. His primary research interest is in British and Commonwealth political fiction. He is the author of *Primal Dream and Primal Crime: Orwell's Development as a Psychological Novelist* and a number of articles.

VICTOR R. S. TAMBLING is a keen student of the life and works of the American author Jack London (1876-1916). He is at present researching the factual basis of London's novel *The Star Rover*, and is working on a biography of Jake Oppenheimer, the man who inspired London's novel. He has had articles published in *The Jack London Newsletter*.

HOWARD WOLF is Professor of English and Associate Chair at SUNY/Buffalo, where he has taught since 1967. He is a graduate of Horace Mann School, Amherst College, Columbia University, and the University of Michigan (Ph.D., 1967). Coauthor of *The Voice Within: Reading and Writing Autobiography* (1973), *Forgive the Father: A Memoir of Changing Generations* (1978), and *The Education of a Teacher: Essays on American Culture* (1987), he has written over 150 literary and cultural essays, short stories, poems, humorous sketches, and a variety of commentaries, reviews, and opinions. A fellow of both the Macdowell Colony and Virginia Center for the Creative Arts, Dr. Wolf was selected as a Fulbright Lecturer in Turkey (1983-1984).

Hofstra University's
Cultural and Intercultural Studies
Coordinating Editor, Alexej Ugrinsky

Walt Whitman: Here and Now
(Editor: Joann P. Krieg)

Harry S. Truman: The Man from Independence
(Editor: William F. Levantrosser)

Nineteenth-Century Women Writers of the English-Speaking World
(Editor: Rhoda B. Nathan)

Lessing and the Enlightenment
(Editor: Alexej Ugrinsky)

Dostoevski and the Human Condition After a Century
(Editors: Alexej Ugrinsky, Frank S. Lambasa, and Valija K. Ozolins)

The Old and New World Romanticism of Washington Irving
(Editor: Stanley Brodwin)

Woman as Mediatrix
(Editor: Avriel Goldberger)

Einstein and the Humanities
(Editor: Dennis P. Ryan)

Dwight D. Eisenhower: Soldier, President, Statesman
(Editor: Joann P. Krieg)

Goethe in the Twentieth Century
(Editor: Alexej Ugrinsky)

Franklin D. Roosevelt: The Man, the Myth, the Era, 1882-1945
(Editors: Herbert D. Rosenbaum and Elizabeth Bartelme)

The Stendhal Bicentennial Papers
(Editor: Avriel Goldberger)

Faith of a (Woman) Writer
(Editors: Alice Kessler-Harris and William McBrien)

José Ortega y Gasset: Proceedings of the *Espectador universal*
International Interdisciplinary Conference
(Editor: Nora de Marval-McNair)